Disenchanted Lives

Disenchanted Lives

Apostasy and Ex-Mormonism among the Latter-day Saints

E. Marshall Brooks

Rutgers University Press
New Brunswick, Camden, and Newark,
New Jersey, and London

Library of Congress Cataloging-in-Publication Data

Names: Brooks, E. Marshall, author.
Title: Disenchanted lives : apostasy and ex-Mormonism among the Latter-day Saints / E. Marshall Brooks.
Description: New Brunswick : Rutgers University Press, 2018. | Includes bibliographical references and index.
Identifiers: LCCN 2017033844 | ISBN 9780813592190 (cloth : alk. paper) | ISBN 9780813592183 (pbk. : alk. paper) | 9780813592206 (epub) | 9780813592213 (mobi) | 9780813592220 (web pdf)
Subjects: LCSH: Apostasy—Church of Jesus Christ of Latter-day Saints. | Apostasy—Mormon Church. | Ex-church members.
Classification: LCC BX8643.G74 B76 2018 | DDC 289.3/32—dc23
LC record available at https://lccn.loc.gov/2017033844

A British Cataloging-in-Publication record for this book is available from the British Library.

∞ The paper used in this publication meets the requirements of the American National Standard for Information Sciences—Permanence of Paper for Printed Library Materials, ANSI Z39.48-1992.

www.rutgersuniversitypress.org

Manufactured in the United States of America

Contents

Preface

In this book, I describe the cultural causes and consequences of religious disenchantment, approached ethnographically and with broad attention to the intersecting influences of history, modern forms of faith, and broader trends in secular society. I aim to show here how complex the relationship is between apostasy—rejecting the central tenets of one's faith—and religious experience in contemporary Mormonism. The book's unifying theme revolves around the idea that disenchantment, as a personal experience and cultural phenomenon, is characterized by an ambiguously conflated intimacy with and estrangement from religion, including the people, places, beliefs, and practices that define it. I draw on descriptions of Mormon church history, spiritual practice, cultural-religious ideology, and (ex-)members' personal experiences to illustrate this dynamic and the ways in which contemporary Mormons leaving the church navigate their departures.

My descriptions and interpretations are drawn from ten years of research and friendship, principally though not exclusively in Mormon and ex-Mormon communities throughout central Utah—the heartland of Mormon culture and location of the institutional headquarters of the Church of Jesus Christ of Latter-day Saints. I first entered these communities as a graduate student in 2008 and continue to regularly visit family and lifelong friends living across the state. Whatever authority or validity my interpretations possess thus stems from my long-term involvement with people in their everyday lives. The ultimate reward and burden of ethnography is indeed bound to the immediacy, and partiality, of such subjective engagements. However, I must be clear that I am neither a current nor a former member of the Mormon Church. Yet I nevertheless hope to have represented the disenchantment experience here equitably and reflexively, without unduly romanticizing or disparaging either religious or secular life.

This book owes its existence to many people who inspired and supported my thoughts and labors over the years. Greatest thanks go to the many friends in Utah, current and former church members alike, who patiently offered their perspectives and insights with a prying ethnographer. Without their having generously invited me into their lives and shared their experiences, both intimate and banal, this book could never have been written. Various insights, descriptions, and interpretations presented throughout this book were first fielded in nascent form with the many undergraduate students at Utah Valley University with whom I had the pleasure of sharing a classroom during my fieldwork. They taught me, as much as I them, through their willingness to turn an unflinchingly critical eye on their own religion and culture. I am especially grateful to the many ex-Mormons, most of whom do not appear in these pages under their real names, whose sophisticated understanding of Mormon history and culture was an endless source of creative, and critical, inspiration. Their words and wisdom pepper each page of this book.

This book has benefited, directly and indirectly, from many inspired teachers. Charles Gattone first compelled me to pursue a scholarly life when he thoughtfully prompted me as an undergraduate student to write an honor's thesis on Mormon men's missionary experiences. His affable presence and intellectual generosity in the classroom and as a mentor set the standard against which I continue to measure my life in academia. I also thank Dorothy Hodgson, who patiently guided me through the rigors of graduate school and the writing of my dissertation. I could not have asked for a more sage and prudent adviser. Parvis Ghassem-Fachandi, Laura Ahearn, and Ryan Cragun were the other members of my dissertation committee, each of whom taught me a unique style of thinking and writing, the fingerprints of which I see throughout all my work. I am also grateful to Rutgers University for providing a nurturing environment to grow as a young graduate student in the late 2000s and for instilling within me a deep commitment to critically engaged scholarship. Equal thanks go to the Department of Family Medicine and Population Health at Virginia Commonwealth University for its support as I revised my dissertation for publication as well as the three anonymous reviewers for Rutgers University Press who shared invaluable suggestions and enthusiasm for this project.

My wife, Katrina, gave more of herself to usher this book into existence than I deserve. Her belief in me and my writing has sustained me through more than one crisis of faith. I thank her with all my heart. Finally, I thank my daughters, Willa and Eleanor, who jointly made their early entrance into the world while I was revising this manuscript and who now, upon its completion, daily remind me what life is all about.

Disenchanted Lives

Introduction

THE "CRISIS OF APOSTASY" IN MODERN MORMONISM

At nineteen years old, Taylor received his "mission call" from the Church of Jesus Christ of Latter-day Saints. The letter arrived in his mailbox in an unassuming white envelope, the official church logo emblazoned in the corner. It addressed him as "Elder," denoting his official station in the Melchizedek priesthood.

Taylor reads the letter aloud to me from across his parents' living room: "You are assigned to labor in the Massachusetts, Boston Mission . . . for a period of 24 months . . . Your purpose will be to invite others to come unto Christ by helping them receive the restored gospel . . . As you serve with all your heart, might, and strength, the Lord will lead you to those who are prepared to be baptized." With a sigh, Taylor gently refolds the letter and tucks it back into the envelope.

Taylor moved out of his parents' home several months prior but offered to meet me here while they were out of town. "You need to see what a Mormon house looks like," he suggested. A faded portrait of Joseph Smith—the founding "prophet, seer, and revelator" of the Latter-day Saint (LDS) movement—hangs on the wall above the couch, a silent witness to our conversation. Taylor impatiently stands up and paces across the compacted pale-blue carpeting. Reading the letter had been difficult. Dozens of family pictures crowded precariously atop a nearby piano rattle with each heavy step he takes. A few pictures show young couples, just married, embracing outside LDS temples. Others are more mundane: high school graduations, family vacations, and newborn infants. Tucked among them, I notice a picture of Taylor smartly dressed in his missionary attire—slacks, white collared shirt, tie, black name tag on his chest—taken the day he left on his mission. Taylor looks young, fresh, and hopeful in the picture—a striking contrast to the sullen, emotionally weathered man I see now. Placing the letter back in a cupboard drawer, Taylor catches my eye from across the room. "This was everything to me," he says. "It was my life."

Receiving that mission call was indeed the culmination of a lifetime of spiritual preparation. Even as a young boy, Taylor knew that someday he would—like his brothers, father, and grandfather before him—serve a mission to preach the gospel. In the six months immediately prior to being called, he followed a strict regimen of personal prayer and scripture study and subjected himself to lengthy private interviews with his local bishop and area stake president, who rigorously assessed his faith, motives, and preparation—in short, his "worthiness" to serve. He then reported to the Missionary Training Center in Provo, Utah, to study church doctrine and strategies for teaching the gospel.

The training worked. Taylor describes himself during the first year of his mission as dedicated and passionate. He baptized nearly a dozen new members and achieved several leadership promotions. He was, as he boasts even now, one of the best missionaries in the area. He never broke the rules and always looked for ways to "serve" the communities in which he worked. When loneliness set in, as it occasionally did, he found comfort in dreaming of the day that he would proudly return to his family and friends in Utah for his welcome home party, get married in the temple, and start a family. At first, everything seemed to be going as planned.

However, on the second year of his mission, Taylor's zeal for missionary work began to fade. While "tracting" on the streets—handing out pamphlets and engaging pedestrians in conversation about God, Jesus, and the Book of Mormon—a person Taylor initially thought to be a potential "investigator" of the church asked Taylor questions he could not answer. Why had God's supposed chosen prophet, Joseph Smith, surreptitiously married other church members' wives? Why was there no material evidence supporting the historical events depicted in the Book of Mormon? And why had his church supported institutionalized racism? "I didn't know what to say. I was blown away," Taylor tells me, the glazed look in his eyes echoing, even several years later, that initial feeling of bewildered impotence. Not only did he not have answers to the man's questions, prior to that day, he had never even known to ask the questions himself. "The guy knew more about the church than I did . . . I just didn't see how that could be possible."

The encounter with the man on the streets prompted Taylor to redouble his efforts to become a model missionary. But since the standard missionary training had not adequately prepared him for such probing questions, he prepared himself for future encounters by reading outside the highly circumscribed list of texts approved for missionaries. Taylor tapped into what he describes as a "black market" network of missionaries sharing unauthorized books, including commentary on LDS scripture and more esoteric chronicles of church history, most of which were not considered "faith-promoting" by traditional church standards. Ironically, this deep dive into Mormon esoterica portended his own emergent skepticism. In these books, he first glimpsed details of his church's history that were at odds with the narrative taught in Sunday school classes and missionary training, which had, as he would later find out, been selectively concealed and distorted by church leadership. "I didn't know what to think . . . Did anyone else know about this? And why wasn't I told?"

"It's only recently that I realized lots of Mormons flirt with this stuff; they just don't talk about it openly," he tells me. "It's too dangerous." Taylor waves me out of my seat and leads us down a hall into his father's study. An old bookshelf leans against the wall. I scan the spines and estimate nearly a hundred texts—a mix of church lesson manuals, scripture study guides, and a few more critical historical analyses I recognize from my own collection, the orthodox and unorthodox volumes mingled together. I also notice the shelves, sagging at the middle, bowing beneath the weight of their heavy load. "It wasn't until a few months ago that I realized my dad had read a bunch of this stuff too, although I think he hides it from my mom," Taylor says. "There was a point a few years ago where he seemed to stop taking the church as seriously as he had before. I never knew why, but I always wondered if he was questioning the church. I don't see how he couldn't."

Staring together at the books lined along the shelf, Taylor says it was not long before he started asking more serious questions about his faith. Could Joseph Smith have lied about everything? Was it possible that his stories of being visited by God, finding golden plates inscribed with ancient writing, and translating the plates into the Book of Mormon were all made up? If true, it struck at the very heart of his and every church members' faith. It was almost too unfathomable to conceive. Cognitive defenses began to kick in. "'Everyone questions a little bit,' I told myself. I thought I could handle it," Taylor says, closing the door to his father's study as we walk out.

Some questions are not meant to be answered in this life, he explains. Instead, Mormons are taught to hold tight to faith and trust in the Lord, and eventually the truth will be revealed. Therefore, questions, especially ones as serious as his, while disturbing, are not to be entertained in public. "We learn to 'put them on the shelf' and keep on acting as if everything's fine." All church members at some point construct a metaphorical shelf in the mind, Taylor confides, a furtive space to conceal their doubts about the church.

Taylor initially was successful in shelving his own doubts and continued with his missionary duties for several weeks. If he just ignored the questions that had crept into his mind, he thought, maybe they would go away. However, he found that his unauthorized study had drained the pleasure he once derived from studying the Book of Mormon. Reading about once firmly held religious truths now potently reminded him of the questions he had left unresolved. The doubts that he thought had been safely shelved unexpectedly protruded into his everyday thoughts—his mental shelf began to bow under the accumulating weight of hastily abandoned questions.

Desperate for relief, he switched tactics. He replaced daily scripture study with more critical investigation, abandoning himself to a search for "evidence":

> See, there's this belief in Mormonism that the church is true, not just because we say it is, but because there's actual evidence and facts that support it. Not

> many people go looking for it though. They just kind of take it for granted that it's there, and, you know, say to themselves "someone else, somewhere along the line did the research for me, so I don't have to do it myself." So, I really thought that if I kept searching I'd find that same evidence. I knew the answers I was looking for had to be there if I just dug deep enough. Then, I thought, my faith would somehow be fixed, and I could go on with my life.

Unable to find "proof" that the church was "true," anxiety and depression quickly set in as he lost control of the morass of information and questions swirling in his head, he tells me with a hint of embarrassment. "I eventually couldn't handle it anymore," he confessed. Bouts of panic, confusion, anger, denial, guilt, and resentment beset him as his once-secure existence in the Mormon faith unraveled with each passing day. In the end, his "shelf broke," and he couldn't bring himself to knock on any more doors or try to lead people to a religion he no longer believed in. "I couldn't keep lying to myself and everyone around me." With only five months left in his twenty-four-month mission, Taylor returned home, a grave dereliction of duty in this pivotal rite of passage for young Mormon men.

We walk back to the living room, where Taylor wearily slumps into a nearby chair. I glance again at Joseph Smith's portrait hanging on the wall and the picture of Taylor in his missionary attire. I wonder if either figure, while caught up in the passion of religious inspiration and devotion, ever thought about what his future, and the future of these religious beliefs and ideas, would hold.

"I knew what people would think of me," he confides. One of his older cousins had come home early several years ago for unknown reasons. "Our family still acts ashamed of him." Taylor's homecoming proved little different. He too was met with disappointed friends and family, who began to speculate about what spiritual misfortune had beset their once faith-filled son. He was now a stranger in his own home.

This is how I first met Taylor, in the throes of what I came to recognize as an acute example of religious disenchantment. It was almost a year since he had returned from his mission. Since then, he said, he had grown bitter and resentful of Utah, of Mormons, and of the church in general. Alienated from all that he had once known, more than anything, he felt isolated and lost. His family refused to discuss his life outside the church or his reasons for leaving and instead repeatedly admonished him to "keep quiet" about matters of religion. Among most friends, he was simply branded an "apostate" and ignored.

However, while research about the church plunged him into existential turmoil, it also introduced him to a new community of other ex-Mormons on an internet LISTSERV for those, like him, who were attempting to "recover" from the church. There, he was able to talk about his experiences, receive emotional support, and begin to create a life outside of Mormonism. With this new group of friends, he began attending parties, drinking alcohol, experimenting with cannabis and psychedelic mushrooms, and having sex—an attempt to, as he described, "forget about the church." He was also introduced to the philosophical underpinnings of atheism and slowly began to replace his reverence for LDS church leaders with his new intellectual heroes of Nietzsche, Hitchens, and Sagan. In general, though, the ex-Mormon groups seemed to provide him with a much-needed respite from the wariness of living in Utah as a former believer. "These people saved me" he told me. "They made me realize I wasn't going crazy."

I originally met Taylor through these loosely organized ex-Mormon groups. Over the course of my time in Utah, we would occasionally get together at ex-Mormon events whenever he made the drive down from Salt Lake to Utah County, where I lived, to visit his family over a long weekend. On such occasions, he would inevitably complain of having to reenter the heart of "Mormondom," a widely echoed characterization of the Mormon cultural-religious stronghold that is Utah County.

As I came to see, despite having "left the church," Taylor in fact lived in a liminal, interstitial space—irreconcilably enmeshed in a Mormon world he no longer believed in, yet one he was unable to fully escape. His presence and very personhood were contested and shadowed. In some ways, this was inevitable, a product of more than a century's worth of Mormonism's largely uncontested dominance in this place. Indeed, everywhere I looked in Utah, I saw the stamp of Mormonism's presence on the physical and cultural landscape—a seemingly unending display of temples, churches, highway billboards, monuments, museums, interpretive markers, bumper stickers, black name tags, and "modest" clothing all working to consecrate and testify to the church's ascendancy in this latter-day Zion.

As a former believer, an apostate, Taylor, and all that he represented, was conspicuously hidden from public view in Utah. His voice was silent, his presence marked only by the disparaging gossip and stereotypes circulating in Mormon neighborhoods about those who "fell from the church." As I later found out, his sudden shift from belief to nonbelief had made him dangerous and uncanny in this area of hegemonic faith and religious certainty. His study of church history and the obvious effect it had had on his "testimony" of the church's truth, rendered him a forewarning of the costs of non-faith-promoting curiosity, a model to others of what happens when faithful church members stray from the "plan of salvation."

However, in contrast to the church's public image of self-certainty, I found strewn about this seemingly undifferentiated plane of religiosity scores of nonbelievers, embodied manifestations of hidden doubt and dissension in a Mormon culture growing increasingly confident amid its meteoric growth as a burgeoning world religion. As anecdotes to a local reality, I came to see that apostates testified about another world beneath the one being portrayed in church ad campaigns and depicted in the popular media and academic writings that celebrated the continued vitality of religion in America (Berger 1996, 1999; Stark 2005). It was this nether world of doubt and disbelief that I set out to study.

Over the course of my fieldwork, I began to see that Taylor's story constituted but one iteration of a theme widely repeated throughout Utah. While apostasy from the LDS Church has existed since its early beginnings more than 180 years ago, the contemporary church now faces a new, distinct wave of detractors. In support group meetings, online social networks, and informal gatherings, I came across many more people, like Taylor, who were struggling to live "in the shadow of the temple." In fact, it seems as if the geographical concentration and cultural ubiquity of Mormonism in Utah has inadvertently produced a counterculture of ex-Mormons yearning to be heard and seen by a religious community that would just as well forget they existed. Indeed, that is why I initially went to Utah to study Mormon apostasy—to understand the historical and social conditions that propelled once staunchly committed church members into this tumultuous undertow of disbelief.

In late 2011, Elder Jensen, official historian of the LDS Church, spoke to a group of students and faculty at Utah State University, where he fielded questions about the challenges facing contemporary Mormonism. Did the leaders of the church know its members were "leaving in droves" over what they "found out [about] church history?" one student hesitantly asked. In response, and in an uncharacteristically open admission from a "general authority," Jensen compared contemporary conditions in the church with an earlier and notoriously troubled era in Mormon history. "Maybe since Kirtland," he said, "we've never had a period of—I'll call it apostasy, like we're having now . . . largely due to these issues."

At the time, I had just arrived in Utah to begin my research on apostasy and ex-Mormonism in the Church of Jesus Christ of Latter-day Saints. Elder Jensen's statement serendipitously validated the topic I was setting out to study. More so, it clarified my task as an anthropologist. I needed to make sense of the constellation of historical and cultural transformations under way in the modern Mormon Church that produced these contemporary apostates as people not only making personal decisions about faith and God but also revealing ominous reflections of deeper tensions in Mormonism.

Elder Jensen's confession and Taylor's experience of faith collapse, apostasy, and involvement in a burgeoning ex-Mormon movement thus provide a prescient introduction to several themes that I explore in this book: how Mormonism's meteoric rise to widespread acceptance has created tensions in its relationship to the past, how history and faith precariously intersect, and how Mormonism's cultural dominance in Utah creates a challenging environment for people who question their faith.

The Restoration of the Gospel and the Mormon Moment

While Mormonism is today inextricably associated with the state of Utah—home to the church headquarters and the greatest geographic concentration of church members—the LDS faith has its origins on the east coast of the United States, among New York, Pennsylvania, Ohio, and later Missouri and Illinois. While the "true" historical narrative of the church's founding is much debated (the topic of chapters 1 and 2), a brief, "faith-friendly" version of events is as follows.

Although Jesus Christ brought his gospel to the world as depicted in the New Testament, shortly thereafter, his teachings were forgotten and the world fell into a "Great Apostasy." False teachings were introduced into the church as the apostolic authority to receive divine revelation was lost: "Without priesthood authority or the full gospel, people had to rely on human wisdom to interpret the scriptures, principles and ordinances . . . and much of what we know about the true character and nature of God the Father, His Son Jesus Christ, and the Holy Ghost was lost. Essential doctrines like faith, repentance, baptism, and the gift of the Holy Ghost became distorted and important doctrines were lost entirely" (Church Education System 2004, 31–46).

However, in 1820, following centuries of spiritual confusion, God began to restore the true gospel to the world through a young fourteen-year-old boy named Joseph Smith. As the story goes, Joseph Smith was confused about which church to join and prayed for guidance. While kneeling in a nearby forest glen, he was miraculously visited by the Heavenly Father and his son, Jesus Christ, who directed Smith not to join any of the existing churches, for all had fallen away from the original teachings of Christ. A few years later, Smith was again visited by an angel of the Lord, who told Smith to venture into the woods near his home and unearth a long-buried set of gold plates upon which the history of an ancient North American people's wars, politics, religious organization, and encounters with Christ had been recorded. Within this sacred record lay the blueprint for restoring Christ's true church. Inspired by God with the ability to read and translate the "reformed Egyptian" in which the plates were originally written, Smith wrote the modern-day Book of Mormon in a few short weeks and then assumed the mantle of "prophet, seer, and revelator" for the nascent Latter-day Saints.

Between 1830, when the Book of Mormon was first published, and 1844, when Joseph Smith was martyred in an Illinois jail cell, the Latter-day Saints grew into a church of thousands of exuberant devotees, united by their belief in the "restored gospel." As Smith and contemporary church leaders have professed, the restored gospel is grounded in the material reality of the Book of Mormon (tangible evidence of Heavenly Father's efforts to commune with and communicate to his people) and an equally distinctive assortment of theological tenets that conspicuously diverge from those of mainstream Christianity. This includes a belief in the flesh-and-blood reality of Heavenly Father, our existence as Heavenly Father's actual spiritual progeny, and the obligation to perform various sacred ordinances in consecrated temples as a prerequisite for achieving an eternal existence in the celestial kingdom. The Book of Mormon and the story of the church's founding has elicited interest and skepticism for the past century and a half, provoking some to convert to and others to outright condemn Mormonism. Its bold reinterpretation of the nature of God, its insistence on the practice of polygamy, and its stories of ancient civilizations living on American soil unfortunately at times has resulted in the persecution of believers, who for much of the church's existence were forced to live in relative exile. However, during the latter half of the twentieth century, Mormonism's relationship with mainstream American culture has gradually, and at times begrudgingly, intensified and improved (Mauss 1994; Shipps 1987), culminating in the so-called Mormon Moment in the early 2000s. This period, beginning with the Salt Lake City Winter Olympics in 2002 and peaking in 2012 with Mitt Romney's presidential campaign, marked Mormonism's rise to popular ascendancy in the American imagination, as evidenced in *Newsweek* cover stories, op-eds in the *Washington Post*, the television series *Big Love*, and a smash Broadway musical, *The Book of Mormon*.

While Mormonism's integration into American culture was a long and slow process, this moment marked a particular kind of relationship emerging between the LDS Church and the larger American public. Patrick Mason, the Howard W. Hunter Chair of Mormon Studies at Claremont Graduate University, explains:

> Interest in Mormonism has waxed and waned over the past 200 years. We could point to other Mormon moments. There's been a lot of attention on Mormonism in the past, but almost all of it was negative. The dynamic has been one where the LDS Church is defensive and the rest of the nation—whether it's religious leaders, the media, politicians—are taking an aggressive stance. In those situations there's not much meeting in the middle, or even productive conversation in the middle. That's the difference about this particular moment. There is a lot of constructive and productive conversation to be had. There's public education to be done. (2012, 20–23)

The Mormon Moment of the 2000s was, more than anything, a period of heightened visibility and scrutiny for the church, during which, as some commentators have noted, Mormonism was put in the world's "spotlight," initiating a process of collective transformation. Some church members felt their faith was "growing up" as it learned to "speak more to outsiders" and "talk about faith in the language of the American public sphere" (Bowman 2012b; see also Lythgoe 1968). More critically, this period also spurred a newfound sense of self-reflexivity and introspective scrutiny among some church members to try "to see ourselves as others see us, [to] think harder about our beliefs and commitments"

(Hardy 2012). In so doing, the Mormon Moment exacerbated deep cultural tensions within Mormonism, in which both church leaders and the membership at large grew increasingly concerned with managing the church's external image while also attempting to stay true to the "peculiar" traditions and heritage that made Mormonism distinctive (Bowman 2012b; Maffly-Kipp 2012; Mauss 1994). Echoing earlier tensions amid Mormonism's reluctant disavowal of polygamy at the turn of the twentieth century, the contemporary church found itself in a double bind as it attempted to reclaim and hold onto foundational pieces of its past (including the church that it once was and in some sense imagined itself "deep down" still to be) while at the same time disavowing and defending itself from the more incongruous and embarrassing historical figures, events, and beliefs that no longer fit into the image it presented to the world.

During my research, pervasive concepts like Mormonism's maturation, burgeoning modern (though in some sense split) self-image, and acquisition of a new language to talk about itself to outsiders revealed the extent to which Mormonism was struggling to create a new sense of collective self in response to its continued incorporation into the larger American public sphere. In the midst of all this, the issue of disenchantment and apostasy was revealed to me not simply as an embarrassing sideshow threatening to detract from Mormonism's growing popularity but as an epiphenomenon of deeper cultural tumult broiling underneath Mormonism's pastoral public veneer.

As the crescendo of Mormonism's century-long integration into mainstream American society (Mauss 1994; Shipps 1987), the Mormon Moment thus figures prominently in what follows not only as the historical and cultural backdrop for the events I describe but also as a potent motivating force for Mormonism's contemporary self-conscious introspection and subsequent reactionary defensiveness over its troublesome relationship to its own history, identity, beliefs, and modes of belonging. Ultimately, it is what has compelled church members to begin the capricious process of asking who and what their faith really is all about as they begin to look at themselves in the mirror of American public opinion. As such, the disenchantment of people like Taylor, rather than reflecting some spiritual pathology or the isolated, individual decision by a disgruntled former believer, is better understood as a complex social phenomenon embedded within and reflective of larger cultural and historical tensions running through Mormonism.

Faith and History

Across the United States, people hailing from diverse faith traditions are moving away from organized religion. Surveys conducted by the Pew research forum in 2012 put the number of "nonreligious" people in the United States at forty-six million (just under 20 percent), up five percentage points from five years prior.

More than thirteen million Americans (6 percent) also now describe themselves as atheist or agnostic. But what social and cultural changes do these transformations of faith reflect?

Religious disaffection is, as many commentators have suggested, an immanently social phenomenon, the product of a constellation of political, economic, historical, and social transformations (Bromley 1998; Roof and Landres 1997), and in many ways, it acts as a barometer of wider patterns of cultural change (Berger 1998). Theories of how this works abound. Some scholars suggest that recent drops in "religiosity" reflect a growing tension among religious and secular principles, ideas, and values (Bruce 2002; Christiano, Swatos, and Kivisto 2002). Others say it reflects the tendency for people in industrialized countries to live increasingly segmented and separate lives, to have less inherent interest in the communal nature of organized religion, or to even simply have less of an existential need for religion, as they live in places where health, wealth, and basic comfort are generally guaranteed (Norris and Inglehart 2004). On a widespread, societal level, these explanations are, at least in part, quite convincing. But how do individual stories of disenchantment, such as Taylor's, complicate our understanding about how this process unfolds? And what can situating such stories within culturally specific modes of faith reveal about cross-cultural differences in the local factors driving religious disaffection?

In this book, I demonstrate how specific modes of faith and religious belonging become internally incompatible and conflicted, attending to the ways in which apostasy emerges as a symptomatic point of rupture amid contemporary Mormonism's negotiation of its mythohistorical past and ongoing assimilation into the broader American society. In doing so, I call attention to both the personal and religious-political stakes of apostasy—its phenomenology and its moral economy, its intimate and collective forms. And I argue that, in light of stories such as Taylor's, anthropologists must do more to interrogate how personal and collective experiences of faith and doubt reflect broader ecumenical, cultural, and political tensions within religious communities.

In order to understand contemporary trends in Mormon apostasy, I attend to how this phenomenon reflects more local and culturally specific tensions overlooked by broader discussions of national-level secularization. In this work, I instead approach religious apostasy as a multifaceted analytic in which culture, history, and the micropolitics of faith intertwine, providing crucial insights into previously unexamined aspects of contemporary religious life. For instance, a central theme of this book focuses on the paradoxical relationship between belief and disbelief as constituting more than opposing ends of a metaphorical measuring stick of religious commitment. As my study of Mormon apostasy suggests, belief and disbelief at times reinforce and precipitate one another. That is, the loss of faith I interrogate here was found to be intimately bound to the multiple and changing ways in which people's "belief" in Mormonism has been predicated on, yet also undermined by, a strong identification with Mormon doctrine and history.

I likewise aim to avoid explaining religious disaffection in Mormonism in terms of an irreconcilable tension emerging at the intersection of public, secular, and private religious spheres (see Gooren 2010), such that apostates' preexisting social marginalization or cultural alienation from their religious communities predisposed them to be led astray by the enticements of secular modernity (see Brinkerhoff and Mackie 1993). By viewing apostasy as an analytically rich crystallization point for underlying tensions within Mormonism, I hope to show how the ex-Mormon disenchantment experience reflects not a lack of commitment, personal pathology, or even a buckling to secularist influences, as it is so often described, but a problem in the LDS Church's handling of its own religious mythohistorical narratives and the way in which these narratives have been retold, remembered, and (mis)represented. I therefore challenge the notion that those who leave religion do so because they have found a "better fit" either in another religion or within secular culture writ large. Taylor's story instead compels us to attend to the ways in which religious apostates do not, as popular stereotypes and some academic descriptions suggest, already have "one foot out the door." Rather, they can be wholly committed and faithful church members, fully entrenched in their religious lifeworlds, before their faith collapses under the load of intolerable internal contradictions, inconsistencies, and betrayed confidences.

Intimacy and Estrangement

Anthropologists studying conversion have established that personal religious transformation always entails a "looking back" to a former faith, even as a new one is entered into (Austin-Broos 2003; Norris 2002). Over the course of my relationship with Taylor, I found that only half of his story about leaving Mormonism chronicled a loss of faith. The vast majority of other ex-Mormons I knew were similarly no longer strictly concerned with matters of religious belief. Most in fact were relatively settled in their "disbelief." The other half of Taylor's story instead unfolded as a prolonged attempt to distance himself from what he saw as the damaging aspects of Mormonism while also maintaining a relationship with the people and places with which he was once intimately connected. Indeed, most ex-Mormons I interacted with were like Taylor, intimately embedded in neighborhoods, families, jobs, and schools where Mormonism was pervasive and dominant despite the fact that they no longer counted themselves among its followers. On a methodological register, this meant attending to a range of seemingly unrelated interpersonal entanglements, following ex-Mormons as they interacted with a religious culture that was now both intimately familiar and strangely foreign.

Much of this is determined by Utah's peculiar religious cultural-political topography, what Taylor and others often referred to as "Mormondom." Mormonism is widely touted as one of the most rapidly growing world religions, with significant populations in other U.S. states, including Idaho, Nevada, and Arizona, and around the globe in Central America, South America, and parts of Africa. However, Utah Mormonism is extraordinarily unique. Settled in 1847 by Mormon pioneers escaping persecution in the east, Utah became the nucleus around which Mormonism began its cultural, political, and religious domination of the intermountain region west of the Rockies (Sells and Berman 2005). It is now the only U.S. state with a single religious group making up the majority of its population, with more than 60 percent of Utah's population claiming membership in the LDS Church.

Just as Mormonism's theological and doctrinal peculiarities encompass believers in a uniquely comprehensive "web of significance" (Geertz 1973), its cultural presence in the state is total and absolute. In this area, dubbed by social geographers as the "Mormon Culture Region," most church members are "born in the faith," living in neighborhoods where they enjoy near absolute religious dominance. As sociologists Rick Phillips et al. (2011) note, the distinction between Mormons in the Mormon Culture Region and those outside it has prompted scholars to describe two different "species" of Mormons. The Utah variant is characterized as "inhabit[ing] a place where the tenets of Mormonism are axiomatic and an LDS identity is inculcated from birth. Their colorful and sensational history . . . is inextricably intertwined with their geography and genealogy" (3).

The Provo and Salt Lake City metropolitan areas, where I conducted the bulk of my fieldwork, are located in the central "Wasatch Front" region of Utah, with the towering Wasatch Mountains to the east, Utah Lake to the south, and the Great Salt Lake to the north. In Utah County, more than 81 percent of the population claims membership in the LDS Church, leading a 2013 Gallup survey to rank it the most religious metropolitan area in the United States. Salt Lake City, home to the LDS church headquarters, is located just an hour's drive north. Although the city has grown increasingly diverse in recent decades, the entire downtown area is visibly, as well as functionally, centered on a cluster of church buildings collectively referred to as Temple Square. On a single ten-acre plot of land in the heart of downtown stand the neogothic Salt Lake Temple, the domed Tabernacle, the 1.4 million-square-foot Conference Center, and the towering twenty-eight-story "Church Office Building." However, the church's influence over state and local politics is, as might be expected, not so well contained. Unchurched residents often jokingly ask visitors if they know how wide the separation between church and state is in Utah. "Three blocks," they say. That's the distance between Temple Square and the state capitol building, where eight out of nine state legislators are church members.

This infrastructural dominance also extends well beyond Salt Lake City. A forty-five-minute drive south along the I-15 corridor, from Salt Lake City down to Utah Valley, passes seven temples (there are a total of seventeen scattered throughout the state), several prominently built on hilltops overlooking the valley, their spires silhouetted against the pastoral landscape. The relatively majestic presence of the temples is complemented by the less ornately built, yet many times more numerous, presence of chapels (also referred to as meeting houses) peppered across the state. In Salt Lake County alone, there is one chapel for every 1.3 square miles of land. And in the three counties surrounding Salt Lake City, there are more than 1,200. To those unfamiliar with Utah, the sheer number of chapels can seem redundant. For instance, it is relatively common to find multiple chapels built adjacent to one another on the same city block. However, such infrastructural tenacity becomes necessary given the sheer density of members in Utah and the need to accommodate the thousands of parishioners in the surrounding neighborhoods heading to church en masse on any given Sunday.

But this is where geography, demographics, and statistics tell only part of the story. While Mormonism's unquestionable cultural ascendancy in Utah is ineffable and profound, the effects of this dominance vary depending on one's relationship to Mormonism. For church members, it contributes to a sense of familiarity and comfort. I often heard Mormons say how easy it was to become part of a new ward (a moniker for local Mormon congregations, akin to a Catholic parish) if they happened to move to a new neighborhood. While friends and neighbors would be missed, the transition was relatively seamless, as ritual practices, worship patterns, and social norms were largely uniform from ward to ward. Almost anywhere you went, you were guaranteed to find a chapel only a short walk away. For non/former members, however, this very ubiquity and uniformity can create a sense of inescapable enclosure. In all inhabited parts of the state, there is nowhere that is not in one way or another Mormon, a unique characteristic that I would later find out has profound implications for ex-Mormons attempting to disembark from the church.

My conversation with Taylor, in which he described being marginalized from everything he once knew and loved, would thus ultimately force me to address the way in which Mormonism's continued presence haunted every aspect of ex-Mormons' lives, from the most intimate to the most social. It would compel me to recognize how deep and expansive the impact of disbelief was while pushing me to address how there is ultimately no area—public or private—external to it.

Yet I also found that Mormonism's continued presence in ex-Mormons' lives manifested in ways more subtle than being estranged from friends and family. For example, I was initially surprised to find that the majority of ex-Mormons I spoke with affirmed Mormonism, to some degree, as a cultural tradition with which they wanted to stay engaged. Most of the ex-Mormons I knew had deep Mormon ancestry, grew up surrounded by an extensive network of family members (all of whom were church members), and had built their entire lives in the faith. So it was not uncommon within the communities I worked for someone to describe themselves as a "cultural Mormon." As I did this, I came to think of divisions between belief and disbelief, as well as what it meant to be a Mormon versus an ex-Mormon, as more opaque and precarious than they often appear.

Apostasy, I argue, therefore presents hitherto unseized opportunity to investigate modern secularization not simply as a process of sociohistorical and institutional transformation but as a "social-psychological revolution" unfolding through people's experience of personal religious disenchantment (Bellah 1970, 66). So although this book focuses on people who largely denounce religion—often describing themselves as secular humanists, atheists, and freethinkers—it is not an ethnography of "secular subjects." In fact, I argue that making such categorical and epistemological distinctions would mistakenly reify the very positionalities and subjectivities my findings confound. This coincides with recent studies of "nonreligion" in the United States, which suggest that most people now "without religion" were not born into "secular households" but were instead raised religious and at some point left their faith (Pew Research Center 2012; Zuckerman 2011). To be nonreligious is therefore to be mnemonically laden with a lifetime of incorporating (to varying extents) the religious beliefs, morals, identities, practices, and conceptions of self from a former faith. I therefore focus on understanding these imbrications as they manifest through memory to explore new ways in which ostensibly secularized people's sense of self and identity is constructed specifically through an ongoing relationship to religion. And I attend to questions of when, how, and to what effect people move between religious and secular lifeworlds.

Over the course of my research, I too realized that ex-Mormons' ongoing emotional, psychological, social, and cultural engagements with Mormonism are easily overlooked if apostasy is focused on simply in terms of division and divergence of belief and belonging (Beck 2006; Morin and Morin 2004; Ure 1999). In thinking about the interconnectivity of ex-Mormons with their former faith, I therefore attend to the many religious experiences, memories, and sensations that people must navigate in their transition from believer to nonbeliever and insist on the persistence of intimate and embodied ties to that former faith. For example, I found that despite ostensibly rejecting their faith intellectually, a tacit psychosomatic impression was indelibly marked on ex-Mormons' lives. Bodies still felt shame for sexual improprieties, minds still reeled from doubt and confusion, and a once-cherished sense of religiously inspired purpose and existential security was achingly out of reach. In fact, it was by attending ex-Mormon support group meetings and parties that I began to identify unexpected, and often intimate, sites of overlap. Learning to drink alcohol, experimenting with new kinds of sex, or nostalgically singing church hymns served as conduits for people to reflect on and critically redefine their lingering relationships to the church in different ways.

Unfortunately, previous studies of secularization, atheism, and deconversion have typically emphasized the influence of Enlightenment-derived values of science, rationality, and reason on people's renunciation of faith, and in the process, have drawn attention away from its emotional, psychological, and embodied dimensions. While scholars often discuss religious conversion in bodily, affective terms—coming to be inhabited by God, feeling his love, feeling a sense of "wholeness" (Harding 1987; Luhrmann 2012)—this has been less explicit in work on disenchantment and atheism. The nonreligious subject is depicted as almost disembodied, reduced to a calculating thinker who is wholly defined by a scientific mind-set and a rationalized body. Former church members across various faiths are primarily asked about the reasons they lost faith or what convinced them that their former religion was false (Albrecht and Bahr 1988; Bromley 1998).

Left unexamined in the isolated focus on reasons for leaving are the ongoing attachments, overlaps, and vestigial remains of religion that hang on to the disenchanted despite their intellectual denunciations and how it is through people's embodied subjectivities that these remains are ultimately dealt with. By attending to ex-Mormons' lives as they are lived, I therefore focus on the ways in which (non)religious subjectivities are ambiguously in process, in a state of liminal flux, as people individually and collectively work through their lingering attachments to, identifications with, and memories of life in the church. Apostasy and disenchantment are revealed as not linear progressions from one positionality or mode of life to another but recursive processes of negotiating both intimacy and estrangement from that which has been ostensibly rejected. This book therefore serves as a reminder that religion, while cognitively compartmentalized, disavowed, or rejected in the formation of secular subjectivities, nevertheless exists in latent form as memory for many if not most secular subjects.

However, in recognizing the lasting connections between the secular and the religious, I do not meant to wax nostalgic over an idyllically more spiritualized past, a period of "porosity" to the sacred, in Charles Taylor's (2007) words, now lost to the ravages of secular modernity. Indeed, much of the literature on "the secular"—as cultural formation, historical epoch, existential condition, or phenomenological orientation—depicts our "present age," as Kierkegaard (1940) phrased it, in a spiritual malaise, a hopeless materialism, or an "immanent frame" in which spiritual passions, transcendent experience, and periods of mystical wonder have all but shriveled into an unimaginative, myopic empiricism (Taylor 2007). That there is certainly a breakdown of "ontological security" amid traumatic experiences of religious disenchantment, I do not contest (Giddens 1991). But we should be weary of prematurely foreclosing the possibility of numinous experience outside of "religion" or in the absence of belief in a divine presence and instead, through close ethnographic attention, look for the ways in which it manifests in nonreligious people's lives as well.

My Own (Non)Religious Subjectivity

No study, especially this one, resists being informed by the particular life experiences and subjectivities of the people who conduct it. Writing on the fraught hermeneutical process that is ethnography, Vincent Crapanzano (1992) reminds us that the anthropologist is inevitably, and forever, caught up in a double (or triple) bind of competing desires. This desire in fact informs (distorts?) the coordinated acts of listening, interpreting, and conveying information in unpredictable, though often surprisingly productive, ways.

I am the product of Presbyterian grandparents and Methodist parents. Some of my most vibrant memories from childhood are ambivalently tinged with the pride of counting myself among "the saved" as I looked down to a world forlorn and lost to sinful pleasures, contrasted by guilt and shame when my Baptist friends at the private Christian school I attended portended my eternal damnation because I had not received the saving grace of "baptism by immersion." That the world was a divided place, broken up into factions of believers and nonbelievers, I learned through Sunday school lessons and Wednesday "youth group" meetings. I was a child of Christ, and as such had a faith to defend. For example, during a lecture on evolution in my AP high school biology class—at the public school I transferred to—I routinely put this faith into action, much to my instructor's chagrin, stubbornly questioning the validity of Darwin's theories.

It was not until my sophomore year of college, while taking my first anthropology course (oddly enough), that I experienced my own crisis of faith. The world, it seemed to me then while gaining my first glimpse of life through the intellectual lens of social science, was ever more terribly complex (and frightening, provocative, and engrossing) than my Christian upbringing had led me to believe. I felt a growing sense of control as I consumed myself in the study of philosophy, sociology, and anthropology. As I felt my intellect grow, faith, ritual, and myth were rendered as social-cultural-psychologically constructed phenomena ripe for critical analysis and deconstruction, stripped of their mystical wonder and power over my life.

The costs and benefits of my own affinity with their experiences (as I saw it) are apparent to me now only in hindsight. As one of my ex-Mormon friends once told me early in my research, "no one can understand what we're going through unless they've been there themselves." The possibility (and potential foreclosure) of intersubjective dialogue and discovery perhaps hinged on, in a pragmatic sense, my ability to say with all honesty, "I've been there too." Attempting to bridge this experiential and existential divide is what anthropology—and, it turns out, apostasy—is made of. Communication across religious or cultural boundaries requires reference to common experience, something the ex-Mormons I worked with found themselves frustrated with as they left the church and tried in vain to explain their experience to their faithful friends and family. "I've been where you are, but you haven't been where I am," one ex-Mormon man told his brother, who was attempting to show him the error of his ways. My having at one point "been where he was" perhaps allowed me to converse with him, paying closer attention to his words and his experiences, in a way otherwise not possible.

My empathy for ex-Mormons' plight, however, had its limits. I often found myself frustrated at their seeming inability to "let go" of the church, annoyed at what seemed to me at the time as their continued willingness to be a victim at the hands of the church. Sitting in ex-Mormon support group meetings that lagged on for three or more hours while members shared their experiences of religious disbelief and personal disarray, I often grew anxious, my leg shaking with foreboding as story after heart-wrenching story was told with nothing seemingly achieved. Couldn't they "buck up" and just get over it? I sometimes thought to myself.

In part, I think, I was discouraged by and reacting to my (assumed) inability to enter into the discussion and provide whatever guidance or support I thought might help their situation. In these meetings, I mostly stayed quiet, intently listening. I felt torn by contrasting desires to, on the one hand, attempt to heal them (or myself?) through whatever therapeutic form of engagement I could offer. And on the other hand, I felt the need to maintain a stoic, clinical distance in order to better apprehend and analyze. Yet my anxiety in these situations (which inevitably bled into all sorts of other engagements) I think reveals the extent to which I was channeling my own experiences of religious disillusionment and repressed anger. Research with spiritually and emotionally traumatized ex-Mormons became an ongoing visceral reminder of my past Christian life, the mnemonic violence they posed for me emerging from (or amplified by) my inability to "fix" them through a critical/therapeutic engagement with their personal situations.

I make these confessions not only in an attempt at self-reflexive disclosure but in acknowledgment that my memories of these experiences shaped my approach to and interpretation of apostasy and ex-Mormonism. This book (like all others), and the ethnography from which it stems, thus in some ways contains as much of me as it does them. In the end, whatever insights and interpretations I have been able to achieve are because of (or in spite of) these contradictory experiences of intimacy and estrangement I experienced with my ex-Mormon friends.

Caveats and Broader Significance

This study focuses on a culturally and historically specific iteration of religious apostasy taking place in Utah as I saw it unfold between 2008 and 2014. Several caveats are thus in order as to what sorts of broader generalizations can be made from its findings.

First, it is not representative of all former church members' experiences in all places or at all times. The people I discuss here do not represent a statistical majority of those who leave the church worldwide. While disparities between church membership numbers and survey data suggest that tens of thousands of people disengage from the church each year, recent studies argue that this is largely reflective of huge baptism rates in places like Latin America, which are then followed by a near 75 percent drop-off rate among such "new members" in the initial three years of church membership (Bryant et al. 2014). Indeed, gathering accurate data on the actual numbers of "apostates" from Mormonism is nearly impossible. While the LDS Church publicly touts its global membership figures, it does not publicize the number of people who are leaving its fold. Similarly, due to the bureaucratic nature of church membership, in which members are "officially" added to or taken off "church roles," they would not necessarily accurately reflect how many people are actually "leaving the church" even if such figures were made available, since otherwise nonbelieving people may still be counted as "members" if they have not officially requested their name to be removed from these lists. Likewise, making inferences from survey-based statistical data in Utah on religious topics is inherently tricky. As Pam Perlich, a senior research economist at the University of Utah who specializes in Utah demographics, has argued, asking Utahns the Gallup question "What is your religious preference?" may result in ambiguous results that do not accurately reflect people's actual religious stances. "People may or may not be actively going to church, but still they would be very connected to the Mormon culture region through their neighborhoods or through their families" (Rosenlof 2014). Similarly, because the issue of apostasy is so negatively charged in Mormonism, survey respondents may give socially acceptable answers to questions about their faith in order to avoid suspicion and stigma, thereby skewing the results. Ethnographically informed, on-the-ground descriptions of this issue are therefore much needed.

Second, in addition to its statistical unrepresentativeness, my study likewise does not reflect the full range of ways in which people may become distanced from Mormonism. For example, I do not account for those who become what is colloquially referred to as "Jack Mormons," people who, while holding a nominal belief and affiliation with the church, are unable or unwilling to maintain the high standard of living and time commitments required by church membership and therefore do not attend church regularly or follow Mormonism's proscriptions against drinking tea, coffee, or alcohol. Similarly, while chapter 3 describes the traumatic existential crisis that can accompany a sudden loss of faith, not everyone experiences this degree of psychological turmoil. The vast majority of people I worked with in Utah were lifelong church members with large, equally faithful extended families, thus their emotional and psychological experiences of disaffection likely differ from former members who either converted to the church later in life or are living in other parts of the country where church membership presumably takes on a different tone and flavor.

Third, while in chapter 2 I return to a theme introduced at the beginning of the book in my description of Taylor—doubt and subsequent loss of faith as a result of uncovering troubling aspects of church history—this is not descriptive of everyone's journey out of Mormonism. Although presumably not representative of all the ways in which someone might lose his or her faith, my focus on this issue in chapter 2 is in response to the pervasive narrative of epistemological doubt and disbelief that was shared, to varying degrees, by all the people I spoke with in Utah. It is also reflective of a prominent upsurge of discussion and debate concerning Mormonism's sacred history among the church leadership and laity over the past several decades. As I discuss in detail further on, this includes a litany of calculated revisions made to church doctrine, scripture, and educational material regarding historical matters; an unprecedented campaign of strategic mea culpas and explanatory essays from church leaders on "controversial topics in church history"; multiple high-profile books by prominent Mormon authors on how to maintain faith in the face of doubt; the proliferation of unrestricted access to uncensored information on the internet and the church's attempt to mitigate this threat; and the emergence of an increasingly visible and vocal ex-Mormon community in Utah and on the internet coalescing around these very issues. This constellation of events and issues does not, in fact, account for every Mormon apostate's disaffection from the church, but it is nevertheless one of the central defining characteristics of modern Mormonism in need of careful study.

Fourth, in several chapters, I discuss the activities of a vocal group of avowed ex-Mormons; however, not everyone who leaves the church or who I discuss in the text is as outspoken as these groups or would even consider him- or herself an ex-Mormon. I therefore discuss the ambiguity, ambivalence, conflict over, and strategic use of this term of self-identification in detail in chapter 6. For now, let me say that while the term *apostate* may, in much of the academic literature, refer to a clearly defined categorical identity of voiced opposition to one's former faith, the semantic heterogeneity of the term inevitably leads to epistemological ambiguity and should thus be handled cautiously by anyone attempting to make categorical or definitional claims about who or what an apostate is (Bromley 1998; Cragun and Hammer 2011). For example, the LDS Church officially states, "When individuals or groups of people turn away from the principles of the gospel, they are in a state of apostasy," prompting questions about the discursive politics of labelling so-called apostates, while the Oxford Dictionary defines apostasy simply as an "abandonment" or "renunciation" of one's religious beliefs. In light of this conceptual heterogeneity, the problem then becomes one of deciding which of the various attributes—apostasy as a decisive act, a categorical identity, a religious positionality, or a state of being—to adopt when discussing this particular phenomena unfolding within Mormonism. However, in this book, I do not plan to achieve any sort of conceptual clarity on this issue. Instead, I take the ambiguity of the term as a starting point to discuss the areas of overlap and intersection among the binary oppositions of member and nonmember and believer and nonbeliever implicit in each of these definitions.

In this book, I am thus guided not by a desire for categorical specificity or definitional accuracy, as seen in much of the sociological and Mormon studies literature on apostasy and deconversion (see Bromley 1998) but by questions of how people living "apostasy" inhabit these zones of spiritual, ideological, cultural, and social liminality (Biehl 2005). This therefore leads to different sets of questions and different modes of epistemological and analytical engagement. In the pages that follow, I ask questions not geared toward simply refining the conceptual models undergirding theories of deconversion and secularization or creating a comprehensive theory of apostasy or disenchantment. Rather, I ask questions that get at the experiential dimensions of *living apostasy*: What might it mean to have a mind intellectually opposed to one's former faith but live with a body that somatically "remembers" ostensibly rejected religious beliefs, practices, and morals? And what is it like to reject the idea of God yet continue to live a life deeply embedded in one's former religious community? My methods are therefore not oriented toward representative sampling, administering structured surveys, or determining the statistical significance of my findings. Achieving some sense of clarity or understanding on the questions I ask instead requires being attentive to the lived realities of people's on-the-ground experiences and recognizing that any knowledge produced through such engagements is inherently partial and open to further interpretation.

Lastly, much of the sociological literature on religious disaffiliation is concerned with treating apostates' stories of disaffection as narrative structures to be objectively deconstructed in order to parse out an internal discursive logic (Payne 2013) or explicitly questioned to determine their "credibility" (Carter 1998; Johnson 1998)—often to be ultimately dismissed, as in one author's description, as self-serving attempts to salvage a "spoiled identity" (Mauss 1998). Other attempts to analyze the rehearsal of apostate narratives on internet message boards as discursive community-building rituals (Avance 2013) are more productive, yet they likewise fail to attend to how stories of disaffiliation emerge from and circulate within people's on-the-ground attempts to negotiate their changing relationships with the church. In contrast, as a cultural anthropologist with a theoretical bent toward poststructuralism, I attend to my interlocutors' narratives in order to understand how the people who tell them make meaning out of their own lived experiences—how they emerge from, critically reflect on, and at times speak back to the sociocultural context in which they were produced—not in terms of how "reliable" they are as objective descriptions of reality.

While this book is a study of apostasy and religious disaffection as it manifests and unfolds in a particular time and place, this phenomenon is nevertheless reflective of more widespread transformations unfolding on the national and global religious landscape. With the advent of increasingly widespread and affordable information technology, an interconnected global citizenry, and science-based knowledge, religious beliefs in every corner of the globe face similar challenges. The historical and social drivers of religious disaffection that I identify in chapters 1 and 2—conflicts in historical narratives, the influence of technology as a carrier of challenging ideas and information, and the increasing interpenetration of contrasting religious and secular ideologies—are indeed transforming a host of other faiths from Southern Baptists and Catholics to small spiritualist movements and Islamic communities (Baker and Smith 2015; Cottee 2012; Sherkat 2014; Zuckerman, Galen, and Pasquale 2016).

Similarly, my descriptions of the consequences of disaffection—dealing with psychological trauma and existential duress, negotiating social stigmas and ostracization, and attempting to identify and inhabit a new secular form of social personhood—while manifesting in unique ways within Mormon culture, are not isolated to this one faith tradition (Manning 2015; Zuckerman 2011). The specific struggles that people from diverse faith traditions actually face, and how they attempt to negotiate them, will largely be shaped by their particular cultural contexts and are therefore ripe for further anthropological investigation.

Chapter Overview

I approach apostasy over the course of these seven chapters as a constellation of experiences, orientations, transformations, and negotiations, following a narrative arc similar to that of Taylor's story described above and moving through the various transition points of faith, doubt, disillusionment, disenchantment, deconversion, stigma, and emergent "ex-Mormon" identity.

Chapter 1 situates the phenomenon of Mormon apostasy in a historical and cultural context. I frame modern Mormonism's issue of apostasy in terms of the church's historical attempts to selectively remember and strategically forget key pieces of its past, leading to what I refer to as a crisis of memory for contemporary Mormonism. This includes not only institutional attempts at internal censorship but, as I discuss in chapter 2, also the emergence of a "mode of faith" that attempts to stay on the "surface" of church history and defend itself from doubt. I examine people's disillusionment as resulting from a historical convergence of Mormonism's attempts to mitigate the threat of its past with the contemporary church's growing self-consciousness as it seeks entry into the mainstream American religious landscape, in which the parameters and foundation of faith have become the object of internal and external scrutiny. Once faithful Mormons begin "digging too deep" into their church's past, leading to a collapse of faith as a self-image developed throughout a lifetime of church membership is undermined by exposure to incongruent pieces of the church's past.

Chapter 3 explores the phenomenological and existential dimensions of religious disenchantment from the perspective of the people who endure it. I draw heavily on the perspectives of a single person who I befriended during the early "stages" of his disenchantment to frame disenchantment as an experience erupting at the intersection of culture and personal biography. My interest is in showing how disenchantment entails certain forms of traumatic loss that are compelled by people's movement out of Mormonism's all-encompassing religious lifeworld. These losses, I argue, complicate theories of secularization that approach changes in religiosity as driven by people's attempts to maximize personal benefit through (de)conversion. More broadly, this chapter addresses the possibilities and problems of recovery by drawing attention to religious disenchantment as an increasingly pervasive, though largely unrecognized, form of social suffering.

Chapter 4 examines the embodied subject as a site of religious deconversion and transformation. Here, I contend with studies of deconversion that focus solely on aspects of belief or identity in order to argue that religious deconversion must be understood as a jointly corporeal and psychosomatic transformation of mind and body. I first conceptualize the body—its affects, sensations, and orientations—as containing residual reminders of a former religious subjectivity that linger even after belief is gone. Then I discuss how embodied experiences of sexuality offer the possibility for a critical reconception of religious self and subjectivity. Finally, I examine how the ideology of atheism serves not only as an intellectual positionality contra religion but also as an instrument of self-inoculation against predispositions to "feel the spirit."

Chapter 5 examines the stigmas and stereotypes surrounding apostasy and apostates in Mormonism. Specifically, I discuss the social and political context of apostasy, focusing on how, through the circulation of rumors, gossip, and explanations about why apostates leave the church, Mormons create and police internal divisions within the church. I examine how the stigmas attached to apostates function as a projective fantasy through which church members expiate tensions and frustrations circulating within contemporary Mormonism. I then discuss how these stigmas create a condition of social alienation and marginality for people leaving the church. I argue that church members occlude apostates from everyday life in order to maintain these projective fantasies and as a defense against the existential threat they pose to the community of faithful.

Chapter 6 explores several ways ex-Mormons attempt to negotiate the stigmas and social marginalization discussed in the previous chapter by examining the micropolitics of self-labeling, a "mass-resignation" march, and a series of "I'm an ex-Mormon" testimonial videos circulated on YouTube. I situate these events within the context of the Mormon Moment and relate ex-Mormons' efforts to achieve visibility and acknowledgement to the LDS Church's own attempt to enter into the mainstream American religious landscape.

Chapter 7 explores the complex dynamics of nonbelieving subjectivities. I compare two case studies—a "middle-way Mormon" and an "angry ex-Mormon"—to discuss how religion is variously identified and disidentified with in the wake of religious disenchantment. I juxtapose how middle-way Mormons attempt to "make it work" by maintaining an intimate engagement with the church, thus blurring the boundary between member and nonmember, with the way angry ex-Mormons come to personify and perform anger as a way of creating and policing boundaries between them and their former faith.

I conclude by pointing to some of the most recent attempts made by the LDS Church to stem the tide of disaffection. I also offer some critiques of Mormonism's current strategy of "pastoral apologetics" by pointing to key dimensions of apostates' experiences that the church must begin to recognize if relationships of mutual recognition and respect are to be restored between it and its erstwhile members.

This book will ultimately do little to remedy the pain and suffering endured by the people who have left, or will leave, the LDS Church under such spiritual and emotional duress. What I hope this work can provide, however, is an addendum to the narratives circulating in Mormonism about who its apostates are and why they are disaffected. Similarly, on a broader level, I hope that this book forces the issue of disenchantment and apostasy, and the effect it has on the people who are living it in their everyday lives, to the forefront of academic and popular discussion about religion, resurrecting the subject from the forgotten recesses of our collective consciousness that all too frequently nostalgically glorifies religious belief and belonging as a quaint refutation of what is unfortunately seen as the alienating and disintegrating effects of secular modernity.

CHAPTER 1

Ambivalent Pasts

SACRED HISTORY AND THE CRISIS OF MEMORY

My duty as a member of the Council of the Twelve is to protect what is most unique about the LDS church, namely the authority of priesthood, testimony regarding the restoration of the gospel, and the divine mission of the Savior. Everything may be sacrificed in order to maintain the integrity of those essential facts.

—Apostle Dallin Oaks (quoted in Anderson 1999, xliii)

Suppose your youth receive their impressions of church history from "pictures and stories" and build their faith up on these alleged miracles [and] shall someday come face to face with the fact that their belief rests on falsehoods, what then will be the result? Will they not say that since these things are myth and our Church has permitted them to be perpetuated . . . might not the other fundamentals to the actual story of the Church, the things in which it had its origin, might they not all be lies and nothing but lies?

—Elder B. H. Roberts, Mormon historian (quoted in Madsen 1980, 363)

There is a statue of Brigham Young, the famed LDS president who took the reins of the church after Joseph Smith died, standing on the campus of Brigham Young University (BYU) in Provo, Utah. Erected in 1961 to celebrate the school's legendary founder, the seven-and-a-half-foot-tall bronze figure depicts Young standing resolutely, his cane in hand and thrust out before him, a knee-length frock coat hanging cape-like from his broad shoulders. An identical statue stands at This Is the Place Heritage Park, a popular tourist site east of Salt Lake City, where in 1847, Young famously proclaimed that the Saints had arrived at their latter-day promised land. In church history, Young indeed rivals Joseph Smith's import second to none. While Joseph Smith charismatically nourished his followers with ecstatic visions and revelations, the whole of Mormon scripture and theology shaped by his creativity and exuberance, Brigham Young was a masterful manager of people and resources who etched out a place for the Saints in the west through dogged determination and ingenuity. Where Smith built the religion, Young built the church.

Figure 1.1. Statue of Brigham Young on Brigham Young University campus, photo by author

I first encountered that statue when Ryan, a BYU student majoring in computer engineering, offered to give me a tour of campus. Like a lot of men at the university, Ryan was several years older than the average upper-level undergraduate thanks to serving a two-year proselytizing mission. Unlike most of his peers at BYU, however, Ryan had not had a testimony of the church for many months and now considered himself an atheist. In fact, it had been through a "secret" BYU atheist club that furtively gathered once a week at a nearby café that we first met.[1] Making inroads into the ex-Mormon community had been challenging, so I was rather thankful for his friendship and offer to show me around.

We met one afternoon at "the quad" next to the library for my tour. Surrounded by hundreds of young, jaunty students bustling to and from class, I eagerly followed Ryan's lead down the crowded campus sidewalk. We began to chat about life as an atheist at BYU, the struggle to keep his disbelief a secret, and plans for life after school. He said he was primarily looking forward to not having to "fake it" anymore, to finally be open about his problems with the church. Then Ryan turned and asked if I had ever seen a picture of Brigham Young. Yes, I replied. "Good. Get out your phone and pull up a picture of him," he instructed. "I have something to show you."

Unlike most portrayals of Young I was able to find, in which he sported rather luxuriant facial hair throughout much of his life, the statue depicted a beardless and clean-shaven man. Pointing to the crux of Young's neck, Ryan commented, "Some people say you can see a scar from where they 'shaved' his beard off when the school outlawed facial hair." BYU's "honor code" has notoriously strict personal conduct and grooming standards for students, Ryan explained. Although he doubted the rumors about shaving, Ryan said he nevertheless wanted to show me Young's beardless chin as an introduction of sorts to the kind of devious representation of history that disturbs ex-Mormons: "Why not just make him how he really looked? Did they think if students saw a statue of Brigham Young with a beard they'd all suddenly start rebelling? It's that kind of stuff that gets to me. Just be honest." Leading me down another sidewalk, Ryan pondered the larger effects that these types of revisions were having on other people like him and his ex-Mormon friends. "You wonder if the church ever regrets getting itself into this mess."

In contrast to the rumors, I came to find out that the statue was indeed originally cast with Young sans beard, as he appeared in his youth. However, this was a deliberate decision, reflecting what increasingly appeared to me as an entrenched neurotic tendency in Mormonism to strategically represent only those aspects of the past amenable to its present principles, values, and desired self-image.

The course of history had, I found out, demanded that Young be presented beardless at the university bearing his name. Following trends in the larger American culture, where facial hair was waning in popularity, the church made an abrupt change from the late nineteenth century, when it required missionaries to grow beards as a sign of maturity and wisdom, to a point where facial hair of any kind was discouraged. Apostle Dallin H. Oaks, then BYU president, explicitly signaled this shift in a campus speech given in 1971, where he argued for the need to make a break with Mormonism's historical grooming standards. "Our rules against beards and long hair are contemporary and pragmatic," Oaks told the student body. "They are responsive to conditions and attitudes in our own society at this particular point in time . . . [and] are subject to change . . . In the minds of most people at this time, the beard and long hair are associated with protest, revolution and rebellion against authority" (Oaks 1971).

Oaks's equating of rebellion and beards is significant. At midcentury, when the statue was cast, Mormonism was attempting to shed its image of pastoral prairie dwellers and become nominally "mainstream." This meant facial hair—symbolically representing "hippie"-inspired expressions of nonconformity and Mormonism's laboriously disavowed polygamous roots at a time when the church was attempting to make inroads into mainstream conservative American culture—had to be literally and figuratively removed. So, ironically, while Mormonism had begun as a radical religious movement, countercultural in its own right, it had increasingly sought to present itself as the clean-faced champion of righteous morality throughout the last half century. As a result, every church president since David O. McKay in 1951 has gone beardless. And in 1961, the church's flagship university, BYU, erected a statue of Brigham Young conservatively—and conspicuously—clean-shaven. From then onward, hairless, smooth faces became the compulsory, idealized image toward which future generations of Mormon youth would collectively aspire.

Collective Memories

The next two chapters are about this peculiar relationship Mormonism has with its past, its effect on church members' faith, and how it has shaped Mormonism's contemporary crisis of apostasy. This chapter in particular focuses on the first part of this conundrum—that is, how an ambivalent attitude toward the past has provoked collective anxieties in Mormon culture that are precariously managed through the strategic revision of core mythohistorical narratives.

Central to this argument is the basic, though easily overlooked, fact that the idea of "history" as the conceptual bridge between the temporal universe of the past and the present stands in for and functions as a sometimes formal, yet always utilitarian, form of collective memory (Assmann and Livingstone 2005; Halbwachs 1992). There are two dimensions to this that inform my discussion of church history. On the one hand, through a group's collective memory, the past shapes and even gives life to the present. Erecting public memorials, like the Brigham Young statue, creates what we can think of as atemporal relationships, "analogous linkages" between past and present that sustain communal integrity and identity (Gregory and Lewis 1988). However, all kinds of collective acts of remembering—whether through the circulation of oral narratives, inscriptions in text, or visual representations—revitalize the people, events, ideas, and principles found in the group's collective history. On the other hand, the past does not always fulfill the needs of the present. What's found there may be antithetical to the collective's contemporary identity and may need to be reconstructed to fit modern needs, concerns, and interests. In collective memory, there is always therefore a bit of deception and fabrication at work, as the past is continuously "corrected" to better fit contemporary conditions.

As we will see, while church history is the virtual lifeblood of contemporary Mormonism, the reinscription, recirculation, and representation of historical memory are also treacherous when the past is found to be at odds with the needs of the present. In such cases, strategic "corrections" and acts of "institutional forgetting" have been called for over the past half century. But there is something more to this issue of collective memory. Inasmuch as memories of the past are carried within individuals, they bestow on group members a sense of self and personhood—to share common memories is essentially to *be* part of the group. And more importantly here, to have different memories is to be a stranger. As I discuss further below in the context of Mormonism's historical development and interactions with American culture, both a lack and excess of memory have come to constitute existential threats to individual church members'—and the entire church community's—sense of self and identity.

Crisis of Memory, Identity, and Self

I met Ryan at the café again several weeks later. He told me he had recently "come out" to his parents as a nonbeliever. It was the hardest conversation they had ever had: "My mother cried." He said that he desperately tried to explain why he was leaving, why after twenty-five years as a faithful member, he could no longer believe its teachings. "But she wouldn't listen," he said. "The only thing she could tell me was that I had *forgotten who I am*."

That Ryan's mother should accuse him of forgetting, of having had a lapse of memory that was somehow tied to his failed identity as a Mormon, intrigued me. It increasingly seemed, over the course of my conversations with ex-Mormons, that the church's own contemporary identity depended on its ability to selectively remember, and strategically forget, the past. Ex-Mormons' loss of faith was indeed explainable in terms of the failures of memory, but not the kind Ryan's mother accused him of.

Like Ryan, most of the former church members I spoke to in Utah had been "living the gospel" their whole lives. They were born, and had planned to die, as Mormons. However, in the course of participating in church activities and developing their "testimony" of the church's "truth," they discovered things that eventually drove them to disbelief. That is what their friends and family did not understand, they said. As one ex-Mormon woman told me, "Everyone says that if your testimony was ever actually real or as strong as it was supposed to be, you never would have lost it. But that's not right. We were doing everything we were taught, as much if not more than anybody else . . . *It's really the best of us who leave*."

Within Mormonism, and most of the academic literature, apostasy is framed in terms of an individual who has lost something vital and distinctive, largely due to a personal decision. Losing faith, or "deconversion," is attributed to an individual's inability to fit into the religious group—being "offended" by a social slight, having a shift in personal priorities, being drawn away by the enticements of "the world," or never really having had a deep faith in the church's teachings to begin with (Bromley 1998; Carter 1998; Mauss 1998). Yet ex-Mormons were saying something very different. Their faith was true and solid. But then it went away.

This assertion that, contrary to popular stereotypes, it is "the best of us who leave" is therefore telling. While a faithful testimony is ostensibly built on members' study and pondering of stories regarding Joseph Smith's visionary encounter with God, his discovery and subsequent translation of golden plates into the Book of Mormon, and the contents of scripture itself, ex-Mormons frequently told me that having "dug too deep" into that fabled past paradoxically inverted its faith-promoting potential for them. They claimed that "researching the church," beyond what was depicted in church lesson materials and from the pulpit, unintentionally uncovered pieces of Mormonism's sacred history that undermined the sanitized narratives they had been taught. They encountered something they did not recognize, something that was never supposed to be seen.

Theirs was then not a problem of forgetting, as Ryan's mother intimated, or having a *lack* of memory about who they were as members of the church. Rather, as I began to understand after hearing dozens of similar stories of religious disillusionment spurred by encounters with Mormonism's repressed history, ex-Mormons were afflicted with an *excess* of historical memory, having discovered pieces of the past that refused to fit within the intentionally altered or distorted narratives they had once relied on as a foundation for their faith in the church.

Over the course of my research, I came to see that the very existence of contemporary Mormonism was predicated on maintaining this elision and that a complex and fraught relationship among memory, faith, and history was broiling beneath Mormonism's contemporary crisis of apostasy. In particular, in the following two chapters, I contend that apostasy in Mormonism should be understood in light of, and as a reflection of, historical and cultural shifts in the internal dynamics of the Mormon faith.

Part of the story of contemporary Mormon faith and apostasy is about the paradox of living in a church in which belief seems ever more precarious and doubt pervasive while the ghosts of Mormonism's past are increasingly resurrected in the present. Yet this is not a story of ex-Mormons' lack or loss of faith. "That pisses me off when people say that about us," an ex-Mormon friend of mine once asserted. "People think that somehow I lost my faith. But I didn't. It lost me." Intentionality is not what it seems. His faith "betrayed" him, he said. The church—its history, teachings, and leaders—betrayed him. So this story is also about faith losing you—how intimacy, knowledge, and understanding invert and subvert themselves, imploding under their own weight. Rather than discussing apostasy in terms of the movement of people and the beliefs they hold *away* from faith, I focus on apostasy in terms of a religious disenchantment effected in a movement *through* faith, resulting from an overabundance of intimacy *with* faith—in this case, one founded on, and undermined by, a particular narrative of the church's past. This movement has created what I term a *crisis of historical memory*.

The historical backdrop of these transformations is, as briefly discussed in the introduction and further developed in this chapter, Mormonism's ambivalent relationship with and fumbling attempt to render innocuous the vexing aspects of its past while it seeks a place on the contemporary U.S. religious landscape as a thoroughly modern, mainstream church. The example of Brigham Young's beard presciently illustrates this issue. But the complexity runs much deeper.

Historian Jan Shipps once aptly characterized Mormonism as, unlike other modern religions, "a faith cast in the form of history" (1987, 165). Mormonism is in fact a religion predicated on, and articulated through the narration of, distinctive historical events such as Joseph Smith's "First Vision" and the historicity of the Book of Mormon as an ancient document describing the pre-Columbian history of North America. Yet Mormonism no longer envisions itself as the beard-wearing, hand-cart pulling isolationists of the nineteenth and early twentieth centuries. Mormons now strive to foster an image of thoroughly modern, business-savvy proselytizers who preach the gospel with cleanly shaved faces while dressed in suit and tie, harnessing the power of the internet to reach ever more investigators of God's one true church. At the center of this transformation, therefore, is a conflicted sense of self and identity, one that seeks to be simultaneously modern and historic. This is manifested most evidently in the church's attempt to draw on the power of collective memory to distinguish and unify an ever-growing collective church body while also disavowing and disassociating from those aspects of the past that threaten to fragment its nascent modern self-image.

As I see it, Mormonism's mythohistorical past—both temporal and celestial—tells a story of its forced disconnect from, and determined attempt to return to, a lost charmed existence. But at the center of this story is an ambivalent struggle between remembering and forgetting. As I discuss in the following section, memory at times brings people closer to their roots and at other times threatens to uproot the meaning of the past altogether. But we should begin where Mormonism itself begins: the cosmological story of premortal existence and the plan of salvation that members believe they must follow in order to return to that existence.[2]

Restoring the Real

> *[The purpose of mortal life for the children of God is to provide the experiences needed] to progress toward perfection and ultimately realize their divine destiny as heirs of eternal life.*
>
> —"The Family: A Proclamation to the World" (Hinkley 2010)

Figure 1.2. Illustration depicting "Our Premortal Life" in the *Doctrines of the Gospel Student Manual* (2000)

In Mormon theology, the plan of salvation (a.k.a. the plan of happiness) is the foundation on which all else, material and spiritual, stands (Church Educational System 2000b, 13–15). It is nominally a cosmic story about Mormons' struggle to live a godly mortal life, follow the church's teachings, and achieve eternal exaltation in the celestial kingdom. Yet told this way, the story is deceptively teleological—unfolding as a steady progression with an ultimate end. If we focus instead on the relationship between its structural components, it reveals something quite different.

The plan of salvation begins in the premortal existence, a Mormon doctrine that builds on biblical reference to a relationship of divine maternal/paternal intimacy in the cosmic womb. "Before I formed thee in the belly I knew thee; and before thou camest forth out of the womb I sanctified thee" (Jer. 1:5; see Church Educational System 2000b, 13–15). Specifically, prior to mortal birth, Mormons believe individuals existed in a "premortal life," as inchoate "intelligences" in an ephemeral state out of time and place, seamlessly joined with celestial parents. Each of the intelligences were then given a spiritual body and became "the spirit child[ren] of God the Eternal Father and his beloved companion, the Mother in Heaven" (Hinckley 1949, 140), living with them "in a perfectly arranged society" and enveloped in a blissful world suited just for them (Smith 1984).

However, Heavenly Father wanted something different for his children. "Finding he was in the midst of spirits and glory, because he was more intelligent, [God] saw proper to institute laws whereby the rest [of the intelligences] could have a privilege to advance like himself" (Smith 2007). This plan included sending his spirit children to earth to obtain bodies of flesh and bone. There, he planned, they would "learn by experience through earthly vicissitudes" yet have no memory of their life with him and would therefore have the "agency to fail or succeed" (Church Educational System 2000b, 13–15). They must, if they wanted to return, successfully fulfill all required covenants and ordinances and obey the celestial order of existence, the sacrosanct law he imposed as their Heavenly Father.

However, Mormons believe that throughout mortal life, memories of the premortal existence come back to us. "By the power of the Spirit, in the redemption of Christ, through obedience, we often catch a spark from the awakened memories of the immortal soul, which lights up our whole being as with the glory of our former home" (Church Education System 2001).[3] Teachings of the prophet, lessons from scripture, or personal revelation all provide further glimpses into this forgotten world.

Ideally, the plan of salvation culminates in eternal exaltation. There is a triumphant return to the celestial kingdom, where Mormon families—past and present, temporal and celestial—will be rejoined to live together "for time and eternity." At this point, "all things shall be restored" (Alma 40:23), including "our premortal memories" (Maxwell 1994). But this is not a concluding narrative climax as much as a rebounding return to our lost forgotten origins. The plan of salvation therefore does not end simply in realizing one's salvation and exaltation but rather in the *restoration*, realized through memory, of a temporarily lost familial unity, a cosmic reclamation of a forgotten former existence.

Untoward Returns and the Uncanny Lack

When I first learned about the plan of salvation, I was struck by its vast cosmological scope. It was a story of humanity's origins in a timeless preexistence and its struggle to return again to an eternal existence in the celestial kingdom.

Yet for all its grandness, it was also a story, humble at heart, about restoring a lost intimate relationship with heavenly parentage and the toils of forgetting and remembering what that life was like. I soon realized, however, that apostates' relationship to—or rather, *departure from*—the plan of salvation and their stories of having discovered untoward pieces of Mormonism's past were intimately related.

This cultural dynamic, in all its complex interplay among the workings of memory, longing for family, and unexpected return of disturbing pieces of the past, reminded me of the concept of the uncanny lack. Specifically, in Lacanian theory, the uncanny is a disturbing experience that arises when there is an untoward return, repetition, and *excess* of what was supposed to be kept hidden and repressed in the process of subject formation—or, as I am drawing a connection to here, Mormonism's grand narrative of the plan of salvation.

According to Lacan (2006), in early infancy, the child experiences a comfortable synchronicity with the world, in which divisions between self and other do not exist. They are suffused in what he calls the "Real," an undifferentiated state "without fissure," largely mediated via the child's nurturing relationship with the mother. However, in order to be engaged in the affairs of the broader social world, a critical division had to be made internally between self and other.

During what Lacan refers to as the "mirror stage," these divisions first take form. The child is granted an awareness of its physical, though at times uncontrollable, body and its inherent visibility to others. Yet it also realizes the way in which its inner life of thought and experience is distinct from, and sometimes at odds with, its external image, requiring increasingly sophisticated manipulations of its bodily shape and movement.

Lacanian theory suggests there is a "phallic intrusion" of a new "symbolic order." Here, the (symbolic) father, by demanding language and order, makes a "cut in the real," a division between the child and its previous womb-like existence. As a result, the child realizes that survival in this world now requires adhering to the father's "Word." Lacan speaks of the "name of the Father" as being henceforth identified with "the figure of the law."

I see clear parallels between the story of the plan of salvation and Lacan's conception of subject formation: the womb-like preexistence, the introduction of and identification with Heavenly Father's laws, and the social/spiritual development realized through an autonomous corporeal existence. However, what of memory, the past, and its uncanny returns?

Although cut off from the Real, memories of that sublimely transcendent existence—an experience incapable of being fully described or imagined—are not entirely jettisoned. Rather, as the subject conforms to the demands of living within its new social order, Lacan suggests that the memories are repressed and transfigured, surviving as a latent fantasy that the experience of fulfillment will be restored in the future. However, untimely returns of the real are occasionally glimpsed in the form of an uncannily distorted memory, vision, or experience. Yet because the subject has adapted to and grown comfortable with its new existence and effectively forgotten that past, the very otherworldliness of the Real—in defying description or imagination—is therefore experienced not as a blessing but as a disorienting trauma.

In a similar fashion, following the plan of salvation is not without challenges. At times, memory becomes excessive and obstructive and challenges faith in this narrative of eternal return. Brief glimpses into the preexistence, "spark[ed] from the awakened memories of the immortal soul," can be enlightening but also traumatic. Mormons say that there are things unwittingly discovered when looking at church history that, although disturbing and doubt-provoking, have an eternal truth to them that has just "not yet been revealed." That is, these discoveries are part of the plan of salvation, but they just don't know yet how they fit in. Such problems can take multiple forms: Why were certain facets of doctrine, though once sacrosanct in the church, later denied or altered? Why were practices or behaviors, though seemingly immoral, sanctioned by some church leaders? How do inconsistencies and mistakes in scripture, although incriminating, reflect a complex yet logical higher order? Although reminiscent of a lost celestial existence, "further light and knowledge" is needed in order to have a "correct" knowledge of these things' significance. This too, Mormons hope, will be provided when their memory is fully restored upon Christ's return. Until such time, however, lest anxiety, doubt, and confusion run amuck, destroying one's faith and undermining progress on the plan of salvation, it is necessary to just forget.

Anxiety of the uncanny is not produced by lack of knowledge or incertitude, Lacan argues, but a loss of the lack that made the social subject possible—a filling-in of information incongruent with present needs. Mladen Dolar (1991) states, "It is the anxiety of gaining something too much, of a too-close presence of the object. What one loses with anxiety is precisely the loss—the loss that made it possible to deal with a coherent reality . . . the lack lacks, and this brings about the uncanny" (13).

Although on one level describing child development, Lacan's conception of the uncanny lack typifies broader dimensions of societal subject formation that inform my understanding of Mormon history and, more specifically, the church's contemporary crisis of apostasy. However, it is not an individual's experience of social development or losing faith that I am concerned with here. Rather, I am interested in how apostasy stems from the workings of cultural patterns. The story of the plan of salvation can therefore be said to resonate on a broader mythohistorical level, crystallizing in succinct narrative form the plot points and central tensions underlying the entire story of church history. It is, to borrow a phrase from Clifford Geertz (1973), the story that Mormons tell themselves about themselves—in this case, a story about the longing to restore a lost mode of existence, the sense of internal fragmentation, the need to control and contain an unwieldly body, and the ambivalence of too much or too little memory when dealing with a sacred past. In effect, as the central grand narrative around which Mormonism revolves, it provides a window into how Mormonism reflects on its own spiritual/psychic development, desires, and vulnerabilities.

However, the conception of the uncanny lack provides more than just a neat metaphor of the pathological forms of remembering entailed in Mormonism's plan of salvation. This story informs all of Mormonism's historical development and shapes how Mormons think about memory, the past, the future, and what is needed to get there. But as with all stories, this one does not simply reflect what is or what has been. Imbued with sacred significance, it is generative of the very reality it describes. It provides the blueprint for exaltation. Restoring memory of a premortal charmed existence takes priority over all else. And as we will see ahead, it has created conditions in Mormonism for everything else, even "true" memories that have inconveniently returned, to be sacrificed in service of maintaining a "correct" memory of the past.

In the rest of this chapter, I thereby attempt to trace Mormonism's historical development by focusing on its response to the many temporal dislocations it has faced in modern life. To do this, I describe the ways in which Mormons have developed from being a people *of* history to a people *with* history to a people with a history viewed as *indispensable* and *dangerous*, capable of both giving eternal life and taking it away.

A People of History

Mormonism initially emerged out of a tumultuous period of religious revival sweeping the country during the first few decades of the nineteenth century, in what is referred to as American Christianity's Second Great Awakening.[4] For the most part, it was a vibrantly emotional and enthusiastic reformation movement that reflected a popular backlash against the skeptical rationalism and deism of the Enlightenment, with Baptists, Methodists, and new denominations such as the Seventh-Day Adventist Church pushing American Christianity away from the more formal, tradition-bound habits of other Europeanized denominations. The early Mormon "Saints" (as they often referred to themselves) shared some characteristics with these other groups, including the practice of speaking in tongues and having spiritual visions. Similarly, each denomination saw itself, in different ways, as enacting a "restoration of the gospel" and returning Christianity to a purer form that God "originally" intended before humankind, as the Mormons claimed, "corrupted the principles of the gospel and made unauthorized changes in Church organization" during the millennia-long Great Apostasy (Church Education System 2018). This moment was, in essence, defined by its attempt to reinstate, and thereby effectively return to, a past unadulterated existence from which humanity had been tragically long alienated.

However, the Saints were unique compared to the other relatively unstructured and egalitarian denominations. In their attempt at restoring Christianity, they directly harkened back to an ancient divine order. That is, to bring about this return to a sacred past, Mormons believed they had to reinstitute an eternal, though hitherto lost, divine law set forth by Heavenly Father. The early Mormons in fact believed themselves to be inheritors of Old Testament mandates to build the kingdom of God on earth and establish a new Zion to prepare for Christ's return. They believed that they could achieve this by consecrating patriarchs and prophets, who would receive revelation directly from God on behalf of "the elect" and restore the "keys of the priesthood" (Smith 1972).

Even more critical to bringing about this return to the eternal, the Saints believed that they had to construct temples for conducting the sacred rites and ordinances that Heavenly Father demanded. The most important of these was the endowment, a ritual in which church members received instruction, through a series of lectures and scripted reenactments, about their eternal journeys from premortal existence through eternity: how the world was first created, what happened in the Garden of Eden and after Adam and Eve were cast out into the "Telestial world," and how righteous individuals could progress to the celestial kingdom by entering into "covenants of obedience with God" and adhering to "Terrestrial" laws. During the ceremony, members learned the spiritual names that they went by in the preexistence and the various "key words" and "signs and tokens" that they would need to repeat after death to gain reentry into the celestial kingdom. Finally, at the end of the endowment ceremony, symbolically culminating their return to an eternal celestial existence, members were granted access to an ornately decorated "celestial room"—a stylized replica of the celestial kingdom—where they were allowed to sit quietly to pray and ponder their eternal life (Church Education System 1975).

Although the temple ordinances only gave church members a taste of what lay in store in the celestial kingdom, early Mormons came to realize that more worldly divisions among past, present, and future were thinner than initially believed. Through revelation, Joseph Smith revealed that Mormons were latter-day "chosen people"—analogous to the ancient Israelites—living alongside Indian tribes who, as Joseph Smith taught, were in fact remnants of a lost tribe of Israel. Similarly, the Book of Mormon itself, as a written record of these ancient peoples and their encounters with Christ, effectively served for church members as a mnemonic connection to and prophetic guide for recreating this fabled past.

As "prophet, seer, and revelator," Smith indeed experienced frequent visions and regularly spoke to God. He would then publically announce to his followers in sermons, newly revealed scriptures, letters, and journals what God had told him and in this way keep them rhetorically immersed in his divine presence. During this early period, Mormonism was indeed theologically inventive and spiritually charismatic. Most of Smith's revelations, no matter how initially strange they seemed, were successfully adopted as "corrections" to contemporary Christianity's most basic tenets, including the nature of heaven and God and the purpose of human existence.[5] Important for my discussion here, these revelations not only reflect the creative exuberance of the early church but elaborate even further on Mormonism's central theme of eternal return to a lost mythohistorical past.

First, heaven was conceived of as containing three distinct "degrees of glory," differentiated by their relative proximity to God, which individuals and indeed entire families could achieve in the afterlife. At the uppermost was the celestial kingdom where God lived. And at the bottom was the telestial kingdom, reserved for humanity's miscreants, "liars, and sorcerers, and adulterers, and whoremongers" (Doctrine and Covenants 76:103), and any others who refused to accept Christ's teachings. Finally, infinitely removed from the kingdoms was a place called Outer Darkness, set aside for those who commit the "unpardonable sin" of "blasphemy against the Holy Ghost"—that is, who knowingly "sin against the Holy Ghost by denying its influence after having received it" (Turner 1992). There, so-called sons of perdition (i.e., apostates) would be severed from God, Jesus, and all humanity (including friends and family) who inhabited the other three kingdoms (Doctrine and Covenants 76:36).

Smith's corrections on the nature of God were equally revolutionary and explicitly thought about in familial terms. Diverging from dominant Christian notions of God as a nebulous spiritual being, Mormons believed that Heavenly Father had once lived as an actual man of flesh and blood with a wife (Heavenly Mother) and family. Because Smith had obeyed Heavenly Father's divine law, he had been granted godhood and now lived somewhere in the heavens on a star or planet named Kolob (Gee, Hamblin, and Peterson 2006). While dwelling in the celestial kingdom, Heavenly Father and Mother were believed to have created spirit children, who would one day, according to the plan of salvation, be given physical bodies and populate the earth. They too had the potential to one day be exalted and populate their own planetary realms. Smith taught, however, that it was only through celestial marriage (polygamy) that they could be exalted to godhood alongside their Heavenly Father and Heavenly Mother. (It is important to note here that Mormons believed it was only by mimetically identifying with the rules and roles set by their heavenly parentage that they could ever truly return home.)

For early church members, temporal existence deeply intersected with the eternal. In both daily life and ritual practice, they were intimately immersed within a timeless existence where the sacred was palpable, new religious truths were continuously being revealed, and spiritual experience was consistently spontaneous, mystifying, and profound. However, this was not to last. Mormonism's "peculiar" beliefs provoked the suspicions of the wider American populace, which was increasingly leery of the insular community and its strange beliefs and "unchristian" marriage practices.

The nascent church never gave up on its hopes of achieving a return to that "timeless existence," relocating several times over the course of just a few decades—from New York to Ohio, Illinois, and Missouri—each time attempting to create a new home. However, each of these sites, largely located within areas densely populated by Christians, failed to provide respite, as intolerance toward Mormonism continued to bedraggle the church community. Their latter-day Zion of unencumbered oneness with the divine seemed ever over the horizon. This persecution eventually culminated in 1844, when Joseph Smith was assassinated by a violent mob while being held in a Carthage, Illinois, jail on charges of ordering the destruction of a newspaper facility that had been publishing material critical of the church. Surrounded and persecuted, the Saints decided to make a final desperate exodus to the location that Smith had prophesied would be their ultimate latter-day Zion in the Great Salt Lake Valley. Led by the stalwart Brigham Young, whose firm presence strengthened the church's resolve during the arduous trek, they were eventually able, upon reaching Utah, to quickly set about settling their newfound land of bounty, transforming it into a place where they could continue to practice their religion unfettered and eagerly await Christ's imminent return in isolation and peace.

Indeed, throughout the mid-1800s, Mormonism's temporal horizons were still consistently defined by its anticipation of an impending messianic return, an event that early church leaders preached would, thanks to their restoration of the gospel and divine law, happen before that "very generation" passed away. To a large extent, this drove the Saints to successfully establish a theocratic mode of self-governance in their territory, which they referred to as the State of Deseret (derived from the word *honeybee* in the Book of Mormon), and produce a bustling agricultural economy and sizeable militia. Yet mounting external political and economic pressures soon encroached. The driving of the "golden spike" in 1869, just sixty-six miles north of Salt Lake City at Promontory Summit, completed the First Transcontinental Railroad and effectively opened Utah to increasing waves of non-Mormons.[6] Meanwhile, the larger American society began to decry Utah's political "theodemocracy"—in which ecclesiastic leaders were routinely elected to political office—and its peculiar doctrine of plural marriage, a practice roundly condemned by the newly formed Republican Party as one of the "twin relics of barbarism" alongside slavery.

Faced with a U.S. government weary of the Saints' military, economic, and political domination of the intermountain West, an American populace intolerant of the practice of polygamy (to such an extent that prominent Mormon polygamists were often forced into hiding); and the possibility of prolonged legal entanglements over the practice of polygamy with the federal government, the church was eventually compelled to conform to the demands of the "gentiles." Realizing that the survival of the church was at stake, president Wilford Woodruff issued the historic 1890 manifesto, which revoked support for plural marriage in the United States and called for Mormons to abide by the laws of the land in which they resided. Reflecting on his decision, a distressed Woodruff would write in his diary, "I have arrived at the point in the history of my life as the president of the Church . . . where I am under the necessity of acting for the temporal salvation of the Church" (Woodruff 1983). Six years later, Utah became the forty-fifth state in the union with a secular constitution and government, and Mormonism developed a religious morality increasingly aligned with Christian conservatism and unapologetically devoted to monogamy and the nuclear family. Its existence forever afterward inextricably entangled with the wider American culture.

Hopes of restoring a seamless connection to and immersion in a sublimely transcendent, messianic way of life had largely collapsed. Mormonism had effectively capitulated to the perceptions, preferences, and demands of outsiders. While an idealized ancient past depicted in the Book of Mormon had once directed their religious labors toward Christ's impending return, Mormonism's temporal horizons progressively narrowed over the twentieth century. Its religious mission would be steadily reduced to a focus on personal exaltation rather than apocalyptic preparation, its sectarian eccentricities tempered into a pursuit of American society's acceptance. As a result, Joseph Smith's discovery of the Book of Mormon, the restoration of the gospel, the religious persecution, the westward exodus, and the settlement of Utah slowly metamorphosed from lived realities into storied mythos, historical reference points in Mormonism's emergent collective memory.

This collective memory of the past became increasingly important in the twentieth century as Mormonism sought to maintain a distinct identity separate from Christians and American culture, provoking Mormonism to intentionally transform, preserve, and perform its past in new ways. Yet in doing so, it found that the past, while giving life to the present, also at times endangered it when the details of that past contradicted contemporary needs and wants.

A People with History

Mormonism has long instinctively sought to document its past. Early church members kept informal personal diaries and records, consisting of both mundane happenings and spiritual experiences, which they dutifully passed down from generation to generation. Folk tunes and hymns were written to commemorate key events, such as Joseph Smith's martyrdom and the Saints' persecution in the East. Official records of church happenings were also kept. In particular, the seven-volume *History of the Church* describes Joseph Smith's autobiographical account of the church's founding. Often cited in church periodicals and sermons, segments of that history have since been canonized as scripture.

Church history early on became a formal course of study in Sunday school classes. With it, church history became distinctively more stylized and depicted in increasingly dramatic form throughout the twentieth century. For example, beginning in the 1930s, elaborate outdoor "pageants" were routinely performed, dramatizing key events—including stories found in the Book of Mormon and episodes from the church's early founding years—replete with ornate set designs, costumes, and musical numbers. In more contemporary Mormonism, images of the church's past have proliferated in a torrent of historical simulacra, including collectible toy figurines, comic books, decorative posters, board games, dress-up costumes, interactive computer simulations, animated cartoons, docudrama films, historical reenactments, monuments, and open-air living history museums.

Throughout the twentieth century, Mormonism's history indeed seemed to have escaped its temporal restraints and been reborn in multitudinous fashion in the present, marking a shift in Mormonism's collective conscious and relationship with the past, which historian Pierre Nora (1996) suggests resembles the dramatized and routinized forms of memory that become prevalent in the modern age. "Memory is constantly on our lips because it no longer exists," he writes. "Precisely because the past has no hold on to the present the compulsion to commemorate is everywhere." Summarizing Nora's argument regarding the shift from a premodern to a modern form of memory and echoing the history of Mormonism sketched out so far, cultural historian Bill Schwarz (2010, 51) writes:

> The operations of memory in the premodern epoch register, for Nora, as what he calls "real" memory: intimate and "spontaneous," imbricated in lived experience such that memory itself exists free from mediation. It is, precisely, immediate with experience. It is essentially collective, most commonly based on rural custom. And it allows the past to be "inhabited" in the present. . . . Modern memory, whether in actuality or in its potential, begins the process of turning inside-out the practices of "real" memory. Memory, real memory, dies at the outset of modernity. But in its place emerge new institutions devoted to recovering what has been lost, creating new, ersatz memory-forms—performed rather than lived, mediated rather than unmediated—that replicate, at varying removes, what had once been vital and replete.

Under Joseph Smith's prophetic leadership and even during the first few decades in Utah, Mormon memory operated, in what Nora typifies as the "premodern register," in an intimate, spontaneous, and "real" form. For early Mormons, the sacred past was indeed "imbricated in lived experience." Whether by receiving revelations concerning forgotten memories from the premortal existence, restoration of an ancient pure form of Christianity, or walking among members of a lost tribe of Israel (Indian people), the past was fully "inhabited" in the present, free and unmediated. However, with its acquiescence to American culture, "real" memory died, producing in Mormonism's collective psyche a disturbing sense of "emotional or psychic loss" as it was "ravaged by its disconnection to the past" (Schwarz 2010, 44). Modern life for Mormonism was indeed increasingly defined by what Nora describes as a "sense of loss, of tearing apart, and of permanent separation [from the past]" that eventually *required* the religion to create an imaginative "restorative harmony" that could bolster its contemporary identity (Nora 1996, xvii).

What we see then is the product of the Saints being progressively forced to think of themselves as a people *with* history that they desperately needed to hold onto rather than as a people living out history. The further they integrated into American culture, the risk of wholesale assimilation stoked concerted efforts to maintain Mormonism's distinctive past as a nostalgic form of self-preservation. And so new generations of Mormons were compelled to rediscover, even recreate, who they were as Latter-day Saints by collectively ritualizing a mnemonic return to the past.

New Mormon History

The most concerted effort to shore up contemporary identities through a restoration of the past came in the 1970s when Mormon historian Leonard J. Arrington was appointed as the official church historian (Prince 2016). The first professional historian to serve in this capacity, Arrington sought to professionalize the newly formed church history division by cataloguing and opening its archives to Mormon and non-Mormon scholars for research, which quickly brought about a golden age of historical scholarship dubbed the era of "New Mormon History." Indeed, this unprecedented access to and exploration of previously protected archival material was motivated by what historian Richard Bushman describes as a "quest for identity rather than a quest for authority"[7] in the pages of history. Torn between conflicting needs to integrate and to hold onto a distinctive identity, Mormon historians turned to the past to better remind themselves, and their fellow church members, who they were as Latter-day Saints.

The New Mormon History era produced two general works on church history, *The Story of the Latter-day Saints* (1976) and *The Mormon Experience: A History of the Latter-day Saints* (1979), which largely achieved these aims. In fact, while the first was written for church members, the second was intended for a wider non-Mormon audience, and together, they sought to broker new relationships between Mormons and outsiders—and between Mormons and themselves—through the pages of history.

However, New Mormon History's mode of scholarship significantly diverged from traditional Mormon history writing. For example, its progenitors referenced original source material instead of secondary texts written by church leaders, analyzed the role of individuals' motivations and intentions in shaping historical events rather than attributing them to divine providence, and demonstrated a scholarly objectivity reluctant to shirk away from controversial topics or interpretations. As a result, they began to produce unflinching depictions of historical figures and events that, in their nonpartisan historicity, challenged official versions of history (Quinn 1992) and undermined its ability to function as a form of collective nostalgia. Three works in particular stand out during this era. Fawn Brodie's (1971) critical psychobiography of Joseph Smith, *No Man Knows My History*, presented a portrait of the beloved church founder that described his prophetic teachings not as divinely inspired revelations but as manifestations of a deep psychological conflict. Juanita Brooks's (1950) *The Mountain Meadows Massacre* chronicled the mass slaughter of more than 120 men, women, and children at the hands of Utah Mormon settlers, a topic which had not been discussed up to that point. And Linda King Newell and Valeen Avery's (1984) *Mormon Enigma* scandalously portrayed the sexual politics of plural marriage in the early church with all its trappings of coercion, manipulation, and deceit at the hands of a few nefarious church leaders, including Joseph Smith.

Unsurprisingly, New Mormon History soon fell out of favor with church leadership, who began to worry that the intensive study of church history, rather than strengthening faith, might unintentionally undermine it. Despite Arrington's proclamations of continued faith and claims that history had "nothing in there for us to be ashamed of," church authorities soon began attacking Arrington's professionalism and issued an unofficial gag order against the beleaguered historian (Prince 2016). Then, in 1982, Arrington was quietly removed from his position as church historian, and the history division, which he had founded, was quietly disassembled.

In a letter to his children, Arrington later reflected on these actions and offered a word of caution to future generations of church members: "The attempt to suppress problems and difficulties, the attempt to intimidate people who raise problems or express doubts or seek to reconcile difficult facts, is both ineffective and futile. It leads to suspicion, mistrust, the condescending slanting of data." The more Mormons "deny or appear to deny certain demonstrable 'facts,'" he told them, "the more we must ourselves harbor serious doubts and have something to hide."

Correlating the Past

New Mormon History's "quest for identity" had effectively threatened to dissolve the historical roots of Mormon identity altogether. However, the church could not isolate itself from the past. Its founding figures and events were still inextricably at the center of its cultural imaginary and collective consciousness—robust collective memory of the sacred past was still needed. However, that memory needed to be tamed and focused in order to avoid further untimely engagements with the past.

In a sweeping reorganization of church operations, President David O. McKay formed a host of "correlation" committees tasked with implementing changes to church ordinances, doctrines, organizations, meetings, and materials (Allen and Leonard 1992; Prince and Wright 2005). On an administrative level, correlation sought to centralize the church's organizational structure under priesthood authority, including local ward functions and meetings, which were standardized to follow a three-hour block of meetings on Sunday instead of being spread out throughout the week as was previously the norm.

More importantly, over the course of the twentieth century, church history and doctrine were progressively simplified, standardized, and protected under correlation. Before correlation, local governing bodies each developed their own unique curricula for Sunday school and other educational programs. However, starting in the 1940s, Church Education System employees began to systematically review the content and wording of all lesson materials to ensure that they conformed to official church doctrine. Sunday school lessons increasingly told truncated stories of early members' devotion to the prophet, religious experimentation, and spiritual piety, exclusively focusing on Mormonism's distinctive historical accomplishments and religious truths. And in order to discourage questions that would detract from the official narratives, "correlated" materials assiduously avoided mentioning details and distractions such as incongruities in scripture and more unseemly aspects of church history—including early conflicts, debates, and controversies (Duffy 2005). Lesson manuals further admonished Sunday school teachers to refrain from incorporating materials or texts from outside sources, stating that teachers should avoid "substitute[ing] outside materials, however interesting they may be" (Perkey 2011). In general, teaching gospel principles and righteous living were prioritized over scriptural exegesis and moral and spiritual instruction over obligations to historical accuracy.

To further ensure that the entire church body adhered to these guidelines, church leaders emphasized the importance of reading only "correct" interpretations of religious teachings as a means to sustain personal happiness and church-wide harmony. To support these efforts, the church printed new materials clarifying what the hierarchy considered to be official doctrine and history and subjected existing materials to intense scrutiny and revision. Official church history records, church leaders' transcribed speeches, published pieces of key figures' personal diaries and correspondence, former iterations of educational materials, official revelations, and scripture itself were all systematically reviewed, revised, and/or suppressed. Inconsistent, conflicting, or unorthodox information was amended or deleted from subsequent printings. In the end, the true meaning of scripture—and correct version of church history—was restricted to what appeared in church-published lesson manuals and other approved texts. In matters of faith, memory, and history, conformity of knowledge took precedence over depth of understanding.

In this way, the church's past progressively functioned as a form of what Jan Shipps refers to as "sacred history"—aesthetically expanded yet narratively flattened. Shipps (1981, 57) states:

> Sacred history . . . is stripped down—in artistic terms, stylized—so that the story is told in blacks and whites, with no grays. The persecuted and persecutors, the people of God and the people of Satan, good and evil are locked in mortal combat in which compromise is out of the question. All the ambiguity and complexity of human existence is shorn away. Moreover, the context is left ambiguous enough to keep the narrative from being either time bound or culture bound; it functions as scripture. . . . By its very nature it can only be retold and defended; not reinvestigated, researched.

Importantly, what I want to point to here is the way in which the correlation program and the creation of an institutionally defended "sacred history" reveals a deep sense of vulnerability in Mormonism, an uncomfortable awareness of the potential power and threat of the past to fragment the church body in the present. So while church history was looked to as a way to mend growing feelings of alienation and fragmentation, a powerful source of inspiration and cohesive energy for the church body, especially as it sought to contain the centrifugal forces of rapid growth and expansion, it also increasingly became a liability, its very sacredness giving it an uncanny power that threatened to fragment and divide.

Uncanny Histories

> *Church history can be so very interesting and so inspiring as to be a very powerful tool indeed for building faith. If not properly written or properly taught, it may be a faith destroyer.*
>
> —Apostle Boyd Packer (1981)

> *Indeed, in some instances, the merciful companion to truth is silence. Some truths are best left unsaid.*
>
> —Apostle Russel M. Nelson (1986)

Reflecting the church's growing concern about its past, Apostle Boyd Packer penned an essay in 1981 titled "The Mantle Is Far, Far Greater Than the Intellect." In a dogmatic censure of church historical writing, Packer admonished scholars to "see the hand of the Lord in every hour and every moment of the Church from its beginning till now" (Church Education System 2003, 646–649). His words are worth quoting at length for the way in which they illustrate the intertwining themes of the benefits and hazards of collective memory regarding the church's sacred past:

> Church history can be so very interesting and so inspiring as to be a very powerful tool indeed for building faith. If not properly written or properly taught, it may be a faith destroyer. . . . There is a temptation for the writer or the teacher of Church history to want to tell everything, whether it is worthy or faith promoting or not. Some things that are true are not very useful.
>
> Teaching some things that are true, prematurely or at the wrong time, can invite sorrow and heartbreak instead of the joy intended to accompany learning . . . the scriptures teach emphatically that we must give milk before meat.
>
> In the Church we are not neutral. We are one-sided. There is a war going on, and we are engaged in it. It is the war between good and evil, and we are belligerents defending the good. We are therefore obliged to give preference to and protect all that is represented in the gospel of Jesus Christ, and we have made covenants to do it.
>
> Those of you who are employed by the Church have a special responsibility to build faith, not to destroy it. If you do not do that, but in fact accommodate the enemy, who is the destroyer of faith, you become in that sense a traitor to the cause you have made covenants to protect. Those who have carefully purged their work of any religious faith in the name of academic freedom or so-called honesty ought not to be accommodated in their researches or to be paid by the Church to do it.

Elder Packer's words presciently reflected a growing nervousness in the church over the increasingly antagonistic relationship between the past and faith aroused in the "New Mormon History" era, an ethos of historical insecurity that would eventually lead to the notorious 1993 "September Six" excommunications and purging of six Mormon scholars who published scholarly work criticizing the church (Ostling 1999; Toscano 2007). But there are also a few things to notice in Packer's words that speak to my earlier discussion of the plan of salvation, subject development, and the emergence of uncanny lack. Importantly, here we see that Packer is speaking to faithful church historians, not to unbelieving outsiders, regarding the effects of their work on the church membership. Historians, with their ability to delve into the past and, through their writings, reinvigorate it in the future, register for Packer as possessing an inherently sacred, though fraught, responsibility. He thus compels them to remember that they "have made covenants to protect," explicitly referring to the oaths they took while learning about the plan of salvation in the temple endowment ceremony. The vital significance of the plan of salvation to all Mormonism is again recalled. Maintaining its integrity through selective forgetting is an unquestionable priority. "We are belligerents defending the good," Packer asserts.

As Packer's words reflect, history in Mormonism was viewed as safe and correct only inasmuch as it served to increase faith. And as the prime progenitor of faith, history had to be protected from potential misrepresentations that detracted from this spiritual goal. As one of Packer's contemporaries argued, "No true Latter-day Saint will ever take a stand that is in opposition to what the Lord has revealed to those who direct the affairs of his earthly kingdom. No Latter-day Saint who is true and faithful in all things will ever pursue a course, or espouse a cause, or publish an article or book that weakens or destroys faith" (McConkie 1984). Such phrasings thus reflected a growing apprehension in the church that its own history now constituted a tool or even a weapon that in the wrong hands could be used against them. The struggle over faith, authority, and identity was quite literally being waged over what was, or was not, appearing on the pages of history.[8]

What we see here is the way in which Mormonism's desire to learn about and figuratively "return to the past" invoked spiritual anxiety through its ability to force the return of long-repressed historical memories. Mormonism had indeed become irritably self-conscious of its past and acutely aware of the inherent ambivalence in remembering it. Indeed, Packer's warnings are directed at an internal threat—that is, church history itself, including its scriptures, teachings, and historical events. But the past for Packer is not inherently evil, however, and this is revealing. Church authorities are not concerned that the historical events or issues being remembered are somehow false, fabricated, or untrue. He does not deny either their existence or their significance—just the timing and conditions under which they make their return. "Teaching some things that are true, prematurely or at the wrong time, can invite sorrow and heartbreak instead of the joy intended to accompany learning." Memories of the premortal existence and church history are here depicted as treasured windows into the sacred but are also, at times, disturbing and pathological. Specifically, it is not the past's existence that Packer brands as dangerous but its potential capacity for destruction when recalled through the workings of untampered collective memory. Remembering too much, even of the sacred, is to "accommodate the enemy" and be complicit in the destruction of faith.

But rather than the grumpy misgivings of a particularly sensitive apostle, Packer's words reflect the ambiguous role historical records have played throughout the church's past.

The Lost Pages

In a most ironic twist of fate, the danger to Mormonism posed by its own past began with the very first pen strokes of the Book of Mormon. In 1828, six months into translating the golden plates, Joseph Smith had produced 116 pages of text. His scribe, Martin Harris, had requested to take the manuscript home to his skeptical wife who wanted to read the text and confirm for herself whether this Book of Mormon was authentic sacred scripture. Smith at first hesitated but eventually granted Harris's request. However, several weeks later, Harris returned to Smith dejected, confessing that the entire 116 pages entrusted to him had mysteriously disappeared.

Upon hearing the news, Smith reportedly cried out, "Oh, my God! All is lost! All is lost! What shall I do?" He had heard rumors that Harris's wife had taken the pages in order to force Smith to prove his prophetic abilities by retranslating the pages exactly as they were first written and demonstrate unequivocally that he was not, as suspected, extemporaneously concocting the story as he went.

Smith then reportedly prayed for guidance, recording in the Doctrine and Covenants what the Lord revealed to him. He was directed to not retranslate the lost pages—the Lord had warned him of a sinister plan at work. Evil men, directed by Satan, had stolen the translation and planned to alter the words. They were waiting for Smith to produce another translation so that they could then produce their altered copy and point out the inconsistencies in a nefarious ruse to make Smith look like a fraud. The Lord told Smith, "And, behold, they will publish this, and Satan will harden the hearts of the people to stir them up to anger against you, that they will not believe my words. Thus Satan thinketh to overpower your testimony in this generation, that the work may not come forth in this generation" (Doctrine and Covenants 10:32–33).

However, Smith claimed that the Lord had anticipated their loss two thousand years prior to the mishap and had instructed Nephi, the ancient record keeper and original engraver of the plates, to produce two sets covering the same time period. The first, longer and more historical in nature, contained the material Smith had originally translated. The duplicate, an abridged version of the same material, contained a message "more prophetic and sacred," which Smith was instructed to translate to make up for lost time. Smith did as he was told and for months after continued to write the Book of Mormon. However, the original text Smith wrote, filled with all the historical detail he had been forced to abridge, was never recovered. For years afterward, Smith would worry about its whereabouts and if it might someday return.

It is important to recognize here the extent to which the pages' absence (or spectral presence) made them dangerous. If one were to look at Smith's actions with a skeptical eye, it demonstrates the very first instance in which Mormonism's past was viewed with ambivalence and even fear. Smith's options for dealing with the lost pages were indeed limited. He could not effectively forget the pages existed—call them a loss and move on with his writing—lest he provoke questions from Harris or others about why, as a divinely inspired prophet, he was not able to retranslate the plates supposedly in his possession. And he could not rewrite the material without the original copy, for he worried his memory might falter and he would not be able to duplicate the details exactly, unintentionally producing a document conspicuously incongruent with the first. The pages' potential to return forever threatened the "marvelous work and a wonder" in which he was engaged.

This dynamic is indeed a potent metaphor for Mormonism's relationship to church history in modern times. Traces of the past threaten to return, out of time and place, and disrupt the present. However, relics of the past are also continuously longed for, and in some sense fetishized, as holding the potential to confirm Mormonism's divine origins once and for all. The church consistently finds itself ambiguously drawn to the past's familiarity and faith-promoting potential yet also at times is repelled by its strangeness. Indeed, throughout Mormonism's history, ambiguous relics of the past, literally unearthed from the ground in some cases and metaphorically disinterred from the written record in others, have caused the contemporary church much dismay.

Faithful Forgeries

Through an etymological analysis of the German term (*un*)*heimlich*, Freud (1919) defined the uncanny as something terrifying that is at the same time paradoxically familiar. "We are tempted to conclude that what is 'uncanny' is frightening precisely because it is *not* known and familiar," he cautioned. The term *heimlich* in fact means "native" or "homelike," so it would only make sense that "*unheimlich*" means its opposite—"unhomelike." Yet having traced the German term back to its roots, Freud found that "homelike," with its connotations of familial intimacy and seclusion, also ambiguously referred to notions of *that which should be hidden from others*. He applied this idea to his interpretations of patient narratives, where he demonstrated that the feeling of the uncanny is often produced by the very repetition of a "homelike" experience—a fear that comes from the "involuntary recurrence of the like"—which he linked back to infantile anxieties over parental relationships. In sum, Freud (1919, 12–13) stated, "This uncanny is in reality nothing new or foreign, but something familiar and old-established in the mind that has been estranged only by the process of repression. This reference to the factor of repression enables us, furthermore, to understand . . . the uncanny as something which ought to have been kept concealed but which has nevertheless come to light."

In 1985, uncanny specters of the past brutally exploded in Utah with the so-called Mormon bombings. In a ruthless attempt to draw attention away from investigations into his illegal forging activities, Mark Hoffman, a renowned dealer in historical documents and a disgruntled ex-Mormon, killed a former Mormon bishop and his wife with homemade pipe bombs. The details of the crime are less important here compared to the significance of what happened to the forgeries.[9]

Earlier in the year, Hoffman had sold the couple a controversial document that they later donated to the church, known as the Salamander Letter. It appeared to be a letter written by Harris that—if it were true—contradicted the canonized account of Smith acquiring the golden plates from an angel. Instead, the letter described how a spirit appeared to Smith and "transfigured himself into a white salamander" and indicated that other forms of folk magic were involved in Smith's early religious activities. The church later revealed that it had spent tens of thousands of dollars purchasing other documents from Hoffman, including documents describing Smith's first polygamous relationships. Gordon B. Hinckley, then church president, along with other church leaders, had been enraptured with Hoffman's findings, reportedly regularly meeting with Hoffman over a five year period, pouring over the documents in rapturous, anxious detail.

While all the documents Hoffman sold to the church were forgeries and many of the details were fabricated—including the tales of a talking salamander—it is important to realize here that actual church history inspired their contents. Hoffman knew and understood Mormon history. He had been granted unprecedented access into church archives and thus was able to accurately incorporate overt references to actual historical accounts and events into his forgeries to entice church leaders' interest and concern. He knew the historical facts that had been suppressed and therefore knew what church leaders would find most inspiring *and* unnerving. The history contained in the forgeries was, to the church leaders and Mormon historians who reviewed them over the years, tantalizingly familiar.

Although the church was eventually forced to release the documents to investigators, while they were in the church's possession, it never publicized their existence, and more importantly, it never destroyed them, even long after they were revealed to be forgeries. Instead, it secreted the forgeries away into what is called the "First Presidency's Vault" for safekeeping. But why?

The vault, a heavily fortified section of the church's archives located in the side of a mountain near where the granite blocks used to build the Salt Lake Temple were quarried is used as a repository for sacred artifacts from church history, reportedly containing hordes of historical records, financial statements, membership lists, and genealogical records. Because of the sensitive (sacred) nature of its contents, the vault is closed to the public, only accessible to select church employees and high-ranking general authorities. It is estimated to be, next to Fort Knox, one of the most safe, secluded, and secreted repositories in the United States—it is, for all intents and purposes, a monumentally-sized keepsake box, a place for the church to store treasured mementos of its sacred past.

The decision to stow such important documents in the vault is not surprising. But keeping them secretly sequestered under a mountain, despite church leaders' belief in their authenticity, reveals the extent to which such historical records provided a paradoxically sacred/salacious connection to the past that Mormonism has long been at pains to repress. Indeed, these hidden relics of the past represent, for Mormonism, the epitome of Mormonism's fraught connection to its mythohistorical origins—to a magical, mysterious time when people practiced celestial marriage and miraculous talking salamanders did not seem out of place. The true motivations of the church leaders at the time are unknown.

But the decision to secret away the documents, rather than destroy them, reveals the way in which sacred history within Mormonism reflects the inklings of a collective yearning for a return to that past, however farfetched it may seem through our contemporary eyes. Yet, burying the documents under a mountain of earth indicated that the past, no matter how sacred, also stood to endlessly haunt the "normalcy" of the present. That which was most sacred was also that which was most dangerous. The decision to keep the documents safely hidden in an underground vault reflects an ambivalent acknowledgement, at least among church leadership, that such history, however true, must be repressed, lest the collective self be exposed to the dangers of its uncanny return.

Indeed, amid the church's rise to popular ascendancy in the eighties and nineties, publicizing the existence, much less authenticity, of the salamander letters could easily have undermined Mormonism's long-awaited entrée to the wider American religious landscape and provoked difficult questions from church members asking why the documents contradicted official church doctrine. And for a time, such documents were safely secreted away into the recesses of mountain vaults and forgotten history. However, as the next chapter discusses, the digital age has made attempts to control information (i.e. collective memory) through such metaphorical burials exponentially more difficult.

CHAPTER 2

"Digging Too Deep"

THE PARADOX OF FAITH

Knowledge does away with darkness, suspense and doubt; for these cannot exist where knowledge is . . . no man can be saved in ignorance.

—Joseph Smith (Church of Jesus Christ 2011, 261–270)

Every true faith is infallible. It performs what the believing person hopes to find in it. But it does not offer the least support for the establishing of an objective truth. Here the ways of men divide. If you want to achieve peace of mind and happiness, have faith. If you want to be a disciple of truth, then search.

—Friedrich Nietzsche

It must needs be, that there is an opposition in all things.

—2 Nephi 2:11

The idea of "depth" is deceptively idiosyncratic. It can denote topographical metaphors of extent, expanse, proximity, and downward distance, as in "deep in the mind" or "deep in the past." Relational metaphors of affinity, intimacy, or rapport can also be conveyed, as in people who share a "deep history" or "deep intimacy." There can also be a certain, though semantically incongruous, degree of high-minded insight, intelligence, wisdom, or discernment, as in "deep thinker" or "deep study." In the Mormon cultural context, these definitions overlap. Throughout the church, one hears references to members who exhibit (or are encouraged to develop) a *deep faith*, evidenced by an elevated sense of reverence, knowledge, or understanding of church teachings. In Mormonism, the confused definitions are indeed fitting. It is primarily through an intimate, sustained immersion in a sacred past and by plumbing the depths of church history and scriptures that one gains the knowledge of the religious truths necessary to achieve the lofty heights of eternal exaltation.

For the ex-Mormons I spoke with, however, faithful study did not result in spiritual enlightenment. Deep faith had initially led them to deep study. Yet I came to see that their faith had effectively undermined itself. While delving into supposed "faith-promoting" scriptures and history, looking for inspiration and answers to questions, they devastatingly found that they "dug too deep." In a sardonic turn of phrase I often heard repeated, ex-Mormons would tell me, "I studied my way out of the church."

In this chapter, I build on the previous discussion of Mormonism's anxious form of collective memory. The LDS Church has historically connected with and strategically repressed aspects of its sacred past that were once fundamental to but became increasingly at odds with its modern self-image. This, we saw, led to the creation of and faith-driven identification with a highly standardized, protected, and sanitized mythohistorical narrative of its sacred past. In what follows, I discuss the consequences of that historical development by looking at how unmitigated access to church-related information—enabled by the internet and provoked by the so-called Mormon Moment—has created and subsequently strained a uniquely modern "shallow" mode of Mormon faith.

I will present several common trajectories, or case studies, of religious disillusionment to illustrate the paradox of faith that is "digging too deep." Though the outcome is the same for each case—a collapse of faith—the paths people take out of the church differ. Each person was motivated for different reasons to research and ask questions, to no longer accept church history at face value, and to dig even deeper. In this way, each case illustrates different "issues" that ex-Mormons commonly say "flipped the switch" for them: an unexpected discovery about the church struck a discordant note with each person's particular mode of faith and ultimately caused the "shelf" in his or her mind to come crashing down.

Betrayed by Faith

Ex-Mormons' disenchantment from Mormonism is often described in terms of an excess of depth and intimacy, which involves a transformation that cannot be described simply as a *loss of faith*. Rather, I think disenchantment is better understood through the language of seeing, experiencing, and interacting with once taken-for-granted truths—ensconced in religious rhetoric, sacred symbols, and historical narratives—in a fundamentally different way. Digging too deep and studying the way out of the church entail a transformation of the dominant modes of signification on which faith in Mormonism is built.

In fact, a common refrain among many ex-Mormons was that they had been "betrayed" by "hidden" information that the church "lied" about. Indeed, betrayal is a powerful way to think about what people experience in "researching the church," for it points to the way in which Mormonism's own particular modes of faith, and its own sacred histories (and attempts to manage that history), have paradoxically undermined members' testimonies. For decades, church leaders have preached that scripture and church history are inerrant and plainly interpreted. The information and lessons found within, they claim, are conclusive, forthright, factual, and unambiguously moral. Studying scripture and church history unequivocally leads to stronger faith, they say. However, ex-Mormons say they found otherwise.

This argument diverges from much of secularization theory, which suggests that enlightenment values progressively colonized, supplanted, and eventually withered away so-called traditional religious sensibilities in the modern age. In contrast to such approaches, I found that among ex-Mormons, research-induced disaffection was not the product of having subjected the sacred to scientific principles adopted, or thrust upon them, from secular society. They did not, for example, believe in the book of Genesis, take a class on Darwin's theory of evolution, and then decide the biblical story of creation was false.

Claims of betrayal point to something different, something more insidiously intimate and duplicitous in the paradox of modern faith. I am informed by philosopher Charles Taylor (2007), who in *A Secular Age* argues that modern-day disenchantment and secularism emerged from transformations internal to ancient Christianity. That is, contrary to popular thought, secularization was not a result of religion's external conflict with the godless ideologies of natural science but rather originated internally within the fundamental principles and lived experience of western Christian faith, a phenomenon that closely parallels much of the conflict in contemporary Mormonism.

In *A Secular Age*, Taylor points to several changes in Christianity's modes of faith, which led to altered experiences of faith and eventually widespread disenchantment. First, aiming to enliven followers' level of religious commitment, early reform movements sought to render the natural material world into a new field through which properly educated and disciplined believers could see God's divine machinations at work. If God designed the natural world, they reasoned, then his divine stamp could be found there. Whereas God was once found by looking up to the heavens, he was now sought by looking down here to the earth.

Through closer and more refined study, Christians hoped to better understand God's nature and ultimately prove his existence. In this new Christianity, rational epistemologies flourished, and empirical study became an act of piety—believers soon developed systematic techniques to acutely observe and assess the divinely inspired properties and processes of the natural world. However, according to Taylor, these efforts failed to find God. As a result of their newfound ability to map, measure, and predict this world, believers instead gave birth to a new sense of anthropocentric self-sufficiency that ultimately opened the door to godless forms of humanism.

Second, Taylor points to a growing self-consciousness in the Christian faith experience. In contrast to the old world, where belief was "naïvely" totalizing and far-reaching, new world Christianity was, as Taylor describes, uniquely "reflective." This stemmed in part from Christian nations' desire to expand knowledge and spread faith by exploring new lands and peoples. However, these explorations put western Christians into contact with new cultures who practiced forms of "belief"—for example, animism, ancestor worship, paganism, and so on—that were entirely bizarre and wholly unrecognizable as "religion." Christians could no longer presume, Taylor argues, that others shared their most basic assumptions about God, the heavens, or earthly existence. And as a result, they were forced, going forward, to include within their religious imaginary the idea that nonbelief was distinctly possible. This was by all accounts a major shift in perspective for a church that, due to its long-term, overwhelming dominance over a relatively small part of the world, had taken its particular understanding of the divine order of existence wholly for granted as somehow universal or natural. In the end, this shift brought about an increasingly self-conscious dimension to Christianity, as it was forced to see itself in relative terms as but one kind of belief comparable to innumerable others. Christianity was therefore for the first time—that is, if it wanted to communicate with or convert others—obligated to clarify, justify, and illustrate why its beliefs were uniquely "true."

Taylor explains that these developments ultimately gave rise to a "new moral order," which we in the contemporary age now live in. We have ceased to be a "vertical world of mediated access" (Taylor 2007, 209), referring to a world in which society's members were held together by their communal gaze upward toward the unquestionable authority of the divine king. Instead, the death of that "old hierarchical order" has given way to a "horizontal, direct access" society, one defined by "impersonal egalitarian" principles. We now look downward and toward each other for answers to divine questions.

I disagree with Taylor's bleak assessment of this new moral order. But his method of tracing disenchantment back to early Christianity's mode of faith is inspiring for my current topic. In this chapter, I attempt something similar. I argue that Mormon apostasy stems from three core characteristics—or vulnerabilities—in its own contemporary mode of faith: (1) an overestimated confidence in the strength of testimony, (2) an emphasis on rational study and evidentiary logic to confirm religious truths, and (3) an emerging self-consciousness in the face of scrutiny from outsiders. Together, I argue, these characteristics have contributed to a situation in which Mormons' identification with a sacred past is rendered unsustainable.

Strong and "Shallow" Testimonies

When we bear testimony, we declare the absolute truth of the gospel message. In a time when many perceive truth as relative, a declaration of absolute truth is not very popular, nor does it seem politically correct or opportune. Testimonies of things how "they really are" (Jacob 4:13) are bold, true, and vital because they have eternal consequences for mankind. Satan wouldn't mind if we declared the message of our faith and gospel doctrine as negotiable according to circumstances.

Our firm conviction of gospel truth is an anchor in our lives; it is steady and reliable as the North Star.

—Dieter F. Uchtdorf, "The Power of a Personal Testimony," October 2006 LDS General Conference

The formula of faith is to hold on, work on, see it through, and let the distress of earlier hours—real or imagined—fall away in the abundance of the final reward.

—Elder Jeffrey R. Holland, "The Laborers in the Vineyard," April 2012 LDS General Conference

Faith means the will to avoid knowing what is true.

—Friedrich Nietzsche

Figure 2.1. Stripling warriors coloring page, LDS.org, https://www.lds.org/bc/content/shared/content/images/gospel-library/magazine/fr10mar35_dots.jpg

Every year on July 24, the state of Utah observes "Pioneer Day," a state holiday commemorating the faith and fortitude of the Mormon pioneers who entered the Salt Lake Valley on July 24, 1847. Although held only a few weeks after Independence Day, Pioneer Day celebrations easily outshine those of the national holiday. Utah Mormons celebrate en masse with picnics, potlucks, dances, and group walks down sections of the Mormon Trail while pulling handcarts, as well as attending an annual parade. As a sometime resident of Utah, I was accustomed to seeing people dressed in historic pioneer garb at the parade and elsewhere. However, at one parade in particular, I witnessed something quite unfamiliar—several hundred of the church's "young men" had gathered—clad in an assortment of leather skins and plastic-molded "steel armor" and wielding toy swords and shields—to march the streets of town. Standing on the sidewalk, I watched boys from eight to eighteen plod by in scraggly rows. Then every few hundred yards, much to my surprise, they stopped, found their place in line, and began a foot-stomping, sword-waving chant before crying out in rapturous union, "We do not doubt!"

As I later discovered, they were reenacting a legendary story from the Book of Mormon—that of the fabled battalion of "stripling warriors" who served in "Helaman's army" (Alma 53–56). In scripture, two thousand Ammonite young men are said to have risen to fight on behalf of the godly Nephite people against its enemies: "And they entered into a covenant to fight for the liberty of the Nephites, yea, to protect the land unto the laying down of their lives." Though woefully inexperienced, they followed the prophet Helaman, whom they called "Father," into numerous battles. However, despite murderous odds, the warriors always emerged from battle unscathed, for as "they had been taught by their mothers . . . if they did not doubt, God would deliver them" (Alma 53–56).

As the boys continued marching down the street, parade spectators could not help but marvel at the strength of their young testimonies. I heard one group of people confidently predict that the future of the church was stronger than ever with such promising youth in its midst. This was surely faith in action, I initially thought. However, while it was certainly an impressive display, I eventually struggled to share their perspective. I did not know exactly why at the time, but their testimony of undaunted faith seemed too self-assured, too energetic, too belligerent—its violent imagery too combative. It seemed too different, I thought, from the normally meek, soft-spoken testimonies I typically saw Mormons deliver.

As mentioned in my introductory chapter, in the LDS Church one sacrament service every month is set aside as a "fast and testimony" meeting, during which members are invited to speak to the congregation from behind the lectern and "bear their testimony." Typically this entails telling an inspiring story, in a gentle voice, of a particularly faith-affirming experience—for example, how prayer or an instance of "listening to the spirit" benefited the speaker. And the speaker then ends his or her testimony with some version of the statement "I know this church is true."

While the tone and volume of the stripling warriors' chant starkly contrasted with the typically reserved practice of bearing testimony, I began to notice several striking similarities that revealed to me hitherto unrecognized characteristics of Mormonism's particular style of faith. I came to see that the stripling warriors' boisterous confidence and allusion to church history was also a more routine feature of people's testimonies than I at first appreciated. First, the phrase "I know this church is true," rather than just a stylistic flourish, seemed obligatory in people's addresses. Young children practicing their testimony at the lectern would, I noticed, often be accompanied by parents who fed them key phrases to repeat. "I know this church is true" was invariably part of the lesson. On a rhetorical level, I began to see that bearing testimony obligated the speaker to claim a faith that was conspicuously free of doubt, question, or equivocation. Second, I started noticing that people bearing testimony would also add other confidently asserted statements referencing historical events and figures or key pieces of doctrine. For example, "I know Joseph Smith spoke to God," "I know the Book of Mormon is the greatest book ever written," "I know Thomas S. Monson (the current president of the church) is a prophet of God," or "I know that we have the restored gospel." Such declarations, while undoubtedly heartfelt, also seemed to tacitly confirm the speakers' consent to the canonical version of church history as a foundational component of their faith. And third, I began to notice that Mormons also bore testimony at other church functions, when spending time with friends and family, and at community gatherings. Faith, for all intents and purposes, seemed abundant and strong.

But I began to question: Why make such public displays of undaunted faith, explicitly absent of doubt, through an overt identification with church history? Was this simply what having deep faith, or a strong testimony, of the church had always been about? Or was this somehow also reflective of more contemporary tensions between doubt and faith?

My questions were further compounded when I talked to Robert, an ex-Mormon man in his midforties, who I met through one of the ex-Mormon support networks I joined on first arriving in Utah. I immediately gravitated to him, drawn to his at times witty, at times caustic, and always shrewd assessment of Mormon culture. In one of our early conversations, while sipping whiskey together at his home after watching the General Conference on TV, he told me that the average Mormon's faith was "thin" and "fragile." This surprised me. Having listened to "average" Mormons speak about their faith at length during sacrament meetings, while they were doing missionary work, and in interviews, their faith seemed to me quite genuine and deep. However, Robert disagreed: "Oh sure, they believe everything they say. And they're awfully committed to it.

But start asking them questions and poking around a bit, and see what happens. They're comfortable talking about the church and giving their testimony, but only if it's in certain situations where they feel safe and in control. Start asking them about topics they're unfamiliar with or really hard questions, and you'll see, they start to squirm."

I had no reason to doubt Robert. He had lived four decades as a faithful church member, both in Utah and throughout the country, and on all matters—from the religious to the political and mundane—he was introspective and insightful. However, it was only later in my research, when I began to clumsily challenge church members' disparaging stereotypes of ex-Mormons by explaining the many historical and theological issues the apostates had found with the church, that I finally witnessed the "squirming" Robert told me about. My efforts to talk about Joseph Smith as anything but a divinely inspired prophet who single-handedly brought about the "restored gospel" were immediately evaded or rejected. The church members I spoke to would, almost invariably, become agitated and defensive or quickly offer glib, at times dismissive, responses before shifting the topic of conversation. I later told Robert about what I had experienced. He first laughed at my naïve attempts to debate with "TBMs," or True Believing Mormons, as ex-Mormons called them. But however foolish, he said, it was useful to my study—I got a glimpse of how delicate Mormon testimonies really were. But Mormons unconsciously recognize this too, he explained. They talk constantly about the need to nurture and protect their testimonies because they implicitly realize that they are vulnerable. Mormons instinctively conform to and accept unquestioningly what the church teaches, so they never unwittingly stumble into uncharted waters and have their faith unexpectedly challenged. "Everything's okay as long you don't venture out of the shallow end of the pool," he said. Shallow faith was a safe faith. And a safe faith was a strong faith.

I was faced with a paradox, it seemed. Faith could not be simultaneously strong and deep *and* fragile and shallow. On the one hand, I knew the survey data. Mormons, especially in Utah, reportedly boast some of the highest levels of religiosity nationwide. Hearing people bear testimony and chant "We do not doubt" was also quite convincing. Yet on the other hand, I was swayed by my conversations with Robert and my unease with accepting Mormons' frequently repeated declarations of faith at face value.

The answer, I would discover, lay in understanding how faith operated in contemporary Mormonism—as Robert claimed—in the shallow end of the pool. That is, Mormonism created the sensation of total immersion while simultaneously safeguarding itself against sinking. I sought to uncover how faith was constructed and performed—and could indeed at times seem deep and strong—but also how collective efforts to maintain its purity circuitously concealed a pervasive and persistent vulnerability.

Collective Faith

In Mormonism, testimonies are what Emile Durkheim (1995) would call a "social fact," a manifestation of distinctive ways of thinking, feeling, and acting shared by the collective. Yet social facts, like testimonies, are not simply behaviors that each group member engages in. They are reverberations of the group's core ideas, beliefs, and values that are "repeated in individuals."

This, Durkheim suggested, creates the conditions where communal action produces a uniquely transcendent, collective-effervescent experience. In such activities, there is an amplified resonance, such that "even when we have individually and spontaneously shared in the common emotion, the impression we have experienced is utterly different from what we would have felt if we had been alone." As Durkheim ([1895] 2014, 25) described, "An outburst of collective emotion in a gathering does not merely express the sum total of what individual feelings share in common, but is something of a very different order. . . . It is a product of shared existence, of actions and reactions called into play between the consciousnesses of individuals. . . . If all hearts beat in unison, this is not as a consequence of a spontaneous, preestablished harmony; it is because one and the same force is propelling them in the same direction. Each one is borne along by the rest."

There is a "compelling and coercive power" at work that imposes itself in such a way that conformity seems natural. Individuals may then, in a scramble to conform, abandon themselves to their totalitarian logic and manufacture an "illusion," such that they have themselves "produced what has been imposed upon [them] externally." But, Durkheim argued, attempts to resist soon reveal their coercive nature: "If an individual tries to pit himself against one of these collective manifestations, the sentiments that he is rejecting will be turned against him" (1995, 22).

Yet this is not to say that testimonies are insignificant to individual church members. I do not dispute that they seem uniquely authentic and powerful, on spiritual and emotional levels, for many people. Indeed, Durkheim claimed that "the forms that these collective states may assume when they are 'refracted' through individuals are things of a different kind." Their very "dint of repetition" instead points to their existence "independent of . . . individual manifestation[s]," their origins and structuring logic dwelling "outside the consciousness of the individual" (1995, 54–56). The Mormon practice of bearing testimony—in its stylistic patterns, its ubiquity, and its obligatory nature—is thus in many ways a social fact par excellence. In its collective reverberations, we are able to see, beyond its meaning for any particular individual, the fundamental mood and disposition of Mormon faith in its entirety.

Performing Faith

Bearing one's testimony is to publically make a statement of faith, but as with the boisterous cries of the young stripling warriors, it also rhetorically signals that one is absent of doubt. I first discovered the relationship between testimonial strength and spiritual uncertainty in conversation with an ex-Mormon woman named Melanie, for whom the act of bearing testimony was once prescribed as a panacea for doubt. Melanie told me that when she first began questioning the church, she approached her bishop for help. He confessed that he too sometimes had questions, but that, instead of letting them "weigh [her] down," he advised her to bear testimony to others whenever possible. "To my neighbors, to my family, anyone who would listen," Melanie explained. "He didn't want to deal with any of my questions about the church . . . just bear my testimony." Indeed, Mormons believe that creating and maintaining a strong testimony is necessary for weathering any of life's unpredictable conditions. "Our testimonies will keep us happy and safe in troubled times," Allan F. Packer counseled in his address, "Finding Strength in Challenging Times!," at the April 2009 LDS General Conference. But why would bearing one's testimony frequently and widely, a practice ostensibly dependent on an already established faith, be warranted in moments of vulnerability and doubt?

A strong testimony, in Mormonism, is both a reflection of cognitively based inner convictions and a stylized dramatization of learned behaviors. Church members believe that they not only gain knowledge of the church's truth through intellectual study but also develop it through repetitive, embodied practice. As one church apostle advises, "We gain or strengthen a testimony by bearing it . . . testimonies are better gained on the feet bearing them than on the knees praying for them" (Oaks 2008). Bearing testimony indeed becomes an example of instrumentally ritualized faith. As Talal Asad (1993) suggests, rituals are meaningful not only for the "content" communicated through them but for the ways in which the ritual instills particular emotive states and affective predispositions into practitioners as they perform (or even simply observe) the set of actions repeatedly over the course of a lifetime. In this way, ritual allows participants to "make themselves" into the culturally ideal person. Thus giving a testimony and repeating the phrase "I know the church is true" is a culturally patterned, self-disciplined practice through which members attempt to inculcate an emotionally resonant sense of spiritual confidence.

"Knowing the church is true" is therefore in some sense unlike other forms of knowledge based on empirical evidence or rational argumentation. Instead, I found that creating a strong testimony in Mormonism is akin to what Raymond Williams (1978) describes as a "structure of feeling"—a unique state rendered through institutional discipline, in which distinctions between affect and cognition are collapsed and intertwined. In fact, in Mormon parlance, "knowing" can be a product of "feeling." A church member once described to me, "When I read the Book of Mormon, or sing at church, or hear the prophet speak, that's when I feel the spirit and I know the church is true." Church leaders teach this as well. "A testimony is what we know to be true in our minds and in our hearts by the witness of the Holy Ghost. As we profess truth . . . we invite the Holy Ghost to confirm the verity of our words" (Bednar 2009, 19). Taken this way, the act of bearing testimony constitutes a unique form of psychophysical experience—"thought as felt and feeling as thought" (Williams 1978, 132)—provoking acute embodied sensations (a "burning in the bosom," as Mormons say) that supplement and supersede more cerebral or cognitive modes of knowing.

In Mormonism, this is most readily achieved by adopting and correctly performing the appropriate bodily techniques and vocal patterns that indicate one is "moved by the spirit." I once observed a particularly effusive testimony delivered unexpectedly by a coarse-looking middle-aged man. It began awkwardly. His heavy frame rested on fisted hands braced atop the lectern. He stumbled through his opening remarks, telling a meandering and uninspiring story of childhood memories attending church with his family. The increasingly distracted congregation reflected, in their absent stares, his entirely perfunctory performance. Then his voice broke. His droll, plodding oration became stifled and breathy; and he stalled. His hand reached up to wipe away a single tear sliding down his graveled cheek. In solemn, pensive, and whispered phrases, he repeated, again and again, "I know this church is true." People looked up from the pews, their interest rekindled. The next speaker, a middle-aged woman, inspired by the man, told of how, unlike at her non-Mormon in-laws' house, she feels the spirit so powerfully in times like these that she too "beyond all doubt" knew this church was true.

When done correctly, bearing testimony results in audience and speaker "feeling the spirit" and having their faith strengthened. Saying the right words and phrases, in the right environment, confirms that the spoken words are "true" and strengthens conviction: The speaker, regardless of his or her existing level of faith, suitably mimics behaviors that he or she has learned through observation ostensibly provide evidence of a strong testimony; the audience in turn identifies the testimony as authentically spirit-filled, responding with affirmation or gratitude for the speaker's efforts. As a result, everyone involved is left feeling like they witnessed or *are* themselves—despite whatever doubts they may have harbored, like Melanie—a person who actually knows that the church is true. Functioning on a collective level, this pattern in essence creates a communal positive feedback loop of self-propagating spiritual conviction.

Additionally, because Mormons believe that bearing and witnessing testimony invokes such feelings and strengthens faith, they are encouraged to frequently bear their own and ask others to do the same on almost any occasion—during fast and testimony meetings, at sacrament, after Sunday school lessons, or during Family Home Evening—and with anybody—other members, investigators, friends, and so on—explicitly attempting to continually create and recreate an environment conducive to feeling the spirit. After several people have spoken during a fast and testimony meeting, for example, it is not uncommon to hear someone exclaim how effectively this has "brought the spirit among us."

To some extent, this is all powerfully productive. Faith has the appearance of sui generis. But there are latent vulnerabilities here as well. First, while Mormons seek to strengthen faith through ritually provoking strong emotions, this is also potentially a liability. By conflating cognition and emotion, the Mormon epistemology of faith perpetuates an illusion of false equivalency between depth of feeling and depth of knowing—that is, between the presence of a psychosomatic sensation and the presence of empirical evidence. I observed another testimony from a young man who—quite unusually—began by listing, in vague terms, problems with church history that he had recently discovered. "I got sucked into that for a while," he confessed. "But I come here, and I hear you all talk, and I feel so comforted . . . I don't understand everything I've learned about, but I know there's an answer. I look at all of you and know that the prophet [Joseph Smith] was telling the truth. Had he not stuck by his convictions [regarding the First Vision story], none of us would be here."

In learning to feel the spirit when bearing testimony, the average church member is led to believe that he or she actually knows something in some empirically verifiable way. The significance of this dynamic will be more apparent when, as discussed further below, we consider church members' beliefs that Mormon theology, doctrine, and history are founded on and evidenced by a material historical record. Yet suffice it to say, this manufactures a potentially inflated sense of confidence in the basis for one's faith that is easily challenged by sojourns into the uncharted depths of Mormonism.

Second, the belief that one "gains a testimony by bearing it," including dramatically performing certain body and vocal techniques, has created a situation in which a potentially pervasive, delicate mode of faith is obscured by doubt-driven theatrics. The collective practice of reciting testimonies, rather than reflecting widespread piety, could be read as a parade-like spectacle of members who whole-heartedly profess their convictions in an anxious attempt to ritually discipline themselves into conformity despite harboring private misgivings. Ex-Mormons often told me how, in the weeks building up to their final collapse of faith, they desperately bore their testimony with increasing frequency and sincerity in the hopes that it would rekindle their waning beliefs. Since the depth of any individual's testimony is, to some extent, dependent on his or her participation in a system that encourages the continual reproduction of dramatized faith performances, the system as a whole can easily produce an illusion of histrionic stability.

Third, the expectation that members deliberately manufacture collective experiences of "feeling the spirit" potentially creates a spiritual echo chamber. As seen with the woman described above, who spoke of her non-Mormon in-laws' spiritless home, the world outside the "Mormon bubble" registers as hostile to faith. As a result, maintaining a strong private testimony is forever dependent on staying in environments where public testimonies are incessantly rehearsed. Outside these environments, faith is left exposed and fragile.

Maintaining Faith

Creating a strong testimony is one thing, but maintaining it is another. Even testimonies that are ostensibly "strong" are also recognized as susceptible to corruption. Members are taught to be vigilant in order to avoid thoughts, actions, and—most importantly—texts that may threaten their testimonies. Avoidance in this way can be a faith-driven ritual practice as well. One of my ex-Mormon friends told me about a church event her daughter attended, where the young women in her stake gathered together to talk about "avoiding doubt." During the lecture portion, the stake president advised everyone to read only information about the church supplied by church leaders or found in approved publications and on the LDS.org website to avoid "exposing [themselves] to contrary information" and avoid "delving into church history unsupervised." He then read an article, written by an LDS general authority, stating that reading anything that provokes doubt in Joseph Smith would put them at risk of losing the spirit altogether, an unthinkable condition akin to "going mad" (a topic I return to in the next chapter). And in an even more ambiguous instruction, they were told that when they confronted a "troublesome question or concern about the church" to "doubt your doubts" before doubting the church.

This discourse has shaped everyday experiences of faith in the church, resulting in a cultural pattern of anxious avoidance of perceived threats. On one of my initial fieldwork trips, I was briefly employed at a deli in a college town in southern Utah where most of my coworkers and customers were members (or former members) of the church. During a lunch break, I pulled out a book I was reading, Fawn Brodie's *No Man Knows My History*, a large paperback about Joseph Smith with a well-known painting of the prophet's face printed on the front. One of my coworkers, a young woman attending the local university, seeing the text in my hands, slid down next to me on the counter where we both were leaning. "Can I see what you're reading?" she asked enthusiastically—I think hoping to start a conversation about the church. She took the book in her hands, recognizing the painting on the front but not the title of the text. Flipping to the back, she perfunctorily scanned the synopsis and blurbs before growing agitated and, hastily handing it back, asked me where I bought it and if it was "church approved." "Church approved?" I asked. "Yeah," she said. "Or is it one of those 'anti-Mormon' books?" I must have looked baffled; a few minutes later, one of my ex-Mormon coworkers quietly took me aside to explain what had happened. "She didn't recognize the book, so she checked for the church's stamp. She thought it was anti-Mormon, and it scared her." Later, as I began to collect books from local yard sales and thrift shops, I saw that those published by the church as official "educational materials" indeed came with a prominent inscription of the church's logo printed on the back. Similarly, other books given or recommended to me by faithful church members were either distributed by the church-owned Deseret Book publishing company or, if published by any other press, typically contained a conspicuous endorsement from an LDS general authority on the back cover. Each of these markers symbolically testified to readers that the contents of the book would not challenge the stories and narratives that they learned in church and that their faith would, in essence, be "protected." Importantly, these are not markers of the text's sacredness. Rather, they indirectly signal to would-be readers that they can safely wade into the book's depths and expect to emerge unscathed.

There are an array of other coping strategies, what ex-Mormons often refer to as "mental gymnastics," that Mormons rely on to maintain a safe, shallow faith in the face of challenging information. As one ex-Mormon explained, writing a post titled on an online message board:

> Every educated, rational, intelligent, thinking person in the world bends the conclusion to fit the facts, right? If you think the world is flat, but sail off in one direction and wind up back where you started, then you bend your conclusion (the world must actually be round) to fit the facts (since I couldn't have come back here otherwise). Mormonism does the exact opposite: The *facts* are bent to fit the *conclusion*. The conclusion is that the Church is true, and all the facts are bent into the most ludicrous shapes to fit this conclusion. . . . If some contrary evidence shows up which would lead one to believe that the Church isn't true, for example, all types of illogical arguments are postulated to discredit or reinterpret the evidence. (Anonymous 2008)

Throughout the course of my research, I heard several of these arguments used by faithful church members. When presented with information that was irreconcilable with their beliefs, they employed a number of intellectual defenses. "There are some things we weren't meant to understand in this life," they might say, implying that an answer to the problem, while not immediately available, will eventually be revealed in the next life. Explaining something as "not meant to be understood in this life" also suggests that the problematic information, in its very irreconcilability with conventional logic, testifies to a higher-order, supernatural, and divine logic at work. It effectively transforms faith-challenging problems into faith-promoting points of spiritual fascination, as the desire for an immediately satisfying answer is forever deferred to the future when "all will be made clear." In regard to dealing with problematic historical information, problems with the past are safely projected to possible solutions in the future. "That's OK with me," one church member told me. "I don't need to have all the answers right now. It's the devotion to spiritual searching, and pondering, and praying that I enjoy."[1]

Another response was that "God doesn't give us all the answers since he occasionally wants to test our faith," which functions along a similar logic. In the face of challenging information—a test from God, which affirms the belief that he pays attention to and cares about his people—the process of fighting off doubt and maintaining faith is turned into an intimate and gratifying performance of obedience and righteousness to a coy and capricious Heavenly Father who, in the event that church members "pass the test," will dole out his divine countenance on the now "worthy" believer.

Some employ a strategy of self-inoculation or desensitization to troubling issues. When I mentioned to my TBM friends that apostasy was in part driven by people's discovery of problems with church history, they sometimes claimed to have already been aware of the "historical issues." Though they had been briefly drawn into the problems and had done a bit of research of their own, they had ultimately found the issues to be trivial and said they had now safely emerged with their faith wholly intact. Yet when I asked where they had done their research, they inevitably told me about briefly perusing one of several Mormon apologist websites that discuss problematic church history, where they had read an article written by a church leader or historian that had satisfactorily "dealt with the issue." However, much of the Mormon apologist writing, when I read through it, consisted of little more than reactionary obscurantism in response to perceived "attacks" on the church—the evidentiary logic and overall narrative at times incomprehensible. I was later told by an ex-Mormon, "That's how [Mormon apologist websites] work. They overwhelm people with nonsense and make them feel as if 'someone' in the church who is smarter than they are has dealt with the problem. They can then go on with their life and feel more secure in their faith."

Members who do inadvertently come across troubling information or have nagging concerns, however, find themselves with little recourse. Without an outlet for expressing doubt, church members are typically forced to "keep it to themselves," I was told. As a result, they have created a unique cognitive space to hold their doubts. "Everyone in the church has a *shelf in their mind* where they put all their questions," Robert explained when I asked him whether he thought anybody else in his previous ward ever questioned or doubted.

> They may not talk about it, but it's there. It's what everyone does to survive. See, you don't have time or energy, or even the courage, to address all the little problems you come across in the church. Like for me, I never understood how celestial marriage [polygamy] could be a part of God's plan. But see, you can't dwell on stuff like that. So you put it on the shelf and tell yourself that it'll eventually be explained, because right now there's more important things to worry about, like making sure you get all of your family into the celestial kingdom. Everything else comes second to that, so you just ignore it.

The shelf, it seems, holds all the doubts and questions that might otherwise weigh down members' testimonies and disable their ability to maintain faith.

However, this still does not resolve the paradox of Mormon faith: Is it truly strong or shallow and weak? One might argue that what I am referring to here as a shallow mode of faith is in fact a strong faith—it just operates according to a different cultural logic. Perhaps the "shelf in the mind" is an effective coping strategy. Or perhaps most Mormons really are not all that concerned about problems with church history. After all, if what one observes at any given fast and testimony meeting is indicative of the state of the church, so to speak, faith seems strong. And I might be persuaded to agree with that argument, if not for the fact that the ex-Mormons I spoke with claimed to have been *betrayed* by their faith—they had thought it was strong until it wasn't. Testimonies, perhaps, mean just a little bit more.

This brings us back to where we started. While I earlier discussed how the act of bearing testimony creates both the experience and the appearance of strong faith, I think the performative component has another layer. I want to draw attention not to its content but its delivery and stylized, repetitive structure. I sat through numerous fast and testimony meetings while in Utah, during which I heard dozens of testimonies. Over the years, I heard many more in conversation with Mormon friends and missionaries and while viewing televised addresses from church leaders. In doing so, I quickly noticed that there was little variation in what people said or how they said it. Even the vocal patterns and tone of delivery were fairly consistent, with church members speaking in measured, solemn phrases, their narrative periodically and predictably interrupted by an eruption of tears or a choking off of the voice, effectively punctuating the emotional and spiritual gravity of their address. I began to imagine how, for someone sitting in the congregation week after week, these individual statements could begin to merge into a symphony of indistinguishable voices proclaiming, in repetitive chant-like fashion, "I know this church is true" (a.k.a. "We don't doubt!"). Yet amid the collective clamor, I found these declarations of faith interesting for what they did not say, what they refused to say, and what they went out of their way to forcefully, dramatically, and repeatedly draw attention away from by declaring the opposite.

While watching these repeated efforts to publically express unwavering faith, I was reminded of the psychoanalytic concept of repetition. Repetition is no mere reoccurrence, where a repeated instance of a particular event or behavior can simply be the product of habit, tradition, or necessity. In Mormonism, bearing testimony is indeed habitual, traditional, and, if you want to stay in good standing, necessary. Young children are taught how to appropriately deliver such an address as a kind of rite of passage. And adults are asked by church bishops to bear testimony in exchange for being granted access to the temple.

Yet the concept of repetition compels us to see these moments as something different. Bearing testimony indeed struck me less as a set of quaint or even controlling social mores oft repeated and more as a culture-wide neurotic obsession. This seemed to function as a compulsion to say, over and over, in the same predictable way, at every meeting, on every occasion, the very same things. As Calvin Hall (1999) suggests, behaviors falling under the concept of repetition are not distinguished merely by their frequency of occurrence but by their notably exaggerated, compulsive, or inflexible character. However, the compulsion is not one of rote obedience or fastidious adherence to custom. Stilted and dramatized, the neurotically repetitious behavior is a defense against an unspoken, even unconscious, anxiety. "[It] must be constantly on display," Hall explains, using the hallmark topographic metaphor of ego psychology, "[for] any failure to exhibit it would cause the contrary feeling to *come to the surface*" (Hall 1954). Reflective of anxieties long unacknowledged, repetition is in this way both symptom and mechanism of psychic repression.

In Mormonism, the collective compulsion to give testimony and the obligation to publicly proclaim "I know the church is true" has developed as a ritualized means through which members mediate the ever-present threat of doubt circulating within the contemporary church.

Two points can be made about this. Viewed as neurotic repetition, the pervasive cultural habit of bearing testimony reflects an equally pervasive collective anxiety about the resurfacing of buried traumas. But does not that faith, so often repeated, seem strong and resolute? Contrary to appearances, the average member is not safely insulated in a bubble of naïve faith, in which dangers are isolated outside a fortified wall of testimony. There are (and will continue to be) threats assailing the church that are unavoidable, no matter how well the defenses are constructed. Indeed, if "everyone has a shelf in their mind," it formed not as a contingency but as a necessity. A question or doubt at some point penetrated the member's defenses and needed somewhere to go, and so the shelf was built. Mormons' habit of repetitively bearing testimony to each other is therefore understood as an unconscious eulogy to lost naïveté, a collective attempt to rebuild damaged faith, and a tribute to their shared scars. But what are the buried traumas that have resurfaced to cause such scars? And why are they so prevalent?

The testimony must be repeated ad nauseam because the threat is ever present. Every member must partake in the ritualized obsession because each has been equally exposed and is equally in danger. Indeed, the threat runs through the very center of the church. And this is where the performative drama of dressing up as the stripling warriors and the content of testimony becomes crucial. Their message is not just "I know this church is true" but "I know" followed by assertions about the truth of Joseph Smith, the Book of Mormon, the First Vision, and so on. Members attest faith in the very things that, due to their centrality to Mormonism's core beliefs and their foundational status in the collective memory, are absolutely nonnegotiable. The force of their testimonies reflects the vital importance of Mormonism's sacred past to the life of the church. Mormonism itself is, in some ways, the thing that the Mormon faithful have to fear the most. Testimonies are inflexible because they have to be. As an answer to the question about the paradox of Mormon faith, the very qualities that give testimonies their appearance of strength also reveal a deeper vulnerability—nothing motivates a spectacle of strength like a repressed experience of weakness.

Yet faith and doubt are not inevitably irreconcilable conditions. As theologians and religious philosophers have long contended, "the confession of doubt is in fact the beginning of philosophy . . . [and] part of a very difficult road to theism" (Lloyd 1907, 27). However, if there is any truth to Nietzsche's suggestion that "madness is the result not of uncertainty but of certainty" ([1882] 2001, 62), such an emphasis on an unequivocally confident mode of faith, as I've discussed here, conceals the extent to which faith is also made dangerously frail and susceptible by virtue of its obstinate rigidity. The shelf in the mind does not break because it was not strong enough but because it was made too unyielding and was ill-equipped to withstand the weight of a deluge of doubt-inducing information rising from the depths of Mormonism's hastily forgotten history. Under the weight of the past, the shelf breaks and faith is broken.

However, the dangerous portions of the past do not rise up spontaneously. They are looked for. As Taylor suggests happened in the lead up to our now secular age, Christians went looking for an imminently rational God at work in the temporal world and devised an epistemology and observational methodology to find him, which unintentionally undermined their faith from the inside out. Why and how Mormonism has mimetically repeated a version of this requires us to look at another dimension of Mormon faith that is concerned with issues of learning and study, which serve as a motivating force for and vehicle through which the past enters the present.

A Love of Learning

Mormons pride themselves on being saints and scholars. I first recognized this in a slightly awkward encounter with my next-door neighbor Brent, who, after seeing that my wife and I were new to the neighborhood, invited us over for dinner. In the first few months after our arrival in Utah, we had received frequent invitations from other young couples wanting, I suspect, either to make friends or simply to learn about the new non-Mormons on the block. Unlike some people's overtures, which seemed primarily motivated by a desire to determine our likeliness to convert, Brent's invitation struck me as sincere, and we readily accepted.

I had recently been on a bout of reading nineteenth-century Russian literature before going to bed—a thoroughly recondite habit that few others shared, I thought. Searching for something to chat about in the postsupper conversation,

I brought this up, noting that I had recently finished a collection of Anton Chekhov's short stories. "You should read this one in particular, about—" I began to suggest. "Oh, yeah, I love Dostoevsky and Pushkin," Brent interrupted knowingly. "The Brothers Karamazov is one of my favorite books," he continued, commenting on Dostoevsky's particular stylistic devices, use of symbolism, and political allegory. He then directed me to his bookshelf filled with novels and thick anthologies of Russian and German literature. "Wow, that's awesome. How did you get into all this?" I asked enthusiastically. Brent briefly paused. Then he politely yet directly asserted, "We read all kinds of stuff. You know, the Church focuses a lot on the importance of learning and education."

I was initially caught off guard by Brent's response. Despite having told him about my research on ex-Mormonism and apostasy when we first met, that night, we had not once talked about religion or even his membership in the church. I quickly realized that, despite my best intentions, Brent mistook my excitement at finding a kindred spirit for naïve astonishment that he, as a Mormon, could be so well-read.

"The principle of education is woven into the most fundamental beliefs Mormons hold about God, about life and about themselves," an official church public relations website attests (Mormon Newsroom 2018). In fact, within Mormonism, knowledge is considered a sacred virtue. Expanding it is both a divine mandate and a divine reward. "Latter-day Saints affirm, for instance, that God is all-knowing, and are taught that 'the glory of God is intelligence, or, in other words, light and truth.'" As children of God, Mormons identify with this idyllic portrait of paternal sagacity, believing that "the objective of all people is to continuously strive to become like Him."

However, acquiring knowledge is an ambiguously sacred and secular affair, with goals of piety and worldly practicality intermixed: "Latter-day Saints recognize that education is crucial for moral and practical reasons that range from the support and upbringing of their families to participation in broader society . . . They are encouraged to love learning and teaching, and they recognize that knowledge is personally empowering . . . [and] ought to have practical value; it should improve one's ability to make social contributions, to be financially self-reliant, and generally to 'act well in the world's work'" (Mormon Newsroom 2018). As Brigham Young testified, it is a conduit through which an authentic existence takes shape: "Education is the power to think clearly . . . and to appreciate life" (quoted in Brimhall 1920, 831).

To seek and acquire knowledge, irrespective of religious intent, is further venerated as an inspired endeavor that values and exercises distinctly nonreligious fields of study: "Church teachings outline a vast field of valuable knowledge, incorporating an unlimited array of secular and religious subjects. Geography, culture, history, science and innumerable other subjects fall within these wide parameters, which extend well beyond the conventional scope of religious knowledge." Boundaries between and the relative utility of different forms and topics of study are inimitably blurred. "Indeed, at one level, Mormons do not distinguish between 'secular' and 'religious' knowledge. They regard all forms of truth as pertinent and sacred" (Mormon Newsroom 2018).

This is not, as might be presumed, a case of secular logic invading the religious sphere. As I describe further in one of the case studies that follow, the legitimacy of Mormon mytho-history, especially the Book of Mormon, is in large part founded on materialist evidentiary logic. Facts are presumed to speak, as it were, in support of spiritual truths. Yet for Mormons, education is also dually, and unabashedly, intellectual and inspirational, seamlessly integrative of "both intellect and spiritual insight." This is especially emphasized when encountering information that is spiritually challenging, where Mormons are reminded to acquire knowledge "by study and also by faith" (Doctrine and Covenants 88:118). However, Mormons are taught that they need not fear scholarship and learning. They believe that "God is actively involved in the education of His children," and as such, careful contemplation and study are neither undertaken alone nor without a solemn guarantee of ample reward for the effort: "He promises that efforts to learn will be recognized and met with His wise dispensations of knowledge. As a person studies the written text with 'real intent,' the power of the Holy Ghost will manifest the truth of what he reads. God's promise is that as we seek diligently from the best books, '[He] shall give unto [us] knowledge by his Holy Spirit'" (Mormon Newsroom 2018).

Scripture Study Tools

Studying sacred texts grants truth and wisdom, Mormons say. "Feast upon the words of Christ" (2 Nephi 32:3). The Book of Mormon commands, "Search [the scriptures] diligently" (3 Nephi 23:1). But successful study involves "more than just quickly reading through the scriptures" (Church Educational System 2000a). It is a skill, like any other, that has to be learned and cultivated. In particular, it calls for rational discipline, the training of mind and habit, and the application of correct methods and techniques. An LDS scripture study manual instructs church members to

- read carefully to understand the scriptures,
- study every day,
- set a regular time every day when you will study,
- study in a place where you can concentrate without distractions or interruptions,
- study for a period of time rather than reading a certain number of chapters or pages, and
- have a study plan.

During scripture study, church members are instructed to ask questions of the material as a learning aid. "Seeking answers to questions is one of the most important ways we gain greater understanding." One might ask, "Why might the Lord have inspired the writer to include this in the scriptures?" Yet scripture study is presumed to be difficult at times; answers to questions might not be immediately forthcoming. "Individual doctrines of the gospel are not fully explained in one place in the scriptures, nor [are they] presented in order or sequence. They must be assembled from pieces here or there." When the meaning of a text becomes opaque, "don't be afraid to stop," the study manual suggests, as extra effort may be required. "*Most nuggets of gold are not found on the surface of the ground—you must dig for them*" (Church Educational System 2000a, emphasis added).

Specifically, digging entails a methodical use of analytical and interpretive techniques. For instance, members are advised to look up the meaning of arcane words and phrases in their root languages to uncover original definitions and true meanings. The guide further suggests readers to "cluster scriptures" by using in-text cross-reference indexes in order to compare and contrast passages from different sources and look for significant patterns and themes. Most importantly, however, members are urged to study the historical background of the scriptures—the events they chronicle as well as those surrounding their composition or translation—by employing "literal hermeneutic" methods. One study guide suggests using maps to visually and empirically "set the stage" for understanding the events in scripture: "The words and stories will have more meaning if you have a better understanding of distances traveled, climate, topography, and other prominent features of the places you're reading about. For example, the story of Jonah in the Old Testament (see Jonah 1–3) gains depth when we know that the city of Nineveh was located close to modern-day Iraq and that Tarshish might have been located in Spain" (Nelson 2018). Similarly, to better understand how divine revelation guided the evolution of church doctrine and the ecclesiastical organization, members are instructed to study the Doctrine and Covenants—a book in the Mormon scriptural canon that originally contained lectures on basic church doctrine and important revelations, or "covenants," of the church as received by modern day prophets—alongside a chronological history of church events.

Several intersecting threads are at work here. To bolster ones intelligence through education and study is to become godlike. Distinctions between religious and secular topics are irrelevant since both are believed to be worthy of study and a benefit to one's temporal and celestial development. Yet this is no mere concession to or assimilation of secular epistemologies; Mormonism conceives of itself as an imminently rational faith. Its scriptures and history—the entirety of its sacred past—is taught to be empirically real and verifiable through reasoned analysis of textual and material evidence.

This state of affairs has been sustainable for decades, especially given the correlation program's success at standardizing and regulating access to church materials, as discussed in the previous chapter. Yet increasing encouragement to study the past and the provision of detailed guidance on how to do so using historiographic logic and methods has proved incompatible with the hollowed-out mythohistorical narratives that members have traditionally been taught. Although intended as a spiritual exercise to increase faith, cross-referencing sources, reconstructing the church's historical development, interrogating geography, questioning the etymology of language, and subjecting scripture to hermeneutical analysis are in fact the stuff out of which "digging too deep" is made. So while Mormonism fetishizes the epistemological equivalence of material proof and religious truth, its own modes of faith have made this pairing untenable in the contemporary church. We must now ask, What triggered this momentous shift? To do so, we look at how the so-called Mormon Moment and the rise of the digital information age have fatefully converged.

The Mormon Moment and Digital Depth

Over the past several decades, Mormonism has risen to an unprecedented level of popularity in popular American culture, often referred to as the Mormon Moment. In response to this heightened visibility, the LDS Church has increasingly taken to television and the internet to strategically negotiate its public image. For example, the stylishly produced "I'm a Mormon" ad campaign—consisting of the creation of the Mormon.org website, billboard ads, TV commercials, and hundreds of short online video clips of "average members" describing their life and their faith in the church—sought to "change the face of Mormonism" and to combat the often "wildly distorted" image of the church, as public relations officials described it (*Washington Post* 2012). In the wake of the church's growing popularity fostered by these new forms of digital media, the hope was, as one spokesman for the church said, to shift public interest from "what Mormons believe," which church leadership viewed as problematic, to "what Mormons do," primarily by showcasing their acts of charity and all-American Christian character. Indeed, in the wake of this public relations shift, church members have increasingly gone online to share their faith and explain to the world who Mormons "really are," uploading digital videos of their testimonies and blogging about their faith. I spoke to one woman who hoped that church members would use the Mormon Moment to "view themselves in the world's mirror" in order to better "present" themselves to curious outsiders.

However, the LDS Church's desire to be accepted as a mainstream Christian religion on a now highly visible public stage has required it to publicly deny specific "peculiar" aspects of religious doctrine that are at odds with "traditional" Christian sensibilities. At an institutional level, church leadership was faced with a dilemma. They could either work at achieving mainstream acceptance—which meant essentially abandoning many of their most fundamental beliefs, as they had done in the 1890s when disavowing polygamy—or retain a sense of religious peculiarity and distinction at the risk of again falling into the margins of Christianity.

This institutional attempt to "step back" some of the church's more distinctive beliefs was acutely evidenced in a 1997 interview that Gordon B. Hinckley, the president of the church at the time, did for *Time*. When asked if the church taught that God was once a man—a particularly ubiquitous and distinctive teaching in Mormonism—President Hinckley—the foremost religious authority in the church, was uncharacteristically at a loss for words, awkwardly waffling in his response: "I don't know that we teach it. I don't know that we emphasize it. I haven't heard it discussed for a long time in public discourse. I don't know . . . I don't know a lot about it and I don't know that others know a lot about it" (*Larry King Live* 1998). A similar episode transpired again several years later. During an appearance on the *Larry King Live* show, King asked Hinckley, "What happens when you die?" Hinckley paused before responding. "When you die? Well, I'm not fully conversant with that. I haven't passed through that yet."

Public statements like these have forced many average members to be confronted with a contradiction between the doctrines they have learned throughout their life in the church and what contemporary church leaders are now professing. One person, after coming across a transcript of the *Time* interview on the internet and watching a YouTube clip, wrote on an ex-Mormon message board:

> I was taught we go to spirit world or spirit prison. Those in spirit prison will be taught the gospel and if temple work is done for them, they can be together. If not they remain single. As for God once being a man, we teach that if you live the laws of the gospel and reach the highest levels of exaltation that we can become like God. How is that for an answer? It was what I was taught at Church for 50 years.[2] So how come GBH [Gordon B. Hinckley] cannot explain that to Larry King. It just goes to show how the people at the top expect the people at the bottom to push the gospel, but those at the top are not going to say a word. (Secular Priest. 2004)

These issues have also become compounded over the past decade by messages from church leaders that contradict the admonitions to "be careful" when wading into church history. Despite warnings against digging too deep into the past, members also observe church leaders testifying to a national audience that church history is indeed infallible, transparent, and ultimately innocuousness. In a 2005 interview with the Associated Press, President Hinckley was directly asked about the discrepancies between the historical record (culled from primary documents) and official church history and how he "reconcile[d] the differences."

Hinckley responded by saying, "Well, we have nothing to hide. Our history is an open book. They may find what they are looking for, but the fact is the history of the church is clear and open and leads to faith and strength and virtues" (Dobner 2005).

Faced with growing confusion about what exactly faithful members of the church are supposed to believe, many members have thus begun asking questions and doing research in order to resolve this growing awareness of the incongruity between public pronouncements and private teachings for themselves.[3] Another online commenter wrote, "I saw what the church was doing and I felt like something was wrong. I thought, something must be up. What else is out there they haven't been one hundred percent honest about? I started getting curious and doing my own research. I wanted to know what the truth was, you know . . . Had I believed something that was really just a false doctrine all along, or was the church just trying to cover up the truth?"[4]

While only a few decades ago church members would have turned primarily to local church leaders or church-produced texts for information, the internet has provided a new medium through which members can investigate doctrinal discrepancies and discover long-buried pieces of their church's past on their own. As I saw with scores of ex-Mormons questioning, researching, and eventually rejecting their beliefs, the internet is increasingly undermining the institutional church's authoritative control over how church history and doctrine are depicted and consumed by its increasingly tech-savvy and intellectually curious members.

The internet is the primary player in the transformation of access to and circulation of historical information, and it increasingly seems that it has its own form of ecclesiastic agency separate from and counter to the church's, because it allows for accidental and unmitigated access to alternative histories through search functions that are not geared toward providing only faith-promoting renditions of sacred history. As an ex-Mormon friend named Tom once jokingly told me, "You want to know the biggest threat to the church? Google." Tom's disillusionment, like that of most of the people I talked to in Utah, had primarily unfolded through his computer screen. "I was glued to my computer for three weeks. That's all I did when I wasn't at work. I'd come home and just start reading, sometimes all night. I was obsessed. Every time I read about one thing, I'd come across three more [that] I had no idea about. I just kept clicking. That's how I lost my faith, one click at a time." As Tom's case illustrates, the internet has begun to democratize access to and control over historical memory in ways not previously possible. Members with questions about church history are no longer restricted to asking church leaders or referencing church-produced publications for information. The internet is now filled with websites, blogs, wikis, discussion LISTSERVs, and YouTube videos where research on the church's past is readily available, replete with hyperlinked citations sending curious investigators to digital copies of primary documents and source material.

I often heard ex-Mormons describe this period of obsession as driven by the need to "see what else [they] didn't know," a phrase one woman used to describe her experience of intense internet searching. After clicking one link, driven by a curiosity to learn more, she found herself faced by exponentially more links, her search for truth driven as much by the structure of web pages as by her own volition. The internet in this way hinders attempts to present history in terms of a linear or unidirectional narrative. Such experiences of religious disillusionment are in fact made possible by the mechanics of the internet's weblike structure, which is networked by an endlessly interconnected chain of hyperlinks.[5] Such features allow for experiences of what ex-Mormons call "digging too deep" or "studying your way out of the church," in which the sacred historical system of meaning becomes bloated and overdetermined.

Similarly, the internet also hinders Mormonism's ability to adjust its theology, doctrines, or historical identity to fit the circumstances of the present. After hearing a church leader make a claim about Mormon doctrine or history that is either unfamiliar or contradictory with what the church member had previously learned, he or she now has the ability to authenticate those statements like never before. The internet functions as a digital form of memory that does not allow for the kinds of "strategic forgetting" necessary for Mormonism to transform and incorporate itself into the mainstream American religious landscape. Indeed, it actually provokes other pathological forms of remembering. In this way, the internet renders Mormonism's collective memory more rhizomatic in nature, decentralizes its voice, and subverts church authority by introducing readers to alternative facts and explanations.

Frank's Rational Faith

A man is saved no faster than he gets knowledge.

—Joseph Smith (Roberts [1969], vol. 4, p. 588)

I met Frank early in my fieldwork at one of the monthly support group meetings I attended. A tall, lanky man with shaggy blond hair, Frank worked as a freelance musician and producer in Salt Lake City. I often met with him at his house a few hours before the meetings started. Sitting in his living room, amid various guitars and other musical instruments, we talked about life in Utah, fishing, our shared love of craft beer, and from time to time, his former life in Mormonism.

Frank always had a deep love for the church. His love, however, was not the effusive, teary-eyed kind often seen at testimony meetings, he told me. In fact, Frank's emotional and spiritual sensitivity was contrasted with, or perhaps complemented by, his ever-curious and penetrating intellect, a fraught combination in a religious culture that values adherence to, rather than critical discussion of, religious truths. Frank remembered going to church and seeing others in the congregation who were "really into it." At fast and testimony meetings, people would pour out their hearts, he said, telling wonderfully faith-building stories of blessings Heavenly Father had given them and testifying how much they "knew" the church was true. "That wasn't me," he said. "How could they know the church was true? For most of them, it was good enough if they got around to reading their scriptures every once in a while."

Instead, Frank connected to Mormonism primarily as a theological tradition with a wonderfully vibrant past. "I loved the gospel. I loved studying the scriptures and reading about the prophets." As a young missionary, he prided himself on having read every assigned book given to him at the Missionary Training Center ten times during his two years of service. He was the "go-to" guy on his mission when a particularly inquisitive investigator had a question no one else could answer. As an adult member in his home ward, he was the local authority on church history and scripture and eventually was called to serve as a Sunday school teacher and later on within the governing three-person counsel of his local ward, referred to as the bishopric.

Frank indeed once had a strong testimony of the church, contrary to popular stereotypes of apostates held by many "active" members. Frank's testimony, however, was strengthened not by the act of publically bearing it but by "getting into the history," as he phrased it. He liked to see how things "fit together," how church history and the gospel "made sense." Reading church lesson materials and what he referred to as "faith-promoting" histories provided the sense of seamless progression of church history that its leaders often touted as evidence of truly being led by the hand of God. Interestingly, it was through reading about the church's origins that not only Frank's faith but also his personal sense of self and collective identity as a Mormon seemed to take shape. "For me, reading stories about the early church was my way of having a spiritual experience, I guess you could say. I loved reading about how Joseph Smith received almost daily revelations . . . I'd then go and read that alongside the Doctrine and Covenants and literally see how the gospel was unfolding as Joseph and everyone else were struggling to build this church. When I read that history, it was like I was witnessing how each individual brick of the church was being laid. It was like watching the hand of God shape who we are today."

Yet despite his love for the church, Frank admits that he had always been somewhat unsatisfied. Coming of age in the 1990s, Frank was a product of the "correlated church" discussed in the previous chapter. The lesson materials and texts that he was given to read in Sunday school classes or found at church bookstores had been "white-washed," as he now describes it, and had begun to feel spiritually unfulfilling. "I always felt like I was missing something. Like there was something more to be learned. I really yearned for that. I was always reading and studying, trying to strengthen my testimony that way. I took it all so seriously . . . probably too seriously, really." Most people's understanding of church history or doctrine was "a mile wide and an inch deep," he said, "but I wanted more."

Occasionally during Sunday school classes, Frank would try to introduce what he described as a more "intellectual" discussion about the day's topic. For him, such conversation was stimulating and enlightening. But he eventually learned he was fighting an uphill battle. Discussing points of Mormonism's history that were "unclear" or potentially controversial was typically avoided in Frank's Sunday school classes, and he quickly found himself marginalized. His interest in and invocation of church history outside of the lesson plan alienated him from the group. "I liked to push the issue sometimes. I don't know . . . I guess it made me feel involved. But no one wanted to hear it . . . It's weird, you bring up something people aren't familiar with, or start talking outside the lesson plan, and no one knows what to say." For example, in one class, Frank unsuccessfully tried to start a discussion of Mormonism and mainstream Christianity's closely overlapping theologies during the early 1800s. His bishop called him into his office later that afternoon. Someone in the class had complained that Frank was "introducing false doctrine," and the bishop was concerned that Frank's conduct was disturbing other ward members. Frank explained what had happened, but although the Bishop ultimately found nothing overtly transgressive about his comments, "He told me that 'a little history can go a long way' and that most people 'weren't ready for it.'"

Shortly afterward, Frank said he became increasingly critical of the church and the way it seemed to systematically reinforce an intellectual naïveté, a characteristic that he says, mockingly, makes most Mormons into "sheeple"—docile, unquestioning followers. In contrast to such people, staying in the shallow end of faith had left Frank unsatisfied and yearning for more. Repeatedly having his quest for more nuance and detail stymied by entrenched religious-cultural defenses drove him deeper into church history, his desire to study the church's historical record sustained by the hope of eventual fulfillment if only he was able to "dig deep enough." Frank's particular mode of faith thus pushed him into the footnotes, into tracking down citations and primary documents referenced in his readings. By searching in this way, he hoped to get "closer to the truth." "I thought I'd find what I was looking for and be satisfied. But that's not what happened," he told me. Instead, Frank found that reading the primary materials on which these carefully constructed narratives were based—the "Journal of Discourses," diaries and letters, newspapers, magazines, original editions of published scripture, and Joseph Smith's own original *History of the Church*—revealed discrepancies and contradictions in the sanitized version of events that he was taught at church.

Amid this search, his religious faith and identity progressively deteriorated. As Frank later told me, reflecting on this period of critical investigation several months later, "the further I dug, the more questions I had, the less I felt like I recognized who I was anymore." The fragmentation and insufficiency of the historical narrative reflected in his personal sense of self. He was in the midst of a movement that was not just "in" or "out" of Mormonism; rather, he was stuck in a perverse oscillation between intimacy and estrangement in his relationship with a church, and indeed a whole way of life, that he once had intimately "known" and loved but now somehow no longer recognized.

A salient example of this dynamic is seen in Frank's research into an iconic image in Mormonism, Joseph Smith's First Vision, as seen in the painting by Del Parson. The story behind the painting is familiar to every missionary, referenced in every church lesson manual, retold at every general conference, and in some way invoked at every fast and testimony meeting. In it, we see the beginnings of Mormonism: a young Joseph Smith, caught up in a widespread religious revival and confused about which religion to join, goes into the woods near his home and prays to God for direction. Because of the pureness of his heart

Figure 2.2. "The First Vision" by Del Parson

and the earnestness of his plea, God the Father and his son, Jesus Christ, appear in a vibrant blaze of light, bringing the astonished Smith to his knees. They tell him that he should not join any of the religions, for they all teach incorrect doctrine, and that instead he must begin restoring God's one true church.

For the contemporary LDS Church, the story of Joseph Smith's First Vision is the cornerstone of the faith, effectively undergirding Mormonism's most basic and distinctive theological and doctrinal claims. It established a divinely inspired mandate to restore God's one true church. It revealed the true nature of God as a physical, though divine, being of flesh and blood. And it clearly delineated a division between God the Father and Jesus Christ as two separate beings, as opposed to mainstream Christianity's three-in-one conception of the trinity.

The real significance of the image, however, is not found in a hermeneutic reading of its contents but rather in the semiotics of its ubiquitous proliferation across Mormonism. Appearing in church buildings and members' homes, scriptures, and lesson materials, the familiar painting of a brown-haired boy kneeling in the woods, greeted by two glowing, bearded, white-robed personages, unwaveringly testifies of this pivotal event's truth despite its unprecedented, unrepeated, and unverifiable nature. Although originating as a young farmer boy's isolated story of experiencing an ecstatic vision in a secluded wood, the event is now recursively reproduced—and thereby imparted with an unquestionable authenticity—to the millions of members across the globe who view it daily.

The story (and the images by which it is circulated) is indeed at the core of individuals' and the collective church's identities. Integral yet vulnerable and, as such, resolutely defended by church leaders and apologists against criticism or scrutiny, its credibility and authenticity act as a functional surrogate for the vitality of the church as a whole. Its truth is defined not in metaphorical or mythological terms but in the language of empirical actualities. Various church leaders have testified (emphasis mine):

> *Our whole strength rests on the validity of that vision.* It either occurred or it did not occur . . . upon that unique and wonderful experience stands the validity of this church (Hinckley 2002).

> That becomes the hinge pin on which this whole cause turns. If the First Vision was true, if it actually happened, then the Book of Mormon is true. Then we have the priesthood. Then we have the Church organization and all of the other keys and blessings of authority which we say we have. *If the First Vision did not occur, then we are involved in a great sham. It is just that simple* (Hinckley 2016).

> *There is no middle ground.* Joseph Smith talked with the Father and the Son or he didn't. If he didn't, then we are embraced in a great fraud, a terrible fraud (Church News 1996).

Frank initially began to study the First Vision story after an experience he had while attending services at a family member's ward in Colorado. There was a man there "fired up" about an argument he had gotten into earlier that week with someone on the internet who questioned the authenticity of the First Vision and had suggested that Joseph Smith fabricated the whole story. "Here was something I didn't know anything about, so I guess it sparked my interest. At the time, I didn't know what I was getting into though. I just thought, here's another thing to learn about."

Yet his search revealed multiple layers of inconsistencies and discrepancies between the tale illustrated in First Vision paintings and what is depicted in the historical record. Frank found that the First Vision account he learned from the church was only one of several accounts told by Joseph Smith over the course of his lifetime, each version differing from the others in crucial ways. Instead of the momentous, miraculous, life-changing event described by the church, some calculations suggested that Smith did not tell anyone about the First Vision until eighteen years after he said it happened, calling into question how "momentous" the event actually was to the young Smith and how accurately he really could have recalled this memory when he eventually put it to paper. Similarly, though the contemporary church looked to that event as the basis of its unique theology, Frank explained that in Smith's retellings, the number and type of "personages" changed from account to account, ranging from an angel to many angels, Jesus by himself, and God the Father with Jesus. And finally, the age that Joseph Smith said he had the vision shifted several times, from fourteen to sixteen years old.[6] "I was devastated," Frank said. "It's so different from what we learn. It's like he was making it up as he went along, adding something here, changing something there. Every time he told the story, it changed."

This issue of peeling away the veneer of a historical tale only to discover inconsistencies, alterations, and artifice hidden within is not isolated to the First Vision accounts. Similar issues have arisen over the method by which Joseph Smith reportedly "translated" the Book of Mormon from golden plates. Church members are led to believe that Smith primarily read the plates with his bare eyes or used a mystical ancient device called an Urim and Thummim to translate the texts from "reformed Egyptian" to English, as depicted in numerous paintings, church history films, and stories. However, personal accounts from people who witnessed his methods indicate that Smith would primarily place a magical "peep stone" into a hat and then peer into the darkness and read the words that appeared.[7]

That once-believing Mormons' faith is challenged by these revelations reflects the extent to which faith itself in Mormonism has increasingly become founded on and articulated through identification with a certain stylized *image* of sacred historical events. Faith has become dependent on these storied images, their consistency, their reproducibility, and their ability to draw the viewer into them by offering a sense of assurance and intimacy. While images are powerful

Figure 2.3. "Joseph Smith Translating the Book of Mormon" by Del Parson

faith-promoting devices that allow church members to "relate" to these foundational events, a faith built on stylized images is also potentially perfunctory and fragile. Images offer the semblance of understanding and intimacy while being predicated on an elision. This is because the image ultimately contains meaning not just for the contents that it displays but for all the other content that it culls out, obscures, and removes. Its power lies in the illusion of multidimensionality and understanding, offering the spectator an opportunity to gaze at its surface and be drawn into the spectacle. Yet its impotency is also found in its static, atemporal flatness. In order for the fantasy to persist, viewers must then maintain a "faithful" distance from the image, a "fantasmic distance" that allows the conjuring trick to work (Žižek 1989). As Frank found out, total fulfillment of intimacy and knowing is therefore made impossible. Coming too close shatters and evaporates the image—and with it, one's faith. Like examining individual pixels that only become visible when viewing an image up close, peering too far into the image of Joseph Smith kneeling in the woods and talking to God or translating golden plates reveals details previously unseen. And like with pixels, the coherency of the larger image disappears when seen up close.

Such problems are in some ways unique to Mormonism. While Christianity faces similar issues with critical Bible studies undermining Western people's beliefs, the foundational events, texts, and figures chronicled in the Old and New Testaments unfolded in a largely unfamiliar (pseudomythical) place; were inscribed in foreign, ancient languages; and are veiled behind the fog of time, all of which partially protects them from popular scrutiny. Mormonism's history is quite different. It took place rather recently in North America and is well documented in modern English. Historians and laypeople alike thus have a remarkable ability to cross-reference diaries, newspapers, journals, and letters written by people who knew and talked to Joseph Smith as these "sacred" events were unfolding. This facilitates researchers' ability to gather and circulate incriminating information about how the golden plates were translated or the First Vision unfolded. Attempts to depict historical events as straightforward, timeless, and unchanging is likewise increasingly less possible with the proliferation of digital technologies and the democratization of information on the internet. Staking the church's legitimacy and truthfulness on the supposed incontrovertibility of a historical record subject to scathing scrutiny is therefore somewhat akin to the biblical tale of the foolish man who built his house on sand: "The rain came down, the floods came, and the winds blew, and beat on that house; and it fell—and great was its fall" (Matt. 7:24–27).

In contemporary Mormonism, there are increasingly fewer options for someone like Frank to function as both an inquisitive, critical-thinking person and a faithful church member who is able to maintain these popular images of church history. As Frank once told me, "I never thought this before, but I really think I am a case of someone who knew too much." Frank's faith, in essence, fell victim to contradictory impulses in contemporary Mormonism. An earnest desire to deepen faith through engaging with history ultimately clashed with the cosmetically coherent yet deceptively fragile images of the past.

Sherri's Faith: Betrayed by the Book of Mormon

I told the brethren that the Book of Mormon was the most correct of any book on earth, and the keystone of our religion, and a man would get nearer to God by abiding by its precepts, than by any other book.

—Joseph Smith (Roberts [1965], vol. 4, p. 461)

> *Take away the Book of Mormon and the revelations, and where is our religion? We have none.*
>
> —Joseph Smith (Roberts [1965], vol. 2, p. 52)

> *For 179 years this book has been examined and attacked, denied and deconstructed, targeted and torn apart like perhaps no other book in modern religious history—perhaps like no other book in any religious history. And still it stands. If anyone is foolish enough or misled enough to reject 531 pages of a heretofore unknown text teeming with literary and Semitic complexity without honestly attempting to account for the origin of those pages—especially without accounting for their powerful witness of Jesus Christ and the profound spiritual impact that witness has had on what is now tens of millions of readers—if that is the case, then such a person, elect or otherwise, has been deceived; and if he or she leaves this Church, it must be done by crawling over or under or around the Book of Mormon to make that exit.*
>
> —Elder Holland, "Safety for the Soul," 2009 LDS General Conference address

As Joseph Smith proudly proclaimed, the Book of Mormon is indeed the "keystone" of the LDS faith. Without believing in its spiritual and historical veracity as inspired scripture, one cannot be a member of the church. For Mormons, the book is literally, as proclaimed in its opening preface, "a record of God's dealings with the ancient inhabitants of the Americas and [it] contains the fullness of the everlasting gospel." It is simultaneously an authoritative spiritual guide and a factual account of two ancient civilizations' miraculous encounter with Christ.

However, although the Book of Mormon effectively serves as the keystone of truth for church members, those who leave the church describe the Book of Mormon as false and fictitious, saying that when this keystone of their faith began to crack, the rest of the edifice collapsed. So while Elder Holland proclaims that those who leave the church can only do so by "crawling over or under or around the Book of Mormon," I found that for the majority of ex-Mormons, disillusionment was developed by traveling straight through the book itself.

A bit of an oddity for Utah, Sherri grew up in a family that relocated to different states every few years thanks to a father serving in the U.S. Air Force. Although raised faithfully in the LDS Church, her seminomadic lifestyle brought her into contact with a continuously changing set of school friends and neighbors unfamiliar with Mormonism. Describing her early relationships with non-Mormons, Sherri told me how they often asked her questions about the church that she was happy to answer: "Was it true we practiced polygamy? Did we wear magic underwear? What did we really believe? . . . At the time, I loved people's curiosity. It made me feel special . . . [that] I was given an opportunity to share the knowledge I had with the world."

As Sherri grew older, married, and had kids, her testimony matured. Yet she also found that the more visibility Mormonism achieved on the public stage, the more her beliefs were scrutinized by skeptical or outright critical outsiders. She remembers in the run-up to the 2012 presidential elections, in which the Mormon candidate Mitt Romney was often criticized for his faith, church leaders touted the slogan "every member a missionary," encouraging members to share the gospel on the internet and create a positive image of Mormonism to the American public. For Sherri, sharing her conviction of the church's truth on the internet became something of a labor of love. She began to participate in several online message boards and online news outlets, defending the church.

Enlisting average members to defend the church's image on the internet has, however, proved detrimental to people's individual faiths. The act of defending the church can easily slip into counterproductive forms of self-reflexive scrutiny and questioning. For example, although the oft-quoted phrase "I know this church is true" resonates on a deep emotional level with many church members, for people like Sherri who were attempting to share their faith online, it proved trite and ineffective. "You can't just tell someone you know the church is true and leave it at that, hoping that they'll get the message. People had questions, and I wanted to give them answers. I knew we had the truth, and I was going to show it to them. Whether they accepted it or not was their problem." The "truth" of the church had to be translated from a solely emotional conviction to something that spoke to the wider populace's more skeptical and evidence-based sensibilities. "They wanted to know how I knew Joseph Smith was really a prophet, how I knew the Book of Mormon was true. They wanted proof, so I went looking for it. That's what ultimately did me in." How is it, though, that a search for "proof" can end up in a collapse of faith? Likewise, how has the keystone of Mormonism also become its greatest liability?

Members of the church do not learn the history of past church events from which they are temporally and geographically removed. Rather, modern-day members believe that the Book of Mormon describes people, places, and events whose existence can be verified by looking for evidence in the contemporary world around them. For example, a central tenet in Mormonism is the belief that Jesus Christ visited the North American continent and preached to the two primary groups of people inhabiting the land, the Nephites and the Lamanites. A recent instructional video depicts Christ's visit to the Nephites with scenes of earthen mounds and wooden structures spreading across the horizon (similar to the Hopewell Mound Builders who once lived in the middle part of the continent; LDS Media Library 2014). The belief that Native Americans once populated the continent as the Lamanite people, with great cities, roads, and armies, has prompted religiously inspired archaeological investigations, linguistic analysis, and genetic research attempting to find objective and empirical proof of these scriptural truth claims.

> After many years of careful study, the real importance of Book of Mormon archaeology has dawned on me. It will take but a moment to explain. The Book of Mormon is the only revelation from God in the history of the world that can possibly be tested by scientific physical evidence. . . . To find the city of Jericho is merely to confirm a point in history. To find the city of Zarahemla is to confirm a point in history but it is also to confirm, through tangible physical evidence, divine revelation to the modern world through Joseph Smith, Moroni, and the Urim and Thummim. Thus, Book of Mormon history is revelation that can be tested by archaeology. (Thomas Ferguson to the First Presidency, April 10, 1953, Ferguson Collection, BYU)

I met church members in Utah who periodically took family vacations to South and Central America to visit Incan, Aztec, and Mayan archaeological sites, equipped with books they had bought at the church-owned Deseret Bookstore that detailed the "factual evidences" supporting these connections. Similarly, LDS scholars have conducted numerous studies of American Indian DNA in order to validate the Book of Mormon's claim that the Lamanites are in fact the "principal ancestors of the American Indians," as stated on the Book of Mormon's introductory page.[8] Similarly confident in the Book of Mormon's scientific as well as spiritual legitimacy, church members have repeatedly sought authoritative authentication from the Smithsonian Institution in Washington, DC, that it is indeed historically accurate and has been used to guide scientific research, including identifying and verifying archaeological sites found in the New World.[9]

While evidence for the Book of Mormon is sought through its descriptions of empirical links to Native American civilizations, many Mormons' faith is supported by the "very reality" of the book's existence (Nelson 1993). However, according to church members, the Book of Mormon also "speaks for itself" with the "*impossibility* of its existence" except by the miraculous act of divine inspiration. In this way, the empirical plausibility and implausibility of the text (and its claims) constitute two sides of the same coin.

When I would ask faithful church members how they "knew" the Book of Mormon was true, they would often explain to me that Joseph Smith could never have written the book "by himself," and must have "translated" the text from some original, though now missing, document, as he claimed (as opposed to having written it originally himself).[10] I only had to look at the first pages of the Book of Mormon to see the statements of eleven witnesses who claimed to have seen the golden plates.[11] Church members also routinely pointed out another faith-affirming paradox; Smith had a lack of formal education, yet he rapidly "translated" 531 pages of text written in "reformed Egyptian" over sixty-five days. To them, this served as logical evidence that he would have literally been unable to complete the monumental task of translating a presumed actual set of golden plates without being divinely gifted with the ability read in an extinct foreign language—the material and the magical properties of the story mutually depending on and confirming one another. Similarly, apologists point to the use of "Hebraisms" in the text as evidence of its ancient Hebrew origins, including the use of chiasmi (an inverted parallel structure that allows for an author to emphasize key points without the use of punctuation) and the use of Hebrew words with "double meaning," which the young Joseph Smith is assumed to not have been familiar with while growing up in upstate New York. For many church members, the transcendent value of the Book of Mormon indeed rests on the ambiguous conflation of its empirical (im)plausibility.

In this way, the Book of Mormon is thought to testify to its own authenticity, leading church leaders like Elder Holland to claim that the Book of Mormon "is like no other book in religious history." In doing so, the book has the ability to draw readers into a world suffused with transcendent spiritual and moral truths as well as a mythohistorical genealogy made up of ancient Hebrew people, gold plates, and the prophet Joseph Smith. Exhibits at the LDS Church History Museum, for example, attempt to demonstrate to visitors the material reality of these historical events while simultaneously collapsing the boundary between a mythical and the literal historical past, effectively rendering the stories depicted in scripture as "uniquely real" (Geertz 1973). While much of the Church History Museum is dedicated to exhibiting relics of Mormonism's "pioneer heritage," including collections of early church writings, journals, pictures, and pioneer-era tools, another purpose aims to specifically "[engage] children in Book of Mormon history." Through large, colorful, interactive dioramas, visitors are invited to "step into Book of Mormon stories," board "Father Lehi's" ship and use the "Liahona" (a magical navigational device) to sail across the ocean,[12] try their

Figure 2.4. Promotional image on the LDS church website depicting a life-size replica of Moroni burying the gold plates at the Church History Museum in Salt Lake City, https://www.lds.org/ensign/2012/01/children-delight-in-the-book-of-mormon?lang=eng

hand at writing in "reformed Egyptian," and even flip through life-size replicas of the golden plates. While primarily geared toward children, the exhibits capture the imagination of young and old alike. One time when visiting the museum, I watched as parents and older kids moved from exhibit to exhibit, turning the cold metallic plates and wistfully running their fingers across the "reformed Egyptian" characters stamped into their surfaces as they achieved the exhibit's expressed goal of allowing museum patrons to "step into scriptural time."

However, relying on the Book of Mormon as material evidence for religious faith brings a paradoxical form of dependency on that evidence. To rely on empirical evidence for bolstering religious truth claims is to play in a high stakes gamble. The prospect of empirical evidence leads some people to feel more secure in the inherent rationality of their faith. If the Book of Mormon in fact provides an accurate description of ancient peoples and places and was translated from gold plates, then the religious truth claims found within it are validated. Yet this is what makes appeals to "evidence" paradoxically both attractive and potentially destructive. Appealing to a logic of "evidence" as a basis of religious legitimacy shifts the burden of proof onto those making the truth claims. In effect, the same evidence that the contemporary church looks to for confirmation and legitimation of its spiritual truth claims also has the capability of undermining them when the evidence ultimately proves lacking.

Sherri once heard a former prophet say that if church history was true, studying it could only strengthen one's faith. Sherri shared this confidence in the church history's authenticity, its potential to serve as its own unique voice proclaiming the truth of the gospel. She knew the church was true—she assumed the evidence was there and had been dealt with by church historians, intellectuals, and ecclesiastic leaders. She had occasionally heard the warnings about "anti-Mormon" literature that "distorted the truth," but her confidence in evidence outweighed the threat of its potential misrepresentation at the hands of the church's critics.

Like many other ex-Mormons, Sherri's journey out of the church began with an internet search in an effort to better answer a critic she ran across in the "comments" section of an internet news article. "Someone asked, 'If the Book of Mormon is true, then where's the proof? If there had been an ancient civilization on the level of the Nephites and Lamanites, wouldn't we be able to see something of their remains?' I initially thought, of course, that's easy to prove."

However, Sherri's search ultimately provided more questions than answers. A website produced by a group of critically minded current and former Mormons called "MormonThink," which discusses the evidence for and against numerous aspects of Mormon doctrine, history, and scripture, popped up in her browser. Intrigued, she began clicking around. Sherri then spent the next three evenings reading its contents, everything from the scientific data that supported or refuted the Book of Mormon's claims to more esoteric discussions of Mormon theological tenets. "I initially thought I was going to find some answers. I had no idea what was there. Once I cracked open the door, I couldn't get out. I was sucked in. For days that's all I did. I couldn't pull myself away."

The evidence that Sherri had initially been looking for overwhelmed her but not for the reasons she had predicted. Instead, Sherri's research fundamentally undermined all the evidence that she had once thought supported the Book of Mormon. "The archaeological record is clear," she explained. "During that time in history, there were no horses, no steel, and no wheels like it says in the Book of Mormon. Nothing that comes even close. If there actually were Nephites and Lamanites running around, you'd think we'd be able to see evidence of them." The genealogical ancestry that the church taught existed between Lamanites and Native Americans also proved to be false. "People have done this research on Indian blood, and there is absolutely no evidence that they're related to the Hebrews." Finally, the sacred reality of the Book of Mormon was undermined for Sherri when she found out that a former church historian once wrote a book called the *Studies of the Book of Mormon*, which detailed the many parallels between the Book of Mormon and another book published prior to Joseph Smith's "translations." In *View of the Hebrews* (1823), Ethan Smith, a Congregationalist minister, argued that Native Americans were descended from the ten lost tribes of Israel, describes the peopling of the New World by sea voyagers from the Old World, and states that Christ preached the gospel in ancient America—effectively predating the historical narrative depicted in the Book of Mormon.

Even more damaging, LDS scriptures contain a copy of the Book of Abraham that Joseph Smith reportedly translated from an ancient set of Egyptian papyri thought to be lost. Sherri told me that the papyri from which Smith translated the Book of Abraham had in fact been found and studied by several non-Mormon Egyptologists, something the vast majority of church members are unaware of. "They were ancient, and they were Egyptian. The only problem was, they don't say a damn thing about Abraham." According to faithful Mormons, the Book of Abraham contains a narrative of Abraham's life along with three facsimiles containing Abraham's visions concerning premortal life and the birth of creation, materials that have informed Mormon doctrine and are taught alongside the Old Testament in Sunday school classes, in institute courses, and at Brigham Young University. Pressured to provide a full translation of the papyri, Smith attempted to fill in missing pieces of the facsimile, eventually describing the scene as depicting Abraham's sacrifice on an altar. However, those leaving Mormonism often cite the Book of Abraham as the "smoking gun" that drove them from the church when they found out that the papyri, rather than depicting the life of Abraham, are actually common funerary scrolls depicting Egyptian characters and figures such as Osiris, Isis, and Anubis. "If you compare the facsimiles printed in the Book of Abraham with the originals, you can see where Joseph tried to draw in the pieces that were missing," Sherri explained. Faced with all this information,

Figure 2.5. Comparison of the original Egyptian papyri and Joseph Smith's illustration printed in the Book of Abraham

the only conclusion she was able to reach was that "he [Joseph Smith] made it all up . . . It was all there! It was just that none of us had ever been looking in the right places. So piece by piece, I began taking apart everything I had ever been taught."

So what began as a seemingly harmless conversation with an inquisitive outsider turned into an internal dialogue and a search for answers to her own growing doubts—and eventually, the collapse of her faith. Sherri's story is shared by many of the ex-Mormons I spoke with. It is instructive, as it reveals how "digging too deep" and "studying your way out of the church" historically emerges at the intersection of a constellation of developments in modern Mormonism. Prior to the Mormon Moment, members like Sherri never had a pressing need to look at the evidence on which their faith and the church were built. Doing so, however, led Sherri to scrutinize taken-for-granted truths. Under these conditions, evidence in support of the church quickly turned into evidence against it.

At the time of our discussion, Sherri had stopped going to church for just over three months. She was in the midst of a divorce and a custody battle with her husband. He did not want to hear anything about what she had learned. "As soon as I began questioning, it was like what I thought didn't matter anymore." Now alone and confused at where to go in life, she was angry at what she considered the betrayal perpetrated by the church. But as we sat talking at her house that day, more than anything, she just seemed sad. "All I was looking for was evidence for what I thought was true," she said, glancing out the window. "I never thought all this would happen."

Chris and the Mountain Meadows Massacre

In a wilderness of pine, sage, and cedar, Chris and I drove mile after mile down a two-lane highway, looking for the turnoff that would take us to the Mountain

Meadows Massacre memorial site. "Have you ever been here?" Chris asked me on the car ride. "You've got to see it," he exclaimed. "This is the biggest scandal in Mormon history, and I bet you most of the people in the church don't know anything about it."

"I always thought the whole point of being a part of the church was it made you into a more Christlike person. You listen to church leaders and what do you hear: 'be Christlike, be loving and kind, patient and forgiving.'" Chris told me this as we pulled into the memorial parking lot. "But you don't really realize what people are capable of." Chris explained how church members are taught that the world outside of Mormonism is a dangerous place—how well-intentioned, sweet, and charming church members are made vulnerable to "anti-Mormonism" in a multitude of forms yet are never held responsible for their troubles. "Mormons have a persecution complex. They're always the victims and never the aggressors."

The history that members learn about the relationship between Mormons and "gentiles" in the early days of the church is indeed tinged with stories of persecution and victimization at the hands of an at-times violent, larger American populace. Stories of the martyrdom of Joseph Smith and his brother Hyrum at the Carthage jail (where they were waiting to stand trial on charges of destroying a printing press), an "extermination order" against the Mormons declared by the governor of Missouri, and the Hawn's Mill Massacre, in which seventeen church members were killed by a mob, are retold as evidence of systematic persecution against believers. In each case, the Saints are depicted as passive, undeserving victims of others' malice, a righteous and well-meaning people beleaguered by religious oppression.

While the "anti-Mormon" sentiments that the early church faced were bigoted and at times violent, the Mormons themselves were also complicit in the growing animosity and violent conflicts with the gentiles. But the details of the Saints' complicity have been strategically obscured from church instruction materials, leaving the vast majority of Mormons unaware of the church's own violent actions. They are left to assume that they were simply hapless victims. For example, preceding the so-called extermination order, a prominent church leader named Sidney Rigdon gave a speech in which he himself incited violence and further hostility, using the term *extermination* and saying, "It shall be between us and them a war of extermination, for we will follow them till the last drop of blood is spilled . . . for we will carry the seat of war to their own houses and their own families." Similarly, in retellings of Joseph Smith's "martyrdom," no mention is made of his violent attempts to thwart his attackers by shooting a pistol into the crowd of people storming his jail cell, ultimately killing two men. Nor is the Hawn's Mill Massacre placed in the context of escalating violence committed by both gentiles and Saints, in which homes and towns were ransacked and destroyed in reciprocal acts of retaliation.

However, at Mountain Meadows, the extent of the early church's violent past is undeniable. Chris told me the story of the massacre as we walked across the ground where it occurred. In 1857, the Baker-Fancher party, a wagon train of more than 120 people traveling from Arkansas to California, stopped to rest in a grassy valley named Mountain Meadows. A group of local Mormon settlers and militia—fearful of outsiders encroaching into the Utah Territory, then a theocratic land governed by church president Brigham Young, and incited by religious oratory specifying the need to "avenge the death of the prophet Joseph Smith"—staged an attack on the travelers, who were rumored to have possibly been at Carthage jail when Joseph Smith was killed (Bagley 2004; Walker, Turley, and Leonard 2011). Hoping to plunder the wagon train's resources without being identified, the Mormons disguised themselves as Paiute Native Americans and launched an attack. After five days of fighting and having exhausted their supplies of food, water, and ammunition, the Baker-Fancher party surrendered to their attackers.

The Mormons began to worry that their true identities would be revealed and that stories of their actions would spread. They needed a solution. Looking across the valley below, Chris pointed out to me the spot where the 120 captive men, women, and children were marched away from their encampment under the guise of being led to safety and then lined up and shot dead, their bodies hastily buried under a thin layer of sand. "Can you imagine?" Chris exclaimed. The only people to survive the slaughter were a few children under the age of seven, their lives spared because they were thought to be too young to remember.

The need to cover up the Mormons' involvement in the massacre subsequently drove the church to completely deny their involvement for decades after. Even throughout the twentieth century, the massacre went largely unacknowledged by church leadership. The rare times that they have been pressed to account for the Mormon attackers' actions, the LDS Church maintains that they were acting independently and that President Brigham Young had nothing to do with the affair, absolving the present church of any inherited sins of the past.

However, as we stood on the hill overlooking where the massacre took place, Chris recited the list of books he had read describing the event along with the probability that Brigham Young, contrary to church claims, orchestrated the atrocity. "I remember reading the reports of how they had all been shot in the head. I was already on my way out the door, but this really solidified it. They were all executed, there's nothing else to it, and they [historians] think Brigham Young ordered it. It's almost unthinkable."

Chris once believed that no other church, no other culture, could instill morality and righteous living like the Mormon Church. Yet he found it impossible to reconcile the image he had of a benevolent church, led by prophets of a supposedly loving God, with the undeniable atrocity of mass murder committed by those very same people's hands. "That was what was so damning. There was no gray area about it. I couldn't explain it away. I think if you study things like this, you really see what religion is capable of . . . There was no reason for any of this. It wasn't like these people were doing anything to provoke the Mormons, and still they were hunted down out of fear and a need for revenge."

Curtis and the Curse of Cain

Curtis knew little of Mormonism's racist past until BYU religion professor Randy Bott made incendiary remarks in a 2012 *Washington Post* article discussing Republican Mitt Romney's struggles running for the presidency as a Mormon (Horowitz 2012). Specifically, Bott addressed Mormonism's so-called racist past, as evidenced by the church not giving black people the priesthood until 1978, only then allowing them to marry in the church, enter the temple, receive temple ordinances, and in effect participate as full members of the church.

In the article, Bott dismisses the charge that the church was racist for not giving the priesthood by saying that blacks were not ready for it. "God has always been discriminatory," Bott is quoted as saying. "What is discrimination? I think that is keeping something from somebody that would be a benefit for them, right? But what if it wouldn't have been a benefit to them?" According to Bott, denying blacks the priesthood effectively protected them from the "lowest rungs of hell reserved for people who abuse their priesthood powers." He continued, "You couldn't fall off the top of the ladder, because you weren't on the top of the ladder. So, in reality the blacks not having the priesthood was the greatest blessing God could give them."

In fact, for more than a century, the LDS Church taught that black people were inferior—spiritually, morally, and intellectually—to white people. This belief in part stems from Old Testament teachings about the "curse of Cain," in which it was believed that God marked those who turned against him with a flat nose and black skin. Mormon scriptures also reflect this teaching. In multiple passages in the Book of Mormon, having dark skin is described as a curse from God, while white skin is a symbol of righteousness, as in 2 Nephi 5:21: "And the Lord had caused the cursing to come upon them, yea, even a sore cursing, because of their iniquity. For behold, they had hardened their hearts against him, that they had become like unto a flint; wherefore, as they were white, and exceedingly fair and delightsome, that they might not be enticing unto my people the Lord God did cause a skin of blackness to come upon them." Similarly, while God is believed to curse with a plague of dark skin, those who confess their inequities and turn to him are believed to have their skin lightened. "And their curse was taken from them, and their skin became white like unto the Nephites" (3 Nephi 2:14–15).

However, these ideas were not restricted to ancient scripture. They informed church lesson materials and church leaders' teachings well into the twentieth century. In an address at BYU in 1954, Apostle Mark E. Petersen stated, "What should be our attitude as Latter-day Saints toward negro and other dark races? . . . We cannot escape the conclusion that because of performance in our pre-existence some of us are born as Chinese, some as Japanese, some as Indians, some as Negroes, some as Americans, some as Latter-Day Saints. There are rewards and punishments" (Petersen 1954). In the 1970s, President Joseph Fielding Smith taught that "there is a reason why one man is born black and with other disadvantages, while another is born white with great advantages. The reason is that we once had an estate before we came here, and were obedient, more or less, to the laws that were given us there. Those who were faithful in all things received greater blessings here, and those who were not faithful received less" (Doctrines of Salvation 1:61). Children in the church grew up learning that in a premortal battle between God and Satan, black people were so-called fence sitters who were then cursed by God with dark skin so as to set them apart from the more righteous and courageous whites.

In the midst of the church's conspicuously multiethnic "I'm a Mormon" public relations campaign, Bott effectively unearthed an issue long thought to have been laid to rest in the church's past. Bott's remarks threatened to undermine the church's efforts to be seen as a part of a diverse global community and sparked a firestorm of response from BYU students and church leaders denouncing his remarks. But for people like Curtis, the commotion that ensued exposed an aspect of his religion's past that he previously knew nothing about and drove him to begin asking questions. "When you start reading this stuff that Brigham Young said, and everything that was taught for so long, it's disgusting," Curtis said.

Curtis's uncovering of these divisive issues revealed to him not only the extent to which the church's past is filled with moral bigotries but also the contradictory logic undergirding its claims to spiritual authority in the present. The Bott affair was not an example of a lone misinformed church member propagating long-dismissed ideas about race. Rather, he represents a tacit tension at the heart of Mormonism between doctrinal accommodation to mainstream morality and the idea that the church "is right even when it's wrong," as a church member once told me. Curtis was unable to accept the idea that God could promote two morally contradictory positions at different points in time. Curtis began to ask, If the church was indeed led by prophets of God who would never introduce false doctrine or lead the church astray, then how was it that such a morally deplorable doctrine was allowed to persist for so long? "If the church is really who it says it is, then why are they always twenty years behind everyone else when it comes to stuff like this? If it really is led by God, then wouldn't you think they'd be leading the charge against inequality? No, instead they have to be pulled kicking and screaming on any really important moral issue. So I finally was able to bring myself to the conclusion that maybe the church wasn't led by God. Maybe God never had anything to do with it."

Curtis's experience, like those of others who shared his disillusionment, is thus the symptom of a larger transformation under way, his disillusionment the consequence of Mormonism's inability to reconcile the contradictory notions of a divinely led church leadership and a morally consistent theology with the undeniable bigotries in the historical record.

Loa and Plural Marriage

At one time in church history, plural marriage was thought to be a requirement for celestial exaltation, as detailed in scripture: "For behold, I reveal unto you a new and an everlasting covenant; and if ye abide not that covenant, then *are ye damned*; for no one can reject this covenant and be permitted to enter into my glory" (Doctrine and Covenants 132:4–6). Modern-day church members, for whom monogamy is the only acceptable form of marriage in the church, now consider polygamy as a somewhat embarrassing (though necessary) past form of marriage. For them, plural marriage was a commandment from God, albeit one that was isolated to the historical period of the early church as a practical means of ensuring the community's survival. Church members are taught that plural marriage was a pragmatic solution to a "lack of husbands" in the early church, a result of incessant attacks by the "anti-Mormon mobs" and the toils of trekking to Utah, which left many women of childbearing age without husbands and orphans and widows without families. It was also considered a means to "raise up seed unto [the Lord]" (Jacob 2:30), increasing the population of LDS faithful and strengthening the church. Some even say that plural marriage was a Utah-centric phenomenon, fully instituted under Brigham Young, and certainly not practiced during Joseph Smith's time. Many Mormons only know about Joseph Smith's marriage to his first wife, Emma.

Church publications and websites are scant on details concerning the practice of plural marriage, discussing it in generalities without mentioning the historical specifics of its emergence and institutionalization and with none of the controversy surrounding it in the early church. On the church-sponsored website JosephSmith.net, Joseph Smith is listed as having only one wife. Whenever I asked believing Mormons what they knew about the practice of plural marriage, they dismissed the topic as a matter of unimportance to the contemporary church. For example, when I questioned one woman on what she knew of Joseph Smith's involvement, she became flustered and declared the whole issue "typical anti-Mormon propaganda."

Loa was one woman for whom plural marriage played a prominent role in her disaffection. Loa always looked to the marital relationship of Joseph and Emma Smith as a model for her own marriage. "I always wanted to marry somebody who would be like Joseph Smith. He was a Christlike man to me, kind and caring. I loved the pictures of him and Emma. She looked so happy and content . . . I wanted a marriage just like that."

Yet when Loa began reading about Joseph Smith's plural marriages to thirty-two other women on an ex-Mormon website, she felt the cracks start to form and quickly widen in her testimony. Most disturbing to Loa was finding out about Smith's marriage to an adolescent girl of fourteen years of age and his alleged practice of sending married men out on proselytizing missions just so he could marry their wives in secret. "I thought, how could he do that? Those men trusted him, and he betrayed them. And then Emma. What she had to go through being married to him."

As Loa read, she found out that Joseph Smith had begun practicing plural marriage in secret several years before he proclaimed it as a matter of church doctrine. When some of his close friends began to find out, he swore a select group of them to secrecy, claiming that his extramarital relationships were a commandment from God that he was reluctantly obeying, having been threatened by an angel with a "flaming sword" to carry out the marriages lest he provoke the fury of the Lord. "That was all an excuse for him to be a pervert and cheat on Emma," Loa concluded.

Indeed, Joseph Smith began to teach that plural marriage guaranteed eternal life to those who practiced it, including the families of the women he married. "If you read the diaries written by these young girls, you see how manipulative he was," Loa explained. "He'd force the whole family to go along with it. It was basically spiritual extortion. He'd tell them if you don't go along with it, an angel with a flaming sword would destroy them, or something like that." As we sat talking, Loa showed me some of her research into Joseph Smith's practice of polygamy, including various quotes from his young brides that she had scrawled onto a sheet of paper, each one bulleted in a long list of incriminating evidence against the prophet. Shuffling through the papers, she pointed down at one written by Helen Kimball, Smith's fourteen-year-old bride: "After which he said to me, 'if you take this step, it will ensure your eternal salvation and exaltation and that of your father's household and all of your kindred.' This promise was so great that I willingly gave myself to purchase so glorious a reward."

"I started seeing how much everything we did in the church stems from Joseph Smith's desire for sex," Loa explained. "Most of the things we do in the church revolving around the family [go] back to plural marriage. Joseph didn't even teach about 'eternal families' until polygamy started. One of the ways he convinced women to marry him was by telling them it would 'seal' everyone in their family together through him, because he was directly connected to God, or whatever. . . . And before that there was none of this 'families are forever' stuff—he taught that marriage ended at death. All of it was just a way for him to sell polygamy."

Loa also told me that the contemporary emphasis on "temple marriages" began with Smith's practice of plural marriage. "He started bringing women into the temple and closing it off from everyone else as a way to make sure polygamy stayed secret. Only people who had been initiated into plural marriage could be a part of or even know about the ceremony." Smith further ensconced plural marriage in sacred secrecy by creating the "temple endowment." What today is considered simply an oath to not disclose the details of what happens in the temple to nonmembers began with men and women who were engaged in plural marriage taking "blood oaths" and swearing to keep the marriages secret or risk facing a number of "penalties" including dismemberment and disembowelment, each of which was ritually performed in the endowment ceremony. "Even the garments church members wear," Loa concluded, "they were only worn by those who had entered into plural marriage. They wore them so they would be able to tell if someone 'knew' the principle or not."

While a faithful member of the church, Loa had looked to her "celestial marriage" with her husband and the "eternal family" they created together as the most important and cherished element of her life. After she began researching the history of plural marriage, however, everything she once considered to be at the core of her faith was stripped away. Her research into plural marriage had effectively deconstructed the key symbols, rituals, and principles of Mormonism, rendering them disenchanted vestiges of what now seemed to her like Joseph Smith's insatiable desire for sex and power. Perhaps more importantly, Smith himself was no longer the much-admired religious prophet, moral icon, and object of romantic desire that Loa had once loved. Her identification with Smith had been the linchpin of her testimony, the foundation on which her faith in everything else rested. Removing him from his position of symbolic ascendancy undermined the entire edifice of her belief:

> When I started finding out about all of that, I think I finally saw Joseph for what he really was. For the longest time, as I was leaving the church, I held onto my belief in Joseph. I had let go of God and the Bible, and even Jesus. Those weren't so bad to get rid of. But I still held onto the thought that maybe there was some truth to [Joseph Smith], you know, maybe he really was a prophet. But once I saw he was just in it for the sex . . . how manipulative he was, how he treated the people who trusted him and loved him . . . I couldn't do it anymore, I just let go of everything.

CHAPTER 3

"The Other Side of Happiness"

DISENCHANTMENT, LOSS, AND WORLD COLLAPSE

The day I met Jacob was also the first day he attended an ex-Mormon support group meeting. I remember watching him walk into the darkened living room of the ex-Mormon woman's house where meetings were held, his face held low, avoiding people's greetings. I attended these support group meetings off and on throughout my fieldwork, eventually withdrawing from them altogether in the latter stages of my work after the stories of existential dismay and spiritual disillusionment became too emotionally burdensome for me. Jacob's first meeting was actually one of my last. I remember him sitting down next to me on a cracked and faded leather couch, nodding hello, and waiting quietly for the meeting to begin. With almost two dozen people in the room that night, the proceedings were slow. As was customary, people took turns introducing themselves around the room and then telling the stories of their crises of faith, their strained relationships with family members, and how they were doing now that they were six weeks, five months, or a year and a half out of the church—"It gets better," the veterans would say. "Just hang in there," they sympathetically counselled the new arrivals.

Jacob's turn did not arrive until two hours into the session. I was growing restless. For two hours, we had all sat patiently listening to how Rick's wife was threatening to take the kids and leave; how Peggy's parents had told her, "It'd be best if we had some distance for a while"; Leann's confession of long-repressed sexual abuse; and Jeremy's guilt for "putting my kids through all this." When it came to Jacob's turn, he introduced himself to the room with an awkward smile:

> I don't really know what to say. I don't know what I'm doing here. I just found out about this group like forty-five minutes ago online. I actually just found out the church isn't true two days ago, so all of this is real new to me right now. I'm still trying to figure out what's going on and what I think about everything. All I can say for now, I guess, is that I feel like I've lost everything. It's like my whole world is slipping through my hands like sand. I guess I came here tonight because I just didn't know where else to go. Thanks for having me.

Over the course of my fieldwork, I would hear some version of these sentiments repeated time and again. Ex-Mormons described how "finding out the church wasn't true" had left their world in disarray. While people often felt anger, sadness, guilt, or disappointment after leaving the church, people's immediate experience of disenchantment was often eerily inarticulate, at times manifesting only in the form of a vacant stare.

When attempting to explain their condition, ex-Mormons often spoke in abstract and apocalyptic metaphor. Jacob would later tell me that life in the church felt like climbing up the side of an enormous rock wall, the vast expanse of its stony face consuming his vision, its craggy holds supporting his weight as he dutifully climbed ever skyward, laboring upward toward the promised destination of the celestial kingdom. But when he lost his faith, it was as if that wall had suddenly collapsed beneath him, and he found himself terrifyingly suspended in nothingness. A proficient rock climber, Jacob's choice of analogy was informed by his previous experience of the risk of falling from a great height. The logic of that analogy, however, was not his alone and seemed more apropos than I think he was aware. Many people spoke of feeling like they were "floating," that their world "literally shook" or was "crumbling beneath [their] feet." Others described their experience as being in a dream where "nothing seems real," while some intimated that they were instead "waking up from a dream" only to find that "the world [they] thought [they] had been living in was all make believe."

Common to each of these descriptions was the expression of an abrupt, unexpected, and cataclysmic change, with the emphasis on a disruption of "vital contact" (quoted in Spiegelberg 1972) to a plane of existence or "lifeworld" (Schutz 1967) in which they once had comfortably existed via their acquisition of tacit competences, practices, and attitudes (Habermas 1985). To use another metaphor, the symbolic scaffolding that had once constituted the entire system of meaning in which they existed—and the social relationships, everyday routines, and sense of self that emerged from it—had collapsed. They found themselves living a life stripped of its familiar anchor points, in which they were forced to "pick up the pieces" of their former existence, as one man put it, and "figure everything out again from the ground up."

Such an experience of world collapse is possible only in unique situations in which a singular ideology, institution, or belief system encompasses the entirety of a person's existence. And indeed, this is the kind of world in which ex-Mormons once lived. For them, church was not just a place you went on Sundays and religious faith was not something isolated to nightly prayers or belief in God or heaven. Church membership had intimately informed every facet of these people's existence, from their everyday routines and life goals to their personal relationships and collective identities.

As the Danish philosopher Søren Kierkegaard described, to "be" entails an ontological awareness of the reality in which we exist, a continual act of "doing" situated within familiar reference points, points that for Mormons are provided by the LDS faith. However, in the absence of such anchoring points, people are thought to experience acute and often severe forms of anxiety—what Kierkegaard (1941) terms a fear of "nothingness," the threat of "meaninglessness." They experience this as a disintegration of the self or a "dissolution of the existence of . . . personality" altogether (Goldstein 1940). In such cases of "existential anxiety," the experience is not one of being afflicted by something that someone "has" but rather what someone "is." Their entire "being" comes to "personify anxiety" (May 1977).

Attempting to observe and describe the experience of "world collapse" in the midst of religious disenchantment is somewhat akin to trying to catch a shadow. The reality of its existence cannot be denied, yet it is intangible and elusive. It is a phenomenon that exists in the negative. It lacks a substantive "thereness" to point to. What I attempt to analyze here is not the presence of culture or the workings of religion—the practices, identities, or systems of belief that together make up the "lifeworld" of a people and that often serve as the "stuff" of which traditional anthropological analysis is made. Rather, I focus on the ephemeral consequences for people's sense of self and subjectivity when the ontological foundations of culture crumble away.

To analyze these issues, I primarily focus on Jacob's experience with disenchantment as it unfolded in the weeks and months following his loss of faith. We discussed his experiences during in-depth interviews and fleeting conversations. Jacob's experiences are both uniquely his own and in some sense shared among all ex-Mormons who were once faithful church members in Utah. Jacob was a single man in his late twenties who had served a two-year proselytizing mission and envisioned himself one day marrying and building a Mormon family. Some of his experiences were therefore different from women and men of an older generation. However, Jacob's experience of loss of the primary functional attributes of religion—ritual, sacred identity, spiritual wonderment, and so on—are not unique to him alone but are widely shared among ex-Mormons.

Jacob's experiences of loss and emotional turmoil during the first few months outside the church do not characterize all that he felt. He, like many ex-Mormons, experienced a great sense of psychological and social liberation. Leaving the church meant no longer living with what some people described as "cognitive dissonance," artificially forcing the complexity of a morally ambiguous world within the confines of Mormonism's binary conception of good and evil; wearing clammy temple garments under his clothes in the hot summer heat; or devoting dozens of hours per week to church activities.

However, such experiences of liberation are countered by equally powerful experiences of *loss*, and this is what I am primarily interested in. For many ex-Mormons, the church had fulfilled their basic needs and more, providing an ever-present community and social network, a coherent worldview, a sense of meaning and purpose, an array of social and ritual activities to participate in, and deep spiritual and emotional comfort. These people had lived in this "world" for their entire lives—one shared with friends, family members, coworkers, and neighbors—which made their decision to leave the church into a daunting and isolating experience.

Beyond mere psychologizing, anthropological analysis of this kind of experience has the potential to serve as a subtle critique of several claims made by theories of secularization. First, secularization in the United States has not resulted in a mode of life inherently crosscut by the secular; people do not move seamlessly between belief and disbelief. Also, religion has not been relegated to a matter of "individual persuasion" or isolated to church buildings on Sunday mornings. For ex-Mormons, disenchantment entails equally disturbing experiences of "world collapse" because their religion—its teachings, principles, values, practices, institutions, and relationships—once *entirely defined* their world. Second, movement between—or, in this case, *away from*—religion(s) cannot be understood using the increasingly popular terminology of "rational choice theory," which describes individuals "shopping" for spirituality in a "marketplace" of religions. The ex-Mormons I talked to did not leave Mormonism for "greener pastures" because life in the church no longer provided enough "benefits." Their *loss* of faith was not immediately recompensed by a relative *gain* in converting to something else. Instead, it was at first existentially, psychologically, socially, and culturally traumatic. Everything and everyone, including themselves, now seemed strange and unfamiliar.

An Unsheltered Existence

I met Jacob at a pizza shop a few blocks away from a support group that he and I had attended one Sunday morning. We were almost unable to locate a restaurant open on a Sunday where we could go have lunch and talk—the town had been hushed under the solemn cloak of the Sabbath. Groups of families going to or from church in their Sunday attire strolled down sidewalks, towing their scriptures along with them in small black briefcases. "It's weird being on the other side of things like this," Jacob said as we stepped into the restaurant. "We never went out to eat on Sunday. I'd see people who weren't dressed up and know that they hadn't been to church. We felt sorry for them. We thought how lonely they must be on a Sunday when everyone else was at church."

Jacob's memory of seeing those on "the other side" as lonely and forlorn objects of pity seemed especially ironic now that he inhabited this place of "otherness" himself. Divisions between those inside and those outside the church had been created and solidified in his mind while he was a member, when the extent of one's moral personhood was determined by his or her adherence to the church's teachings. Church members were, by following the "plan of happiness," inherently "good," while people who had left or never accepted its teachings were believed to be stuck in a life of sin. Falling away from the church meant falling into this world of loneliness, isolation, and evil, an existence cut off from the warm embrace of church membership. Worse yet, he had believed that those who left were sometimes complacently unaware of their spiritually corrupt condition, having been deceived by Satan into following a path of self-destruction.

Listening to active members give their testimonies of belief and obedience to church teachings, I often heard people exclaim how "thankful" or "blessed" they were to have the church. They punctuated this with stories of the stark contrast they saw between themselves and those they knew who had left. For example, I watched a woman one Sunday afternoon exclaim to her fellow ward members, "Looking at all of you gathered here, I just know this is where I belong. I see my sister-in-law who lives in Colorado [who left the church] and I know she doesn't have this. It seems like she's running around confused all of the time, making bad decisions and whatnot. I know that personally, if I didn't have this church, my life would be like that."

The effects of this logic create what ex-Mormons refer to as a "bubble" around the church community where the meaning and value of everyday existence only makes sense when enclosed within it. "I always thought that somehow life wasn't really worth living outside of the church," Jacob explained to me as we sat down at our table that afternoon. "You think that everything that's worth anything only exists in the church. I mean, really, you feel like it's the only source of good or happiness." Leaving the church, he feared, meant losing a community of moral, spiritual, and social support outside of which life might ultimately prove unbearably chaotic and unfulfilling.

In this way, Mormonism, as it exists in Utah, creates for its members a total worldview that actively defines and controls the very reality it teaches its members about. There are a number of givens about the world that this mind-set affords. Everything—including the meaning of past, present, and future events; the purpose of life; the moral code members are supposed to live by; and individuals' places in the order of existence—is laid out and rendered comprehensible. This cultural-religious cosmology is then overlaid with a sense of eternal significance, in which conformity is believed to produce divine blessings, while disobedience results in both temporal and spiritual consequences. All this affords members a sense that their worldview is the only one possible, while everything outside of it is nonsensical and unsafe.

Like other ex-Mormons I knew, Jacob said that this led Mormons to live a "sheltered" existence. Jacob's life had indeed been routine and predictable. His weeks were structured around church duties and activities and filled with a combination of prayer, scripture study, Family Home Evenings (FHEs), sacrament meetings on Sunday, time devoted to "service," organizational meetings with other ward office holders, and visits to the temple. The "correlated" church lesson materials he read, the schedule of sacrament meetings he attended, and the bureaucratic authority structure in which he served as a priesthood holder had all granted his life a measure of mechanical conventionality.

As Jacob contemplated the repercussions of leaving the church, a kind of tautological logic grew clear. His family had warned him that he was "making things harder on himself," that he could turn back if he wanted to and "make things right." The warning, which Jacob had received from both his parents and the church, seemed to be coming true. Friends stopped calling, and his family treated him as an object of pity. They had effectively made him into the social pariah they had predicted he would become.

Mostly, however, Jacob described feeling vulnerable and exposed. He no longer felt comfortably sheltered and was forced to come face-to-face with the inherent unpredictability and ambiguity of life. He had already begun to feel isolated from friends and family and worried what he would do if he faced an insurmountable problem, such as contracting a debilitating illness or suddenly losing his job and being out of money. He feared that he would prove incapable, unable to cope with a life utterly foreign and perilous outside the church. Potential obstacles found in everyday life now took on inflated significance for him that he found paralyzing. "I wonder sometimes, what if all this doesn't work out? What if I can't deal with it all, you know?" The vague ambiguity in Jacob's pronounced fear of "it all" referenced and encapsulated the entirety of his existence, which could ultimately prove problematic "outside the church."

These issues weigh heavily on those who leave the church. As we sat eating our meal at the pizza shop, the den of noise in that restaurant on that Sunday afternoon punctuated the reverent silence outside. Jacob told me that he worried about whether he was "making a mistake." A lifetime spent living in a world of only two modes of being, two categories of personhood, had stymied Jacob's ability to think outside "the bubble." "What if they're all right about everything?" he asked. "Sometimes I just can't shake the thought that maybe Satan really is deceiving me, and I'm making a mistake. I guess I'll only really know after I die."

Divine Emplacement

Jacob often visited the majestic and rugged landscape of southern Utah where, staring up at the cragged red rock of Zion National Park's canyons, he could ponder how Heavenly Father created and set aside this place in which the Saints could flourish while they restored his one true church. Proof of this existed, he told me, not far from his house. Once while on a walk together through Jacob's childhood neighborhood, he pointed up to a concrete structure built into a nearby hillside. "That's the 'dream mine,'" he said. "I was always told there was tons of gold left in the mines, but it would only be found in the end times." Mormon folk stories tell of economic calamities during the future apocalypse and how the dream mine, filled with untold riches, would indefinitely sustain the church. For Jacob, however, it had always served as a potent reminder that the present and future prosperity of the Saints was intimately connected to this land. It was their home, their refuge, and their sanctuary.

However, this feeling of divine emplacement situated Jacob not only within his immediate Utah surroundings but also out into a broader cosmological realm as well. In the church, Jacob was taught that science would eventually prove what Mormons already knew about the preexistence, the afterlife, and other tenets of Mormon cosmology such as how other planets, circling other faraway stars, were perhaps home to entire civilizations of people Heavenly Father had created. Jacob told me about his memories camping in the wilderness of Utah's backcountry mountains—the stars gleaming in the darkened sky—wondering if he could catch a glimpse of Kolob, the star fabled to sit closest to the celestial kingdom, where Jacob had once believed he had lived alongside Heavenly Father in the preexistence. He remembered longing for the day when Heavenly Father would provide "further light and knowledge" and finally explain the mysteries of the universe, granting his followers a "pure intelligence" through which they could understand the riddles of existence and their role in its supernatural unfolding.

In disenchantment, however, the world seemed drained of its vibrancy—placid, imminently material, and dull. As the enchantment of Mormonism's belief system faded, a world once transfigured by celestial meaning slipped into a harsh, pitiless material reality. "There's no more mystery," Jacob complained when I asked if he missed thinking about that otherworldly existence. "Now I know this is it. This is all we've got," he muttered. "And I think in some ways there's something sad about that, you know, no mystery." The four-dimensional world in which Jacob had existed was reduced to three. There no longer seemed to be an aura of spiritual significance or sparkle of divine transcendence overlapping with the base material world in which he now felt stuck. "Before, anywhere I'd go, I was reminded of Heavenly Father. The trees, the mountains, the rivers, all of it gave me peace and comfort because it was as if it had all been put there for me. I mean, everything still looks the same, but now it all just feels kind of dull and dead."

The world around him now seemed alien and disquieting, dangerous and unforgiving. He explained to me once how "in the church you feel like the whole universe is on your side. Like everything fits together and is somehow looking out for you." However, on a recent rock climbing trip, he found himself suddenly acutely aware of the change in perspective he had undergone as he hung above the earth, grasping the bare rock. "I got scared. And I never get scared climbing; I'm usually just in a zone. And when you get scared, you have problems. It was like I knew that I could get hurt, like that was a real possibility now. It's weird to say, but I realized that the rock wouldn't care if I slipped and fell."

Jacob now faced new questions about the ultimate meaning of human existence that he was unprepared to answer. In the church, he explained, "if there's something that doesn't make sense, you always have this hope and confidence that you'll understand it someday. Like if you just hang on long enough and trust Heavenly Father, any question you have will be answered." However, Jacob now seemed unnerved by those questions that, though they had always perplexed him, had seemed trivial in light of the grand scope of Mormon cosmology:

> I learned about evolution in school. That was one thing, I always knew about this other stuff that was out there. But I never really gave it much thought. I never had to think about what it meant to think that we might have evolved from apes or whatever. Now it's like, if we're just like apes, just like any other animals, then really nothing makes us any better or different. If that's the case, we're really not that special; we just do a good job of telling ourselves that. We're just basically animals who eat, shit, and die like everything else.

He especially struggled with coming to terms with death. Untampered by Mormonism's teachings about eternal life and the celestial kingdom, death's inevitability and finality was singularly unnerving. In the church, Jacob had believed that death simply marked the passage from one state of existence to the next, that the very materiality of human bodies would be reconstituted in perfect form in the celestial kingdom. Yet in disenchantment, he came face-to-face with a new kind of mortality, a frailty he didn't know how to manage. He now found himself trapped within a body hurtling headlong into inevitable decay. I remember Jacob staring down at his hands one evening as we sat talking on my front stoop. With his fingertip, he gently traced the contours of the bones, tendons, and veins running down the back of his hands, observing his flesh as something foreign and fragile. "It's amazing to think, you know, that someday all this will just rot away. That's it; I'll be gone. It's weird, really. I never really thought about it like that before . . . Whenever I used to think about death, I always imagined what it'd be like to, you know, be in heaven, or whatever, and there'd be no more pain or anything. It can be really depressing if you think about it too much. We're all just destined to sit underground in a wood box."

In addition to the strangeness of his own body, Jacob also began to question the ontological status of existence itself. He no longer felt grounded in the reality of the world. It had in some ways lost its solidity and transformed into something ephemeral and fragile. There had been a subtle yet undeniable shift in perspective, in which things in the world, though appearing the same, had taken on a fundamental sense of strangeness. "I sometimes feel like I'm living in a dream. Like all of this will go away, and I'll wake up somewhere else. I don't know where, really, but not here. It's like everything is real and not real at the same time." Similarly, the people in Jacob's life with whom he was intimately familiar also no longer seemed "real." In the church, he had felt united and connected to his family—his reality and theirs intersubjectively interwoven, as if he understood and appreciated each of them on a deep, sacred level. "I thought we were meant to be together. Like Mormonism teaches, that we knew each other in the preexistence." However, in disenchantment, that deep familiarity and sense of common origins and substance had turned strange: "I looked at my dad, and I was just sad. Here was this person who used to mean the world to me, and I guess he still does on some level, but I remember one time catching myself staring at him and feeling like I was looking at a stranger. Here, I've known him my whole life. I mean, he's my dad, and all I can think is how distant I feel from him now. It was like I knew him but didn't know him at the same time."

When I asked Jacob to explain this, he described how he and his family cannot talk to each other anymore, as they no longer shared a common language or familiar reference points for communication: "We have nothing to say to each other. Their whole world revolves around the church, and that's all they talk about. It's like they're trapped in this other universe that only they know exists, and unless you speak the same language they do, and talk about things the same way as they do, you don't fit in. When I'm with them now, all I hear is the church's indoctrination speaking through them."

For Jacob, the world and people around him no longer felt authentic and instead had reemerged as a "hyperreality" of superficial, mass-produced reproductions, hollow and empty. He described people as manufactured reproductions or simulations of Mormonism's teachings, rendered nonexistent in any "real" sense by virtue of their religious "programming." He stated, "Part of me feels like everyone around here is missing something, you know, that makes them fully human. They all look the same, dress the same, talk the same . . . Everyone thinks they're an individual. When you're in the church you think, 'Oh, this person is really good at the piano, and this one likes to cook, how diverse we are!' But that's not really the case. Once you get out, you see it. We're all just little robots, trained to think and act the same way. We all have the same programming."

The Perils of Uncertainty

While in the church, when Jacob felt stressed, confused, or anxious, his faith gave him a feeling of control and security. The rituals of daily prayer and scripture study provided frequent opportunities for personal reflection and meditation, to commune with God, and to seek guidance from the Heavenly Spirit. Inevitably, while reading and pondering over his scriptures, answers to his most pressing questions would be revealed—why his brother had died in that car accident last spring or why his new employers now routinely overlooked him for promotion. "I'd pray about something, ask God to tell me what to do, then flip open my scriptures," Jacob told me one day as we sat in my living room. As we talked, Jacob picked up a cheap copy of the Book of Mormon that sat on my coffee table.

He opened its cover and flipped through the pages before pressing his finger onto a random passage of scripture, demonstrating. "I'd always find something that *spoke* to me," he said. In these times of quiet contemplation, he found solace, reassurance, and inspiration, a means of understanding the seemingly inexplicable accidents and traumas that afflicted him, and a road map for making sense of life when his path seemed uncertain.

Being attentive to the "promptings of the spirit" is another way in which Mormons can mitigate uncertainty. Jacob said he had learned to experience the Heavenly Spirit's presence in his life by the time he was twelve years old, a supernatural relationship he continued to foster for the next several decades. When gathering in his living room for family prayer, singing hymns at church, or visiting the temple, he would feel a calm assurance wash over him, a sense of clarity and peace as the "still small voice" of the spirit "whispered" to his heart. Listening to the spirit in this way tapped him into a constant source of divine inspiration and guidance. He would ponder and pray over the significance of every interaction, thought, or experience, trying to deduce the message contained within it, what God was trying to tell him. "I used to pray about everything. Big stuff, little stuff, it didn't matter. The church teaches you to listen to the spirit. I took that very seriously. I was always connected." Eventually, all of Jacob's emotions, sensations, and feelings became spiritually significant. "Warm feelings" while watching a movie, visiting a friend, or witnessing a sunset were interpreted as a message, a prompting, or an inspiration from the spirit and gave him the confidence that "all was right with the world." In such a mind-set, feelings of nervousness, guilt, or apprehension were for him blatant "reminders that I wasn't doing something right."

"Having faith" in this way became a means of mitigating the inherent risks built into everyday life and the existential quandaries evoked by it. The sense of invulnerability provided by faith was built on believers' ability to bracket off negative possibilities and instead maintain a generalized attitude of hope. It also, however, produced in Jacob a propensity to habitually analyze his feelings and sensations as "promptings" from the divine, without which he felt "lost." "I remember when I would start messing up, living in sin or whatever, I'd feel like the spirit stopped talking to me. That was all it took sometimes to get me back on the right path, I was so scared of making a bad decision."

Jacob said that when he realized that the Heavenly Spirit did not, in fact, speak to him, it was one of the most unnerving experiences of leaving the church. "When everything really went to shit was when I realized the spirit was just my own voice inside my head. I realized that for the past twenty years, I had just been talking to myself, and there really wasn't anything there helping me. After that I just remember feeling so alone . . . and then I started to panic."

Without a divine source of guidance, Jacob lost the ability to feel secure and confident.

> Things didn't used to faze me. I didn't use to worry about things the way I do now. You know, bad things would happen, but I felt like I could always handle them. Now I feel like the littlest problems quickly blow up into something much bigger than they need to be . . . Like last month, rent was due, and I was freaking out because I didn't have the money. See, so before I would have been worried, but deep down I knew God would be there, I knew I'd have the money in time. It all worked out eventually, but it's stuff like that that can get to you.

Problems like these began to crop up for Jacob more frequently as time went on. He described his life as now stuck in a "harsh reality" that people in the church were "sheltered" from. He now felt as if the future was full of unknown risks that he felt ill-equipped to handle, a stark contrast to the bold confidence he had felt before. "Reality" now became a chaotic and unpredictable enclosure from which he could not escape, yet which he felt powerless to effectively deal with. Everyday life had to be confronted in all of its immediate ambiguities and complexities, leaving Jacob emotionally and mentally exhausted:

> That's really hard, you know. I miss feeling like I have something to fall back on. Even if it's all just make believe. That's one of the hardest parts about all this and I think what scares me about becoming an atheist. It's like you're stuck in reality and never get a break. I hear other people say that, like, after they leave the church, there's no more happy place to run to in your mind. It's so much easier when you can just put your head down and your blinders on and say, I'm going to follow the prophet. When I was in the church, life was so much easier that way. You don't really have to think about things as much. It kind of just is the way it is. It makes it easier to be hopeful about everything when you believe everything is part of God's plan. Really, all you have to do is stay in line, do what you're supposed to, and you're set. People really take that saying seriously, you know, "hold tight to the iron rod." You get in this mind-set that if you let go, everything will go to hell. And in some ways, I think that's true. If you can stay trapped inside the bubble, life isn't so bad. You always know things will work out the way they are supposed to. You're never really alone because you always have the church or God or someone to look after you.

In addition to hope, Jacob's faith had provided him a ritual means of pacifying the inherent anxieties of daily existence. As a priesthood holder, Jacob was able to give blessings to those in need—the fear and pain that accompanies sickness and death were tempered by his hand. For example, Jacob told me how once, when his mother fell sick with pneumonia, Jacob anointed her with oil and prayed a blessing over her, an act that he said brought her comfort and, as he believed at the time, a speedy recovery.

However, dealing with such matters was very different after Jacob lost his faith. Three months after telling his parents he was leaving the church, Jacob's father fell gravely ill. He had been diagnosed with stage three lung cancer and started chemotherapy treatments at the Utah University Hospital in Salt Lake City. Even months after the diagnosis, Jacob largely avoided discussing his father with me and would typically change the topic when I mentioned him. However, during one conversation when he did open up about his father, I noticed Jacob playing nervously with a small metal vial hanging on a key ring, which contained a small amount of oil used by priesthood holders to give emergency blessings. "It's times like these that I really miss the priesthood," he told me. "It's like, I can't do anything. I can't comfort him the way he wants. When he's sick [from chemotherapy], all I can do is sit there and watch him suffer. Every time I go up to see him, he looks worse. He's skinny and pale and just wants to sleep." Jacob watched as his father's friends in the ward came over to the house to give him blessings, his loss of the priesthood preventing him from joining in the group of men lovingly huddled around his father's bedside. "I knew what they were doing wouldn't cure him, but at least it's something, you know?" More so, the possibility of losing his father for eternity haunted Jacob. The finality of death hit him as he described the lost opportunities to connect with his dad, the lost prospect of someday having a relationship made whole after death, which was all made grossly evident in what Jacob feared were his dad's waning moments on earth. The pain of the loss of a once-promised future weighed heavily on him. "What am I supposed to do? This is it. There's nothing else after this. I wish I could just tell myself it'll all be OK no matter what. But it won't."

Sacred Self and Identity

Mormonism gives a sense of meaning and purpose to life because, in many ways, it provides a comprehensive prepackaged identity and eternal goals toward which worldly labors and activities can be directed. This is articulated most evidently in the plan of salvation and the collective effort to "build the kingdom of Zion." Indeed, Jacob had fully embraced the idea that his primary station in life was to "do the work of the Lord," defined in scripture as "to bring to pass the immortality and eternal life of man" (Moses 1:39). Doing temple work, dutifully tithing, converting new members to the church, strengthening others' testimonies, and providing service to fellow church members all contributed to these goals. They all provided Jacob with a daily sense of direction and purpose that was comforting and fulfilling. "You really feel like you're working towards something. Like God is depending on you. It felt good to know there was a purpose to everything I did."

Jacob's daily and weekly schedule had been fastidiously planned around various church activities, a set of labors and duties that he took great pride and satisfaction in while a member. On Monday, he met with his parents and young unmarried siblings for FHE, where they read scriptures, sang hymns, and prayed together. Throughout the week, he worked on his duties as a Sunday school teacher, assisted another ward member in organizing activities for the young men's Boy Scout troop, performed proxy ordinances (baptisms and endowments) in the temple, and held his own personal scripture study every morning. On the weekends, he attended ward picnics, served as a home teacher to a family in his neighborhood, and attended Sunday sacrament meetings where he also led Sunday school lessons.

Mormonism similarly bolstered Jacob's sense of collective pride and purpose by providing a mythohistorical narrative of persecution and redemption in which church members were staged as key players in a great struggle to restore Christ's church in these end times. In the church, Jacob was repeatedly reminded that the Saints were a persecuted people, subject to being misunderstood and viciously maligned by a jealous and fearful American populace. Yet they were guided by a prophet of God who revealed God's truth to his chosen people. Jacob believed that the Mormon people served, as he was taught, as a "city upon a hill" (Hinckley 1990) and that the larger society would eventually turn to them for guidance as the world slipped further into moral decay. "I really thought everyone looked up to us. They may have made fun of us or criticized us, or whatever, but really they were jealous of what we had." Jacob remembers the feeling of quiet confidence this gave him while vacationing with his family on the South Carolina coast. "We'd walk down the street, and I'd see people who were obviously not Mormon. If they happened to look at us, I would think, 'Yeah, they know who we are,' you know, like they could feel something different about us, like we were special." Jacob later told me that he knew one day the rest of the world would come "knocking at our door" for help in the end times. "You get this feeling that everyone [else] will be proved wrong, and we'll be proven right. You know, that someday they'll get what they deserve and then we'll be the ones calling the shots. It's really an addictive thing to believe. It makes you feel almost invincible."

In this way, Mormonism also gave Jacob an understanding of the significance of his personal identity. In moments of quiet spiritual contemplation, Jacob had tried to imagine what life was like before he had entered into this mortal, temporal world. He would often experience a sense of transcendent wonderment when flashes of "memory" from the preexistence came back to him, when he felt like he *knew* what it was like to live as a spirit and to have a "full" knowledge of Heavenly Father's plan of happiness before the veil had been pulled over his memory when he entered mortal life.

This knowledge of the preexistence had not only positioned Jacob in a grand Mormon cosmology but also provided him with an immediate sense of pride and purpose that he could draw on in everyday life, as it situated him within a continuously unfolding supernatural narrative in which he personally played a central role. Specifically, church leaders had often told Jacob and others in this "chosen generation" about how in the preexistence they had proven themselves in great battles fought in heaven against the forces of Satan and how now on earth, they were expected to continue that battle as they "wielded the power of the priesthood" against the "forces of immorality" and "deception" by "restoring" the Heavenly Father's truth to the world. With a slender frame and a passive, at times awkward demeanor, Jacob was hardly a model of strong-willed masculine virility, much less a heavenly warrior. But as he told me about the church's teachings on the great "war in heaven," I saw an image of the man he longed to be and had in part become through his imaginative play as a heavenly warrior in the preexistence. "Church leaders would talk about what we had done and how we had earned the privilege to be born in the end times. I loved hearing that," he said with a self-conscious smile. "I guess because I always felt like I'd done something, you know. Like I was special. I was proud of that."

While he was a member of the church, this cosmological narrative of divine purpose had become inextricable from Jacob's personal biography. Ever since he was a child, Jacob had envisioned a future for himself in which he not only was a faithful church member but would also play a leadership role in "building the kingdom." "You know, my parents, they always thought I would end up being some sort of general authority. Not the prophet, but probably either an apostle or one of the seventy. They were really grooming me for it. I don't know what it was; I don't think they told that to my brothers. Maybe they were just trying to keep me in line, you know? But it worked. That's what I really thought. I was destined to be somebody big in the church. I really took that to heart."

In Mormonism, Jacob's autonomous sense of self was indistinguishable from the collective myths and stories shared throughout the church. That is, Jacob had only ever been able to think about himself, in some kind of self-reflexive awareness of individuality, through the cultural narratives and symbols provided by Mormonism. His only sense of worthiness, purpose, identity, or selfhood came from the church, and it was only achievable through active, faithful membership in the church. Without this, he was, in essence, nothing.

In disenchantment, Jacob felt that sense of fearless confidence and purpose fall away. The world no longer felt "given" to him, his place in it no longer guaranteed by stories of being part of a "chosen generation" or a "chosen people" who occupied a "city on a hill." Jacob began to see himself as part of a global society filled with tremendous diversity, in which he and his religious community's position at the center of a divine historical narrative was undermined by the growing awareness of a multiplicity of actors on a global stage. I first became aware of this while talking with Jacob about his experiences serving as a missionary, in which he reflected on why the people to whom he was proselytizing seemed indifferent to hearing the gospel:

> They [church leaders] had always told us that when people closed the door on us, it was because their hearts were hardened. They knew we had the truth; they just didn't want to have to hear it; they didn't want to have to change their

> lives . . . It was hard having literally thousands of doors closed in your face for two years. But that also kind of gave us confidence. It made us feel like we had something powerful to offer, and people just weren't able or willing to handle it. Thinking back on it, though, I think that was the beginning of all this. I think about all the people I talked to. They were all just living their lives, you know? It was like, here I come, a twenty-year-old kid, knocking on their door telling them I have the truth. And I didn't even stop to think what their life was like . . . There are so many people out there, all doing just fine without me and without the church. They didn't care what I had to say; they didn't think I was special. I was just annoying to them.

When a sense of self is totally wrapped up in a religious lifeworld, the loss of religious beliefs can result in a loss of self in its most basic terms. "I don't know who I am anymore," Jacob once somberly confessed. "All I've ever been is Mormon. I don't know how else to think about things. I realize now that everything I did wasn't because I really wanted to, it was because that's what the church taught me to do. Everything I was going after, I wanted because Mormonism told me to want it. So really, what's left? That's something I'm really struggling with right now. I'm just afraid that I'm nobody without the church. But now that I don't even have the church, being nobody is all I've got."

As the German existentialist philosopher Martin Heidegger theorized, what we may think of as the self (or what Heidegger refers to as *Dasein*) is formed through the practical engagements of people caught up in meaningful labor. While social scientific conceptions of identity and personhood are externally mediated, the self is that which emerges in the midst of internally mediated goal-directed activities and practical engagements with the larger world. Without such activities, Viktor Frankl ([1946] 2006) writes, the self risks falling into a state of anxious depression. Existential disillusionment and suffering arises when life no longer seems to have an intrinsic meaning and the self has no purpose for its existence.

Jacob at times complained to me that since leaving the church, he had felt an unrelenting cloud of misery hanging over him. "It gets unbearable sometimes. I have to stop myself when I get [to] thinking about it too much. I get really down sometimes, you know." Throughout our relationship, Jacob was often difficult to contact; at times, it seemed he purposefully avoided my phone calls and emails. When he did respond to my calls (which he eventually always did), he would give a terse apology, saying that he sometimes closed himself up at home and "ignored the world." He had turned ruminating on his purposelessness into a full time occupation, which only served to further amplify his misery. It seemed that dissociation had become Jacob's strategy for dealing with a world that no longer was the object of meaningful engagement. He had lost the focused direction that Mormonism had given his life. At the end of the day, he could no longer feel a sense of righteous accomplishment or that he had been "part of something" and fulfilled his duties as a member of the church, a steward of Heavenly Father's restored gospel. "That's something the church really does well: it gives you purpose. Because, now, like, what's the point? If there's no celestial kingdom, no reward or anything at the end of the rainbow, you're left having to decide all this stuff [about what to do with your life] on your own. And at that point, I sometimes just say who cares."

However, it was not only a lack of a singular direction to follow that unnerved Jacob. In disenchantment, he was confronted with a dizzying array of possibilities for his life that paralyzed his ability to choose any one direction over another. The loss of a singular sacred identity meant that he now could do anything he liked. However, facing such an "abyss of freedom" was a daunting experience, as Jacob no longer felt comfortably constrained by a prescribed path to follow (Kierkegaard 1981). "How are you supposed to know which way is the 'right way'?" he pondered while discussing what he would do next. "I don't know where to go. I feel like I should stay in Utah because this is where my parents are. But really, there's nothing here for me anymore. So where am I supposed to go? What am I supposed to do?" The fragmentation of one "right way" into an infinite assortment of possibilities meant that Jacob was confronted with the ability to choose any "way" he liked yet was without a means of deciding which one was the best.

Loss

Jacob and I attended a support group meeting one evening where Nathan and Laura, a middle-aged couple who were both "born in the covenant," told their story of leaving the church together. "We feel so fortunate to have gotten through it all together," they said to the audience of other ex-Mormons gathered for the meeting. But as Laura continued to explain, their disaffection had left them "emotionally scarred."

> There's so much we feel like we lost, though. That has been really hard for us, to see everything we worked towards taken away. I think that's important for all of us to recognize. Some might say we "willingly" gave our time and money and energy to the church. I don't think that's 100 percent correct, though, because everything we gave was under false pretenses. And that's how we feel, like we lost everything. The church promises you everything under the sun if you just do what it says. Then at some point, you realize, like us, you've given your whole lives all for a lie.

Others in our circle nodded in agreement. The sensation of loss encapsulated a shared mode of feeling that people experienced in leaving the church. For these ex-Mormons, disenchantment was characterized as the loss of a unified belief system or a church community and as a feeling that their lives had been taken away from them. The charmed existence they once saw themselves living as members of the "one true church" was replaced with a feeling of unmitigated loss as they reflected on the many decades, dollars, and deeds they had selflessly donated to a religion that had now lost its supernatural luster.

In disenchantment, people's personal pasts—memories of childhood, adolescence, and momentous life events—no longer held a sense of nostalgia but only regret and disappointment. "When I think about all the years I spent in the church, I just get angry," one man said. He described how the church had taken away his youth, something that he knew he "[would] never get back." He said he spent his childhood a "nervous wreck," worried that any little sin would jeopardize his future. "Let me tell you, so many humiliating times sitting in my bishop's office telling him about my 'chastity issues.'" He felt like his adolescence was stripped away from him, "co-opted by the church." "I could have gone and done anything. Instead, when I was nineteen, I went on a mission and I spent two years, two years when I should have been out meeting girls and enjoying life, instead feeling miserable." Another woman described her marriage in the church as a "sham," a relationship that had proved emotionally abusive, entered into only because "we thought we were doing the right thing, we were building our eternal family." At nineteen, she had no idea that she was "throwing [her] life away" by forfeiting the possibility of going to college or building a career. "We got married and started having kids. That was it. I was living the perfect Mormon life. I guess at one time that meant something to me. Now it just feels like I was living the life someone else wanted for me, not the one I would have chosen for myself."

The cost of disenchantment could also, for some ex-Mormons, literally be measured. I often met with Tom, a bus driver for the city of Provo, who told me how one day after he left the church, he calculated how much money he had given in tithing. At fifty-two years of age, Tom had been giving 10 percent of his income for thirty-eight years, ever since he began earning a paycheck at fourteen working at the local supermarket. "I forget how much it was exactly, but it was over a hundred thousand dollars," he said—enough that "if I had it all back, I could have probably retired in a few years and sent my kids to college." Instead, on the meager wages and retirement afforded by the city, he said he would probably be working well into his sixties just to make ends meet.

In disenchantment, the past then becomes measured in disappointments and lost opportunities, such that life in the present becomes an incessant reminder of what could have been. "What am I going to do now?" one man asked. "I'm almost forty, and all I've known is the church."

Split-Self and Hyperreflexivity

Human experience oscillates between periods of engrossment in everyday behaviors, thoughts, and reactions and periods of distanced self-reflexivity in which those same behaviors, thoughts, and reactions become the objects of critical reflection. Religion is attractive not only for the comprehensive worldview it provides but also, in part, for its provision of ready-made responses to everyday situations so that such moments of self-reflexivity can be kept at a minimum, thus granting life a relative sense of ease or coherency. However, in disenchantment, ex-Mormons found that the balance typically struck between immersion and reflection becomes unhinged. The usual taken-for-granted foundation of everyday assumptions and practices disappears, ultimately leaving them in a state of perpetual reflection and alienation from the self and the self-evident. Once-routine behaviors, decisions, and interactions now become the objects of intense scrutiny and deliberation.

For Jacob, this loss of what Anthony Giddens (1991) refers to as a "living spontaneity," or a preconscious awareness of how to handle once-routine behaviors, proved taxing. "It gets really tiring to have to think about everything you did before just kind of naturally. It's like, you can't go on autopilot anymore." One way Jacob experienced this was his inability to engage in sustained conversation with friends and family after his disenchantment. "My mind was either racing all the time, or it was like, nothing, like nothing was there. It was like, what do I say? All these things are going through my head all the time. My whole world was going up in flames, you know, everything I thought I knew for certain was just gone . . . it was all constantly buzzing through my head, and I couldn't talk about it with anyone. I knew they wouldn't understand. And then other times I felt like, nothing. Just nothing. Numb. Not good, not bad. Just numb." Jacob said he had to "consciously remind" himself that there were still things he cared about, otherwise he found himself "slipping" into a state of passive removal from everyday life. "I really didn't care about anything. My job, my friends, or my family. It was like nothing really mattered. I literally had to force myself to kind of just keep on with living, even if I didn't understand what that meant anymore."

Jacob also felt unable to deal with everyday social interactions outside of the church. "This sounds bad, but I realized how much I suck at flirting. I mean, dating in the church was awkward as shit too. But at least I kind of knew what to expect. You just make them think what a great priesthood holder you are, and bam, that's all it takes for half of them to be in love with you." Outside of the church, however, he found that the typical rules of dating in the church were no longer applicable, resulting in an overly self-consciousness demeanor that led to failure in dating. On his last date, he said he became awkward and shy, second-guessing every possible move he could make. "I went on a date last week with this one girl I knew from college. She wasn't Mormon, so naturally I was stoked to see how things went with someone that hadn't grown up in the church. Then I realized how stupid I am about dating. The whole time I'm just worrying about what to do or not to do, you know. If I hold her hand, what will she think of me? Is that too forward? Or is she expecting something more and I'm just not getting the signals?"

These experiences of hyperreflexivity lead to what psychologists refer to as a loss of self-affection, or "ipseity," in which there is a loss of the sense of existing as a self-possessed subject of awareness or activity (Sass 1994). While the logic of mainstream psychotherapy was founded on the idea that discursive self-scrutiny will restore a lost sense of self (such that a patient becomes "aware" of the conditions of his or her existence and thus gains some sense of control over them), ex-Mormons in the midst of disenchantment often seem to become counter-productively hyperreflexive. As Louis Sass has written regarding the psychopathology of psychosis, "[an attempt to] reassert control and reestablish a sense of self by means of introspective scrutiny may end up exacerbating feeling of self-alienation and fragmentation" (Sass 2001, 254).

This can manifest in the form of a temporal disruption in narratives of self, in which the biographical continuity of the self becomes fractured and broken into unarticulated discrete moments (Laing 1965). For ex-Mormons, this often manifests in the form of a disjuncture between "when I was in the church" and "since I left the church." For most ex-Mormons with whom I spoke, "when I was in the church" denoted a time in which they were unconsciously caught up in religious enchantment, when all of their thoughts and actions were shaped by the church. They at times seemed to disown that person as deluded, under the effects of "mind control," and often referred to life in the church as being "trapped in a cult." While such temporal divides allow for a disavowal of the former person, and in effect inaugurate the birth of a new one, they also sometimes unexpectedly trigger an awareness of the self as incongruent, internally divided, and having the propensity for self-delusion. One woman at a support group meeting worried that if she could be "fooled" into believing in Mormonism in the first place, how would she know if it was happening to her again. "*I* don't really trust *myself* anymore," she said.

While for some people, unshackling Mormonism's "mind control" resulted in feeling free and mentally unfettered, Jacob often felt paralyzed by his vacillation among alternative frames of reference, points of view, and systems of meaning—what Foucault (1970) has referred to as the affliction of the "heteroclite." "I lost my keys the other day," Jacob recounted, "and my immediate thought was to pray about it. I didn't. But then I had this really strong feeling like I should go outside and look for them. And there they were, in the driveway, where I must have dropped them. And I thought, OK, that could be one of those things you say is a blessing, you know, like the spirit told me to go outside. But I also knew it could just be a coincidence, or an intuition, or whatever." Such instances reflected Jacob's sense that he was somehow neither here nor there, stuck in-between two modes of reality, two conceptions of self that were fundamentally irreconcilable. A sense of self-continuity was thus disturbed, and the singular, autonomous self that typically functions as the seat of awareness fragmented under the weight of multiple heterogeneous modes-of-being that seemed to intersect in and divide

Jacob's psyche. "Sometimes I can't decide who is the real me, you know? How *I* really think about things. You can really drive yourself crazy trying to track it all down."

In response to all this, Jacob began to dissect his life, looking for remnants of Mormonism, searching for and hoping to parse what was uniquely his own and what was "implanted" by the church. For example, Jacob found himself no longer able to enjoy playing the piano, which he was quite proficient at. "I used to be able to play for hours. That was my thing, you know. Now I sit down to play, and all I can think about is the lady in my ward as a kid who taught me to play or how my mom always said my playing was 'inspired.' Then I question whether I ever really enjoyed playing the piano at all or if it was just something I thought I liked because it was what everyone did in the church." Yet the effect of such self-dissection is a crippling sense of self-alienation because becoming conscious of something is to perceive it as separate from the self, an object that can be critically analyzed and deconstructed. It was almost as if Jacob had become aware of himself as a product of cultural determination and therefore was divorced from the sense of being his own "authentic" self.

For most people, this self-dissecting search for authenticity revolved around the issue of personal morality. Although once guided by a moral code provided by church teachings, Jacob now found that the once-stark contrast between right and wrong appeared unnervingly blurred. Basic questions of morality had to be painstakingly reconceptualized outside of the moral horizons provided by notions of sin and righteousness. "It sounds silly, but you really go through this process of thinking about everything you ever thought was right or whatever, and asking yourself, 'Why do I think that?' Some stuff like not killing is easy, but most of it isn't so cut and dry." Jacob at times worried that without the church, he was at risk of unknowingly slipping into immorality. "I really worried that I'd somehow become this horrible person without the church, so it was really important to figure out how I wanted to live my life."

That he should be concerned with things like sin, moral pollution, and personal purity (and the people, places, objects, and events typically associated with them) no longer seemed obvious. Morality and righteousness had lost their "self-evident" truthfulness. Jacob scrutinized every decision he made outside of the church, attempting to analyze the origins and logical repercussions. Deciding whether to try drinking alcohol, a habit strictly forbidden within Mormonism, for example, proved to be an exhaustive exercise. Was drinking inherently harmful? Would it "pollute" his body and cause illness in unforeseen ways? Was it giving into his base human desires for debauchery? Were people who frequented bars or shopped at liquor stores looking for a "way to escape" their problems? Would it change who he was or how he treated friends or lead to his use of "hard" drugs? As we discussed these issues one night over beers, Jacob grew increasingly dismayed. Then in a moment of self-conscious crescendo, he pointed his fingertip to his head and blurted, "I just want to know when we're going to be able to measure all this in the brain." He continued, "When are we going to be able to say this is why we should do this thing or not do this thing? I want a quantified explanation of morality." I was not sure what Jacob meant by "quantified explanation of morality" or how exactly he thought morality could be "measured" in the brain. At the time, I was content to take his proclamations at face value and let his anxiety subside. When I think about it now, though, it seems he was looking for a way out of his paralyzing hyperreflexivity and indecisiveness. He longed for a solid, irrefutable, and unchanging explanation and blueprint for life, even if that meant searching for it in the dehumanized recesses of the material brain. Or through another few beers.

Someone to Show Him the Way

In the first few months that I knew Jacob, he considered himself an atheist because, as he said, "the idea of God just doesn't make sense anymore." And despite his introspectiveness in private, when around other ex-Mormons, he at times displayed a bold, unselfconscious bravado.

Despite this, he could be paranoid and insecure. In the first several months I knew him, Jacob often questioned whether I was really, as I claimed, a nonreligious anthropologist studying ex-Mormons or was, in fact, a closeted Christian—more specifically, a Baptist—surreptitiously infiltrating the ex-Mormon ranks in order to win converts. Though he never articulated what exactly made him feel this way about me, and despite my stern denial, when I asked him about it, he told me that it was "just something that [he got] the sense of."

"Baptists were always really proud about *being Baptist*," he said somewhat scornfully when talking about his mission in a part of the United States where the Baptist denomination was prevalent. When I asked him why he thought I was Baptist, he said it was because I was "nice to everybody," seemed "confident" and "sure of myself," and acted like I "know something that no one else does." He sometimes teased that he could see me "being a Baptist underneath, sitting back and watching us, then going home at night, laughing with all of your Christian buddies about us ex-Mormons."

Yet despite Jacob's paranoia, he was not entirely dismissive or weary of my presence. After visiting a mosque together in order to "observe" Islamic services, an outing Jacob invited me on as a part of a study of world faiths he was undertaking—and coincidentally during a time when he was fantasizing that I was a Baptist—he told me about a recent dream. In the dream, Jacob had been at a party at a friend's house somewhere in Provo where we both lived. When he left the house on foot, however, he didn't know where he was and found himself wandering the streets of town. After walking down unfamiliar streets and past unfamiliar houses, he saw my wife and I sitting on our front porch. Relieved to recognize us and our house, he hurried toward us. As he approached, however, we got up from our seats and walked inside, leaving him outside by himself again, though now with his bearings returned and thankfully able to find his way back to where he had parked his car. Then the dream ended. When Jacob told me the dream, I joked that I was sorry for walking inside without him and that he was of course welcome over to my home anytime. He laughed, replying that he was just grateful for us "being there to show me the way."

Together, Jacob's paranoia about my being a Baptist Christian and his dream about me showing him "the way" are evidence of a subjectivity destabilized by disenchantment and ever grasping for stability and safety. He had projected his loss onto me by creating a fantasy of a closeted identity and a hidden agenda that nevertheless reflected his most prescient feelings of lack. I was to Jacob an embodiment of that which he felt he had lost—pride, confidence, community, and a secret knowledge of truth—when he left the church. In his paranoid, fantasy-driven identification with me as the closeted Baptist, I think he demonstrated a continued desire for religiously inspired certainty that those who have been recently disenchanted feel like they lack in their postreligious lives. In fact, many ex-Mormons I spoke to longed to live in the "bubble" of "naïve faith" I discussed at the beginning of the chapter. During their transition out of the church, they described trying in vain to "make it work," to bring back the sense of comfort and security they had felt when they were believers, before eventually realizing that "once the bubble bursts, it can't be put back together."

Lasting Trauma

As a final thought, I want to point to several ways in which the loss and trauma of religious disenchantment is exacerbated in people's lives even after the initial shock has abated. First, those leaving the church feel isolated by the lack of sympathy or support they receive from friends and family. While their experience of disenchantment has left them emotionally and psychologically reeling, depressed, and at times suicidal, the only response they get from loved ones is that they should "come back to church"—in effect, that they should return to what they feel like is the source of their trauma. As Jacob explained to me once, "It was like, OK, my only options are to (A) throw away everything and everyone I've ever known. Or (B) try to shut my brain off, keep quiet, and go back as if nothing was wrong so everyone else would be happy. But really, what kind of choice is that?" Often, others' responses are coupled with dire warnings that if they should choose not to return, they are individually responsible for the eternal consequences, which leaves them feeling even further isolated. When Jacob told his family he no longer had a testimony of the church, his mother made herself into the victim. "She kept emailing me for weeks afterwards, telling me how much *I* was hurting *her*. Then my sisters would call and tell me how ashamed they were for me, that I could be this selfish and do this to our family. Somehow I became the bad guy, and all I felt was helpless as [I] was watching my whole world fall apart."

Ex-Mormons are often told or made to feel that they deserve to be suffering, since a lack or loss of faith is interpreted by the church community as a matter of individual responsibility and a reflection of a person's individual virtue and worthiness. Losing faith is seen as a result of spiritual laziness or rebelliousness, and former members are considered failures, unable or unwilling to commit themselves to the forms of righteous living that would ostensibly result in them having maintained their faith. Further, the anxiety, depression, and misery former members experience is interpreted as having been brought about by their choice to leave the church. As such, they are labelled as exemplars of what can naturally be expected to happen to someone who rejects truth. Such forms of religious suffering are therefore suffered in silence and isolation, unseen or unacknowledged by people's former communities. Attempts to talk about the suffering result in social marginalization and rejection, while keeping silent sentences the unbeliever to a life of intimate estrangement, where he or she perhaps coexists with friends and family but is unable to express his or her deepest fears, hurts, and grievances.

Jacob's inability to talk with friends and family about his disenchantment was not just a product of his growing social estrangement. Like other ex-Mormons I talked to, Jacob was often frustrated by his inability to capture the experience of disenchantment in words. Despite its profound effects on him, he often resorted to the woefully inadequate term *lost* to describe how he was feeling. The lack of a language to describe his experience proved especially unnerving and isolating, thrusting him into bouts of depression, as he described it at times. My attempts to empathize with his experiences only served to punctuate the near incomprehensibility of his condition. When I prodded him to better describe what he meant by "lost," asking if it made him feel scared, he replied, "You can't understand what we've been through unless you've been there yourself. How do you describe something like this? It's not like anything I've ever felt. It's not like you're scared. There's times you're scared, I guess, but there's something else. Everything you've ever known changes, and no one can see it but you." Unlike other kinds of experiences of trauma, there is not a singular event or object that can be identified as the "cause" of dismay and thus "worked on" through therapy—there is no clearly identifiable object of fear that provokes a recognizable feeling of being scared. Rather, disenchantment manifests as the attenuation of what Husserl referred to as an "intentional horizon" within which certain kinds of experiences had once been possible but now seemed out of reach (Smith and McIntyre 1982). As such, the "cause" of the trauma is both everywhere and nowhere at the same time, ever eluding precise identification or description and therefore only further amplifying its anxiety-inducing effects.

The lack of a set of concepts and terms to describe feelings of religious disenchantment or to identify the experience of religious trauma is further exacerbated by the normative status religion holds in American culture. Religion is held up as a bastion of moral values so that those who disavow it and become openly critical are made to feel as if they are shortsightedly ignoring the values of goodness, kindness, generosity, and so on that ostensibly stemmed from their religious upbringing. As a result, many former members feel as if their experiences are somehow unique to their personal situation or are tacitly dismissed altogether as a case of them "overreacting." Once, one of Jacob's non-Mormon coworkers noticed Jacob drinking coffee, an obvious breach of Mormonism's Word of Wisdom, and began talking about Jacob's recent disaffection. The coworker, though not actively churchgoing, had been raised Christian. He had been sympathetic at first to Jacob's situation. "You could tell he wanted to try to understand. But all he could say to make me feel better was how 'it couldn't have been all that bad' and how 'you can't focus on the negative stuff.'" The coworker told Jacob that he knew lots of other church members who all seemed to be happy and enjoy being Mormon, which left Jacob feeling personally challenged to "explain" his disaffection and stifle his complaints. "What do you do in a situation like that? I'm not going to sit there and argue with the guy; he doesn't know any different."

Jacob's coworker is the product of an American culture in which religion is both pervasive and viewed, if not with outright esteem, then as quaintly benign, consequently creating a lack of discursive space for stories of the damage that religion can inflict on people's lives. In the United States, an ethos of individualism and free will holds the individual personally responsible for his or her "decision" to be a member of the religion in the first place. This can be tremendously frustrating and a continuing source of alienation, even outside of the religious community. As one man explained, "When I try to tell people what Mormonism did to me, how it made me feel constantly guilty, made me waste two years of my life on a mission, forced me to play mind tricks on myself just to fit in, or caused me to have this anxiety and depression, they say, 'Why didn't I just leave before?' 'Before what!?' I want to tell them. It's like they think I somehow chose all this, as if somehow I could have seen it coming and gone somewhere else."

Finally, while the initial shock of disenchantment can be unnerving in the short term, the experience is often prolonged and amplified indefinitely by the ubiquity of religious symbolism surrounding the formerly religious in their everyday lives in Utah. Ex-Mormons living in Utah find themselves inundated with reminders of their former religious life and in some sense are forced to daily relive the trauma of disenchantment. They find that the psychological act of "leaving" the church and efforts to "get over it" are routinely undermined by the church's pervasive presence. Jacob described this feeling of being hemmed in by Mormonism: "Everywhere you go you see churches and temples . . . When I meet somebody new, you can bet they'll ask if I'm a member . . . you can try to get away, but it sometime feels impossible. Everyday I'm reminded of what I used to be, of everything I lost."

There is no easy solution to the issues I've discussed here. Finding a sense of purpose, identity, and intersubjectively constituted sense of emplacement in the world (Heidegger 1977) is a lifelong struggle that everyone, not only those who have undergone a "crisis of faith," must contend with. The road to "recovery" for those leaving the church is sometimes long and arduous, involving much "soul-searching" and personal experimentation with new ideas and new ways of living when ex-Mormons find themselves without the guiding (constraining) influence of the church. How they "recover" from these experiences of loss and disenchantment is a theme I deal with explicitly in the next chapter as I discuss how sex and atheism help mitigate feelings of loss and vulnerability and to a lesser degree in the following chapters when I turn to the politics of identity-making outside the church.

CHAPTER 4

"I Lost My Body to the Church"

SEXUAL AND SPIRITUAL (DIS)EMBODIMENT

For the ex-Mormons I talked to, membership in the church had been all-encompassing. It gave meaning and purpose to their entire sense of self and identity and defined who they were as members of their families and the broader community. In their daily lives, they strove to fill themselves with the Lord's divine presence, to "choose the right" in all actions, and to imbue within themselves a permanent disposition toward "righteous living." They did not experience this as a forced indoctrination but rather as an intimate and sacred form of embodied inhabitation. As members of the one true church, they had learned to attune themselves to the "promptings of the spirit," to treat their physical bodies as sacred temples, and to devote all of their worldly and sexual labors to building a "celestial family."

Upon leaving the church, however, ex-Mormons found that these embodied dispositions long outlived their quickly jettisoned spiritual beliefs. While ex-Mormons regularly talked with each other about why they left the church, the evils of religious dogmatism, the "evidence" against the church's teachings, and how Mormon beliefs are based on "logical fallacies" that they could now "see through," they said they still *felt* Mormon at times. Mormonism "gets into you," they exclaimed. It left an imprint on their lives in often quite stubborn ways.

When I started my research, I initially intended to study how, as disaffected ex-Mormons, people remembered life in the church. How different was life on the outside? What did they think of the church—and religion in general—from their new vantage point as presumably secular subjects? However, I quickly found that intellectually renouncing the church's teachings did not mean that they had successfully rid themselves of the feeling of *being Mormon*.

Ex-Mormons continued to inadvertently remember what they longed to forget. Even long after ex-Mormons thought they "were over it," they told me they were constantly surprised by the things that popped up in the midst of daily life as reminders that "we're all still Mormon." As one man told me, "You're driving in your car, and you hear a song on the radio, or you go someplace you haven't been to in a while, and a memory or a feeling will pop up . . . it might make you feel guilty for leaving, sad, or lonely, and you say, 'Whoa, I didn't realize that was still there.'"

The turn from religious to secular subjectivity is therefore not as straightforward as believing or not believing. As I found throughout my research, transitioning from a religious to a more secularized orientation of the world is not clearly demarcated by people's assent to or rejection of certain religious beliefs. Rather, for ex-Mormons, the transition unfolded through an ambivalent negotiation of ongoing embodied and affective memories of Mormonism and the morals, values, sensibilities, and habits that continued to inhabit them even though they no longer professed belief. We must therefore recognize how shifts in spiritual sensibility are experienced not only in the register of thoughts about cosmology or theology but also on a personal level due to Mormonism's ability to "get under the skin."

Anthropologists studying religion have long understood how the body is used by religious practitioners as a semiotic resource to communicate with the divine (Capps and Ochs 2002; Lester 2005) as well as how embodied practices are linked to particular ideologies, such as order, discipline, purity, or restraint (Simon 2009; Starrett 1995; Yafeh 2007). However, research on secularization and deconversion has yet to focus on the embodied subject as a particularly salient locus of disenchantment. Typically, the body is, as Drew Leder (1990) writes, concealed, hidden, or made "absent" in its everyday banality—and, I would add, it is made secondary to the institutional, political, and sociological fields in which these processes more readily seem to unfold. Yet for ex-Mormons in the midst of the psychological, emotional, and existential upheaval of religious disenchantment, I found that the embodied self was made to "dys-appear" (Leder 1990). It would tacitly reemerge as the psycho-affective field on which ex-Mormons struggled to fully divest themselves of religion and to negotiate the intimate and often ambiguous dimensions of their disenchantment. We must therefore look at how secularization entails what Charles Hirschkind (2011) refers to as the reconfiguration of an embodied and affective sensorium, a reorientation to "self" and "other" mediated through the vague palpability of one's emotions, the struggle to overcome one's unconscious inhibitions, and the efforts to use one's body, to harness its desires, in pleasurable new ways.

This issue of religion continuing to shape nonbelievers' sense of self long after faith is gone means we must also look at the crucial role of how embodied memory as sensation and affect connects the past to the present. The philosopher Henri Bergson, believing that our whole past exists within us in latent form, taught that physical sensation, embodied practice, and memory are inextricably intertwined. Memories can reinvoke bodily sensation, just as embodied experience can evoke long-forgotten memories (Valsiner and van der Veer 2000).[1] In fact, scholars have long described how religious ritual, by effectively harnessing the link between memory and embodied practice, instils within practitioners a powerful sense of symbiotic unity between the self and the collective. Ritual patterns of embodied movement and sensation effectively "entrench religious ideas in memory" (Barsalou et al. 2005, 49), while ritual practice, repeated over time, reinvigorates those memories well into the future. The individual and the collective thus come to reciprocally reflect one another, strengthening their connection and interdependence.

However, for ex-Mormons, a lifetime of ritual practice created a disturbing sense of being haunted by vague embodied memories that reemerged from time to time—an inhibition, anxiousness, or fear—as the church surreptitiously reasserted its control over them. They complained of lasting sexual deficiencies, frequent fluctuations between emotional panic and detachment, and occasionally being lulled into experiencing unwelcome sensations of "feeling the spirit." The intractability of these embodied memories, their continued presence despite the absence of belief, unnerved the ex-Mormons I spoke to. It's a traumatic experience, they told me, not only because of all that was lost but also because of everything that still hung on and refused to go away.

In their early work with "hysterics," Freud and Breuer (1895) found that the affective force of psychical trauma—"fright, anxiety, shame or physical pain"—stemmed from unwelcome, unconscious memories burrowing into the depths of the psyche. The traumatic experience, whether originating from a singular event or a chronic condition, lodged itself into the unconscious mind and "[acted] like a foreign body," which long after the fact continued to function as an autonomous "agent that is still at work." Trauma became a disease of embodied memory. "Hysterics," they concluded, "suffer mainly from reminiscences."

Yet psychical trauma's origins are often ambiguous, untethered from any particular event or experience that can be narratively reconstructed or pointed to, and indeed any one event may not have been experienced as traumatic at all. Instead, as Cathy Caruth (1995) describes, these diffuse memories' traumatic nature stems from their ability to overwhelm and possess the subject:

> The pathology cannot be defined either by the event itself—which may or may not be catastrophic, and may not traumatize everyone equally—nor can it be defined in terms of a distortion of the event, achieving its haunting power as a result of distorting personal significances attached to it. The pathology consists, rather, solely in the structure of its experience or reception: the event is not assimilated or experienced fully at the time, but only belatedly, in its repeated possession of the one who experiences it. To be traumatized is precisely to be possessed by an image or event. . . . The traumatized, we might say, carry an impossible history within them, or they become themselves the symptom of a history that they cannot entirely possess . . . history occurs as a symptom. (4–5)

For ex-Mormons, the church's persistent ability to "inhabit" their daily lives, long after recanting their beliefs, indeed registered as a persistent, colonizing form of psychosomatic trauma. Yet at first I struggled to understand this dynamic.

Early in my fieldwork, a group of ex-Mormons organized a public event at the Salt Lake City Public Library's auditorium, where they planned to sing a set of old Mormon hymns together, the kind that "stirred the soul," and critically discuss each hymn's historical and cultural significance in what seemed to be a truly ambiguous, if not contradictory, admixture of nostalgia and satire. At the rehearsal, I admitted to Ian, one of the choir members, that I didn't understand why *ex*-Mormons would want to do this. Wouldn't it just bring back bad memories? Picking up a page of sheet music, he turned to me matter-of-factly and said, "You have to realize, we're all repressed." When I started to attend support group meetings, I began to appreciate what he meant. Renouncing one's belief in the church was only the first step. Ex-Mormon support groups existed because leaving was not easy; it required many months or even years of working through lingering attachments to the church.

I found that ex-Mormons' psychical traumas only lasted as long as people feared confronting them. After the sing-along, I asked Ian how he felt. These types of events were beneficial, he said. "While I was singing, some of those old feelings came back, but we were with other people who have left the church, so it was a safe space . . . and in the end, I felt better. I think it gave me the opportunity to play with them and realize I am in control."

If religion is written on and embodied in memory, then it is through embodied experience that we must look to see how it is undone. In this chapter, I first examine how ex-Mormons continue to be plagued with embodied memories of the church and trace this back to the church's teachings about sexuality. I then discuss how sex, as embodied practice, also serves as an avenue through which ex-Mormons go about disenchanting the church's ideological hold over them. Second, I discuss how sensations of "feeling the spirit" can be felt even after faith is gone and present a case study of an ex-Mormon man's response to feeling overwhelmed by an acute form of embodied nostalgia.

"I Lost My Body to the Church"

Gesturing with an open palm over her midriff and breasts, Sara told an ex-Mormon support group how her body changed after giving birth to three children within the first four years of her marriage. "I lost my body to the church," she declared. "I wasn't always like this." She used to be proud of her physique—at one time, young, firm, and fit with a trim waistline and "perky breasts." However, she now felt sunken, heavy, and unattractive. It was not that she did not want or love her children dearly. "They're everything to me," she stated. But the choice to have as many as she did, and when she did, felt like it had not been hers. "I never got a chance to just be young and beautiful," she lamented. Other women in the group sympathized with her. Each had her own story of loss, her own embodied memories of sacrificing her figure to the church.

"I lost my body to the church" became a common refrain among many of the ex-Mormon women I spoke to. Inevitably, talk of loss was paired with descriptions of lives spent in the church in which they felt "trapped" in their bodies—"locked behind the bars of patriarchy," as one woman put it—constrained by frumpy clothing, a demeaning self-image, and teachings that slotted them solely as childbearing mothers attached to priesthood-holding men. Most importantly, though, loss was a language of the enduring and ambivalent absence of self in their post-Mormon lives, brought about by the church's continued constraining and controlling presence. Although they could begin wearing more flattering clothing, they said, it was not as easy to ignore the stretch marks and drooping breasts that are immutably etched into their flesh, constant reminders of a body transfigured in service to the church.

For those like Sara, the body became a potent mnemonic device that stubbornly reminded her of what was lost (in the form of a youthful buoyancy) and what was gained (in the form of wrinkles and stretch marks) during her life in the church. She now found that even mundane practices such as looking in the mirror, provoked anger, sadness, and memories of a life lost. "Every day I can literally see what the church did to me!"

However, these mnemonic triggers were not isolated to the presence of visible markers on the body. They also registered as an unshakeable awareness of absence and deficiency. For ex-Mormon women, loss was a polysemic metaphor that pointed to feelings of not knowing how their sexual bodies worked, of realizing that for decades they had been unable to use their bodies as they wished and had been trained to look at them as an enduring source of sin, not pleasure. Ex-Mormon women described lifetimes of "not knowing" their bodies, feeling unable, or unwilling, to fully explore their pleasure potential. For Patti, this registered as a continued lack of control and ownership, a colonization of self that scared her away, even now, from exploring what was ostensibly "hers." "The church did a good job of drilling into me the idea that even thinking sexual thoughts was a sin. Touching myself was a sin, talking about sex was a sin. I got lessons regularly about chastity and staying pure and protecting my temple. Even though it was my body, I had no control over it. It's sad, but I know so many women who never knew they could achieve an orgasm before they left the church. It took me over a year before I was comfortable enough to have one myself."

Patti's description of self-alienation, manifested in her relationship to a body that was strangely hers yet not hers, reveals a more enduring and elusive dimension of ex-Mormons' experiences of continued religious embodiment. To be Mormon is to internalize a highly proscriptive set of habits and dispositions (as discussed below). While these prohibitions may envelope individual church members within collectively held ideas, morals, and values, they essentially operate beneath any individual's active consciousness. The implications of this for ex-Mormons attempting to break ties with the church are profound. Because the values and beliefs that tacitly inform habits are entrenched in people's modes of conduct with themselves and with each other, they may continue long after the rationale supporting them has been forgotten.

Among ex-Mormons, a prominent, lingering form of this was talked about in terms of having "God in the bedroom." Despite rejecting the church's teachings, ex-Mormons often found that God may have left their day-to-day thoughts but had somehow stayed between the sheets, appearing and reappearing during their most intimate moments. For example, John and Lana could talk about sex easily and openly with me and each other, but they were unable to put that talk into action. Over drinks at their house one evening, Lana described what it meant to have "God in the bedroom." "Sometimes when we try something new, I literally get nauseous. I don't know what it is . . . I try to talk myself out of it, but it's always there. We'll talk about trying something new, but when it comes to it, I always end up crying." Lana no longer considered sex as sacred. It was a matter-of-fact part of human existence and even something ideally to be enjoyed. The physical act of sex, especially John's attempts to "try something new," however, made her question whether leaving the church was the right thing to do, the affective power of guilt for using her body "inappropriately" in these moments of sensuality drawing her back into what she described as "a Mormon mind-set." "I can go into the room feeling one way, but as soon as we start going, something changes and I'm sucked right back into it."

On a later day, in private conversation, John gave me his perspective on God's continued presence in their bedroom. He told me how Lana's reluctance to experiment, her frequent bouts of guilt for being "unclean," had been an enduring source of tension in their relationship since leaving the church. In the months and years following their disaffection, they had spent hours talking about sex with each other. He tried to reason with her, to talk through her feelings of shame, fear, and guilt. But in the end, he confessed, "I'm just arguing with thirty years of indoctrination."

The labor of these recurring conversations—each one a reinvigoration and reinsertion of the church back into their relationship and into his life—took its toll. John said he loved his wife but didn't know how long he could keep this up. Being denied time and again had made him start to feel guilty, as if maybe he was, in fact, actually doing something wrong. He began to question whether he was really transgressing a moral boundary, whether he was indeed leading them "down a path of destruction," as he had frequently been taught about in the church. "It's really sick!" he exclaimed. "But that's what it is. It's like God's always in the corner, watching you do it." Frustration about their inability to escape the church's hold on them had depleted his patience. He didn't know what to do. He loved his wife, but he didn't want to "share her with the church" anymore. "Something's gotta give . . . it's either God or me, but one of us has got to go. I spent over thirty years letting the church tell me how to fuck and I'm not going to do it anymore. I'm not."

An understanding of ex-Mormons' religious disaffection is therefore incomplete if all that is taken into consideration is their rejection of particular ideas and beliefs associated with the institutional church or its formal doctrine. Even after rejecting the church's teachings, Mormonism's presence in some ways lingers on in the form of a persistent, tacit embodied ontology that divides one's sense of self between a polluting body and a sacred spirit and creates an aversion to sex in its libidinous forms and a leeriness of the bodily pleasures sexual activity may produce. This inhibition no longer takes the form of an explicit ideology but a tacit colonization of the coterminous mind/body subject. As Katie Stewart writes, the body is not "incorporated into the self as inert substance or bodily 'self-image'" but rather manages to "retain an affecting agency all its own" (1996, 132). Ex-Mormons know this "affective agency" all too well, as the body persistently reemerges as a problem in the process of deconversion. The embodied habits, dispositions, ways of feeling and moving, and internal divisions and external boundaries have all been crafted and disciplined through years of envelopment in church activities, families, and doctrinal teachings, resulting in a persistent "interpellation" of self as "Mormon" (Althusser 1971).

Sacred Bodies, Sacred Sex

Understanding how ex-Mormons like Sara, John, and Lana came to experience this embodied memory of the church requires a closer look at Mormonism's teachings on the body and sexuality.

While walking down a snow-laden sidewalk after church one day, next to a park where children busily played in the snow, I asked one of my Mormon neighbors (a particularly enthusiastic member with four young children) why it seemed that people in the church got married so young (for women to marry at nineteen and men at twenty-one is quite common) and why sex before marriage was so taboo. All I wanted to know, he said, would be clear if I only understood one thing: "Everything the church teaches, everything it does, is about building eternal families."

Earlier that morning at church, sitting in a classroom full of adult couples, I learned what it meant to think about one's "divine purpose" as a father or mother. "The most sacred of all our divine powers is to become a cocreator with Heavenly Father in providing physical bodies for His spirit sons and daughters," we read. "Nothing is more holy; nothing deserves more reverence; nothing is more central to the plan of happiness. And our very souls are at stake" (Bednar 2001).

As I listened to the lesson, I felt something empowering and portentous about the thought of using one's sex, the most carnal and basic aspect of our humanity, for divine ends. I must not have been the only one, for several members of the class eagerly recounted stories of receiving great joy and blessings in their lives by heeding these instructions.

However, while procreation is certainly at the center of Mormon theology, the mention of sex as anything but "sacred" was conspicuously absent in our discussions. Sex as an embodied act was replaced with sex as a sacred ritual and divine mandate. Imbued with an aura of sacredness, in Mormonism the sexed body must be approached with "reverence," a spiritualized sentiment that covers its more libidinous and corporeal dimensions. In the midst of that morning's lesson on celebrating the transcendent act of "building eternal families," I was reminded of how starkly different many of my ex-Mormon friends had come to think about sex and how they regarded the church's teachings on sex as "manipulative" and "damaging." I therefore began to wonder how thinking about sex as "sacred" had shaped the very sense of religious subjectivity and embodied self these ex-Mormons were now so desperate to escape.

I am inspired here by Bourdieu's suggestion that "the most fundamental structures of the group" are rooted in "the primary experiences of the body," or what he calls bodily *hexis* (1990, 71), describing how individuals come to "live as natural, through their very body movements, the basic principles of an 'ideology'" (cited in Starrett 1995). However, Bourdieu makes clear that "what is 'learned by the body' is not something that one has, like knowledge, that can be brandished"; rather, it is something "that one is" (1990, 73). This is because bodily hexis gains its affective force through the workings of embodied memory. Through careful discipline and training, society molds in each person "lasting dispositions" or "structured propensities to think, feel and act in determinant ways" (Wacquant 2004, 316) that continue to exist throughout life "below the level of unconsciousness" (Bourdieu 1990, 73). As such, these determining structures for the most part go unnoticed despite having untold influence on our daily thoughts, actions, and sensibilities.

> If all societies . . . set such store on the seemingly most insignificant details of dress, bearing, physical and verbal manners, the reason is that, treating the body as a memory, they entrust to it in abbreviated and practical, i.e. mnemonic, form the fundamental principles of the arbitrary content of culture. The principles embodied in this way are placed beyond the grasp of consciousness, and hence cannot be touched by voluntary, deliberate transformation, cannot even be made explicit; nothing seems more ineffable, more incommunicable, more inimitable, and, therefore, more precious, than the values given body, made body by the transubstantiation achieved by the hidden persuasion of an implicit pedagogy, capable of instilling a whole cosmology, an

> ethic, a metaphysic, a political philosophy, through injunctions as insignificant as "stand up straight" or "don't hold your knife in your left hand." (Bourdieu 1977, 93–94)

Within Mormonism, this bodily hexis most evidently takes form, and reaches full expression, in the roles and activities of family life, the "ideological nucleus of society" (Reich 1945, 25). Being a father or mother, husband or wife, is a divinely sanctioned role. One learns to be a good member of the church not in addition to these roles but through them. The "plan of salvation" explicitly calls on members to fulfill these roles in pursuit of exaltation, as the church lesson I attended taught. In this way, the topic of sex in Mormonism constitutes the primary avenue by which lessons about church membership, gospel principles, sin, purity, and "eternal happiness" are most fully and intimately articulated.

However, understanding that a Mormon sense of self takes shape by learning to direct embodied sexual capabilities toward building eternal families—what may be considered a positive identification with Heavenly Father as a "cocreator"—gets at only half the picture. The other half consists of learning to correctly "bridle the passions of the flesh," to protect them and constrain them so that they can be used for procreation. I would therefore like to complicate my friend's assertion that Mormonism is best understood in terms of its explicit emphasis on building eternal families. In addition, we must look to how there exists a concomitant negative identification with the sexual body, achieved through a denial and negation of the embodied self, as an equally potent means by which church members incorporate the values and ideals of Mormonism.

In Mormonism, sex is legitimized only inasmuch as it succumbs to the sterilizing power of religious reason; it is not celebrated for its materiality or sensuality but for the way in which, through sex, members of the church put into action their commitment to the gospel. Sexuality is thus treated as sacred because of the central role it plays in the most fundamental principle of the Mormon religion, the plan of salvation's edict to build eternal families. And like most things sacred, it is "set apart and forbidden" (Durkheim [1915] 1995, 47), treated as sublimely powerful yet dangerous, and requires protection from polluting or profaning influences (Hubert and Mauss 1981).

But sexuality in Mormonism is not talked about as "private" or shrouded in secrecy in the same way that sacred rituals or sacred knowledge are. Instead, because it expresses the religious community's most fundamental beliefs and commitments, it is made a matter of collective concern. Couples getting married in the temple learn that they are bound as a unit not only to each other but also to God, their relationship forever constituted by and through his enduring presence in their spiritual and sensual lives: "Physical intimacy is not only a symbolic union between a husband and a wife—the very uniting of souls—but it is also symbolic of a shared relationship between them and their Father in

Heaven" (Holland 1998). Having sex with one's partner should serve as a regular and abiding reminder of this tripartite union and commitment.

Similarly, during obligatory interviews with their local bishops, members' sexualities are routinely made the subject of institutionalized moral oversight. As a part of a series of questions concerning the interviewee's "worthiness" to receive a "temple recommend," members can be specifically asked about their sexual propriety and fidelity, whether they masturbate or have sex outside of marriage, or even what kind of positions and erotic techniques they use within the marital relationship. Such questions reiterate the fact that membership in the church involves both accepting a set of prescriptive beliefs and abiding by a set of proscriptive rules concerning how member use their bodies. Yet these examples also underline how Mormons are taught to think of themselves as powerless to control themselves without divine or ecclesiastic intervention. There is something inside that is powerful and not entirely your own, that is a matter of collective concern and thus is subject to external control.

Church authorities also dictate the appropriate clothes and appearances of members. All members (especially women) learn to cover their shoulders, thighs, and chests with "modest" clothing so as not to provoke lust in others and cause them to sin. Members who have received their "endowments" (a ritual rite of passage conducted in the temple when marrying or before embarking on a proselytizing mission) are instructed to wear a set of knee- and shoulder-length temple garments that serve as a form of sacred underwear, a symbolic reminder of the covenants they made in the temple. Those who dress "immodestly" or do not wear their garments are subject to criticism, gossip, and ridicule. Learning to maintain one's "modesty"—wearing clothing that conservatively covers the chest, arms, and legs—becomes a potent culturally mediated technique for inoculating the latent potentials of the body to provoke sin and points to the ways in which the body is seen as polluting and shameful when inappropriately constrained.

We can thus begin to see that in Mormonism the body and its sexual abilities are marked by a pervasive ambivalence. While heterosexual, procreative marital sex is glorified and celebrated as sacred and divine, sexual bodies and acts are also invariably suspect and dangerous. Church members are taught that the "very elements" out of which their bodies were created are "by nature fallen and ever subject to the pull of sin, corruption, and death" (Alma 39:5) and that sexual sins are more serious than any other sins except murder or denying the Holy Ghost. So even while being told to seek "eternal progression" by harnessing their "divine powers" of sexual reproduction, church members are simultaneously warned that their sexual bodies are the quickest route to eternal downfall. As in the story of Adam's fall from grace in the Garden of Eden, members are taught that Satan affects them most directly through their physical bodies. The eternal rewards of correctly controlling these sacred powers are equally matched by the everlasting punishment for abusing them. One church leader warned, "Your future may be burned; your world could go up in flames" (Holland 1998).

This duality of human existence and everyday embodied experience constitutes the very core of Mormon theology, culture, and religious thought. As simultaneously natural and cultural, carnal and sacred, the Mormon body sits precariously at the confluence of two competing modes of existence, one worldly and one divine. As one church leader succinctly explained, "for at the same time that we inhabit a physical body that is subject to the Fall, we also have a spirit that represents the eternal part of us" (Bednar 2001). Mormonism thus draws an ontological distinction in its conceptions of the self between people's active volitions, seated in their faith and strength of character, and their passive perceptions, sensations, and pleasures, seated in the corporeal body. The embodied flesh, in its profane state of nature, is thought to be susceptible to the influence of Satan and so is directly antithetical to the spiritual self that Mormons seek to groom, thus creating a divided self that is constantly under attack. "Where is the adversary presently directing his most direct and diabolical attacks?" members are rhetorically asked. "Upon our beliefs about and uses of the physical body and upon the family."

Inhabiting a world in which spiritual and embodied selves are under constant attack from evil forces, church members are given strict lessons on keeping spiritually pure and are admonished to be constantly vigilant in renouncing any "tempting influences," including avoiding people, places, and interactions that may pose a danger. As a church pamphlet on "sexual purity" cautions, church youth are to stay attuned to "the spirit" to "help [them] know when [they] are at risk and give [them] the strength to remove [themselves] from the situation" (LDS Church First Presidency 2016). The predisposition to avoid anything eliciting an embodied erotic response—a word, an image, or a song—so as not to provoke the temptation to sin was made quite clear to me once while teaching an introduction to anthropology course at a Utah university. During the showing of an ethnographic film on the !Kung—a hunter-gatherer society who live in the African Kalahari Desert—several of my students stood up and left the classroom when images of bare-breasted women came on the screen. When I asked them about it the next class, they said that the film was too "pornographic" and that it "just didn't feel right."

Similarly, the way that members learn to avoid other people's sex due to its inherent danger and sinfulness is brought into sharp relief in the lessons taught to young men and women in the years prior to marriage. For example, during one object lesson commonly used in Sunday school classes, the teacher brings out a tray of cupcakes, one for each person in the class, and licks one before handing the tray around. Inevitably, the last person to receive the tray is stuck with the licked cupcake, which he or she refuses to eat. Meant to illustrate the value of personal virtue and sexual morality, young members are told that should they give into sexual temptation, they too will be like a licked cupcake, dirty and unwanted.

Yet the greatest danger to a virtuous self is not located out there in "the world." Avoiding pornography is primarily about members controlling the impulses within themselves that pose a risk—their own unconscious desires and unruly appetite for the flesh. As one former church prophet instructed, drawing a direct link between the psychical and the physical, "Be clean in mind, and then you will have greater control over your bodies" (Hinckley 1996). Living with such a divided self means asking whether "my body [will] rule over my spirit, or . . . my spirit [will] rule over my body," as another church general authority explained. The primary purpose in life is to "learn to bridle all of the passions of the flesh" (Bednar 2001).

Avoiding temptation and developing spiritual strength are perhaps effective forms of self-discipline through which church members can suppress their latent, ever-present desires. Existentially, however, thinking about one's entire purpose as defined by learning to "bridle" an inextricable part of one's self made for quite a conflicted existence, as ex-Mormons saw it. If true selfhood is only possible by using one's God-given agency to make correct decisions based on gospel principles but the body is believed to be inherently fallen, as Mormonism teaches, then true selfhood can only emerge when put in opposition to one's own corporeal existence and embodied passions. Having effectively drawn internal divisions between the part of oneself adhering to gospel principles and the thoughts, desires, passions, and appetites that do not align with that idealized sacred self, Mormon subjectivity can in some sense be seen as internally conflicted and narrow. Ex-Mormons would explain to me that the only part of self that can be embraced as authentic in the church is that which has been successfully disciplined by and aligned with a closed set of doctrinaire beliefs. As a result, there is no room for creativity, exploration, or experimentation; all that one can acceptably know about one's body or sexuality is that which has already been identified, defined, and regulated by the church. As would be expected, staying in this narrow perimeter of safe sexuality is apparently, according to church members, easier said than done.

Sexual Sins

When I first arrived in Utah, I would often ask faithful Mormons, "Why do you think people are leaving the church?" On quiet Sunday mornings, I would walk with dozens of other smartly dressed parishioners down sidewalks to attend sacrament meeting in the unassuming redbrick, steeple-crowned chapel where my ward met for services, only two blocks from my house. I often accompanied my neighbor, the ward's elders quorum president, who would explain nuances of church doctrine, ward politics, and his personal views on life in the church as we walked. When I asked him my question about people leaving, he at first admitted that one could never really know other people's real reasons. But from what he had seen, he said, most apostates were unwilling to resist temptations to disobey the "law of chastity," the set of moral rules governing members' sexuality. They had grown lazy—or worse, licentious—and now sought only the vapid pleasures of the flesh. The former members he knew had given themselves over to carnal desires, tragically misusing their procreative abilities, the "most sacred gift" bestowed by Heavenly Father.

As I would learn throughout my research, many ex-Mormons did indeed sexually "let loose" when they left the church. When attending ex-Mormon support group meetings, parties, and informal gatherings, sex was quite frequently a topic of conversation. I heard ex-Mormons talk of having felt sexually repressed in the church and how now, outside of the church, they were actively exploring their sexuality, including different erotic techniques, toys, positions, and partners.

There was an ambivalent transgressive tone to such talk, however. It was often entered into hesitantly, cautiously, as if dangerous. But as conversation progressed, it inevitably turned explosive, explicit, and—it seemed to me—cathartic; the descriptions of sexual experiences both before and after their disaffection became more vivid, emotional, and at times flippant in ex-Mormons' increasingly informal treatment of what had been, in the church, a most hallowed and private topic. Sex seemed to move from something that was taboo, often shameful, and even regretted—as when telling stories of repressing desire, being addicted to pornography, or being a victim of abuse while in the church—to an object of philosophical and scientific contemplation as well as an aesthetic source of enjoyment in their ex-Mormon lives.

In contrast to the moral stereotypes that I often heard projected onto ex-Mormons (e.g., their heathenish desire for the pleasures of the flesh drove them away from the gospel), I began to wonder if sex played a more nuanced role in people's deconversion from Mormonism beyond what my faithful friend considered to be apostates' weakness for bodily pleasure. Could ex-Mormons' focus on sex outside the church be understood as foundational to the process of deconversion itself (rather than as a cause or result of their rejection of church teachings)?

In the rest of this section, I focus on embodied sexuality as it operates at the intersection and overlap of the cognitive/rational and emotive/affective person. I discuss how sex serves as the embodied, affective, and symbolically laden conduit through which a latent religious subjectivity is contested in ex-Mormons' lives. While sex can be constraining, debilitating, and alienating, it is at the same time potentially liberating and empowering, serving as a means by which people can begin to make sense of life outside their former church.

Freeing Sexual Subjectivities

Breaking the hold of an embodied disposition to feel guilt, of thinking of sexuality only in Mormon-centric terms, is not as easy as simply rejecting the church's teachings. Instead, those bodies and sexualities must be carefully reconceived outside the umbrella of Mormon morality. Anthropologists have discussed how religious healing practices successfully address both the cognitive-discursive and the embodied aspects of self (Csordas 1994), bringing about a change in people's patterns of attention that, in the example of trance healing, "deconstructs" the self and "repairs" it in ways that ameliorate distress and physical suffering (Seligman 2010, 314). In this section, I thereby discuss how ex-Mormon bodies reemerge as the political and symbolic terrain on which a reinterpretation of moral and sexual selfhood unfolds in a form of embodied healing practice.

During my fieldwork in Utah, I attended dozens of ex-Mormon support group meetings, parties, book clubs, and discussion groups during which members of the "ex-Mormon community" would gather to socialize, meet new people, and discuss their experiences leaving Mormonism. At one particular meeting, several dozen ex-Mormons gathered at Richard and Ann's house to discuss "Sex outside the Church," as the email invitation titled it, a two-hour-long session set aside to talk solely about sex. When I arrived, all of the furniture had been pushed away from the center of the living room, an assortment of metal folding chairs and plastic patio chairs standing in its place. By the start of the event a half hour later, the seats were filled and the floor space was covered with people splayed out and chatting noisily. Richard, a confident, upbeat man in his early forties who had been out of the church for almost a decade, unlike most others gathered, led the discussion.

In his opening remarks, Richard decried the church's treatment of sex and expounded on an understanding of sexuality seated not in a moral discourse of good and bad but in a scientific rationale of human evolution. His words were savvy; they spoke to the gathered ex-Mormons' collective anxieties about a topic that he suggested was systematically obscured in the church. "We're trained to be sex stupid," he began. "My hope is that after tonight we all come to a place where sex doesn't scare us anymore." In his talk, Richard naturalized sex, situating it within an understanding of human physiology and evolutionary development that was explicitly amoral: "People need to understand that sex operates in one of the oldest parts of the brain. You can go back to amoebas, way back in evolution, when things were first reproducing. Our sexuality is an old, old instinct. Instincts that had to be kept strong to keep the species from dying out. You see, sexuality goes beyond thought, it's subordinate to thought. The only reason we do anything else in our lives, like eating, is to make sure we can reproduce."

Over the course of his lecture, Richard compared humans to other higher-order animals, like dolphins and apes, who have a "genetic disposition" for both pair-bonding and finding multiple partners. More than just a natural history lesson, Richard and Ann described male and female sexual anatomy in great detail, saying that despite the way they looked, they were actually quite similar in form and function. In a humorous sort of "show and tell," they reviewed where various erogenous zones could be found on the body and the physiology of an orgasm, including what kinds of erotic techniques and sex toys could be used to produce one.

Finally, Richard and Ann spoke about the problems associated with the moral imperative for practicing monogamy, a particularly salient issue for many people leaving the church, since marriage was no longer a divine mandate. It was normal and healthy, they said, to have seemingly random thoughts, feelings, and fantasies come up during sex. Rather than continue to repress them, the audience was encouraged to explore what they meant as a way of developing their post-Mormon sexualities. Humans were not "wired" to have sex with the same person, the same way, every few days for the rest of their lives, they said. Being open to and exploring these parts of sexuality was both expected and healthy.

Richard's talk spurred fervent conversation. I sat on the floor next to several couples in the midst of processing the new information who were telling stories and sharing insights with each other. "It just dawned on me," Rachel proclaimed. "Sex is such a basic instinct. It's a survival mechanism. Our urges and thoughts are unavoidable!" The church targeted these instincts and tied one's self-worth to impossibly high standards of behavior, she claimed, all in order to create a cycle of guilt and need for repentance. "It's really impossible to be 'good' by the church standards. That's why they do it!"

Such talk constitutes what psychologists and psychological anthropologists refer to as "cognitive reframing" or "restructuring," a process where events, concepts, or ideas thought to be "maladaptive" or harmful are transformed or otherwise rendered "positive" (Beck 1997). Richard's talk did not directly confront Mormonism or its particular views on sexuality. As evidenced in Rachel's comments, what Richard did was provide semantic tools for the ex-Mormons in the audience to begin reframing their own sexualities and embodied experiences for themselves. Rachel's comments reflect what I heard many ex-Mormons refer to as an "awakening" to their sexualities. They began to see themselves as long-subjected to externally mandated rules governing sexuality, which they were now empowered to fight. Bringing sex out into the open and talking about it frankly, informally, and in a pseudoscientific manner inverted the moral logic regarding sex that had been at work in the church. It was a way of subverting their fear of "uncontrollable passions" and temptations to sin and converting that fear into an understanding of themselves as having natural "instincts" that superseded Mormonism's teachings on sexuality.

There was a therapeutic dimension to the sexual reframing ex-Mormons were undergoing. For example, they contended that Mormon sexual morality held members to an "impossibly high standard" that subjected church members to a pervasive form of sexual repression. Several men confessed to being obsessed with pornography and masturbation while in the church; the desire to masturbate had driven them into deep bouts of self-loathing and guilt, as the temptation to sin seemed to erupt from within themselves rather than some external source (which they could ostensibly avoid). In their discussions at the group meeting, however, ex-Mormons asserted that the true source of pathology was in the church's compulsory restrictions on sexual expression. Natural sexual instincts, they said, worked outside of any conventional understanding of morality and should not be subjected to repressive religious control. Attempting to suppress desires created the transgressive pleasures the church sought to extinguish and led to the pathological mind-set and behaviors that plagued them. "It was like magic," one man asserted. "Once I realized that what I was feeling was natural, I didn't need it anymore. The addiction went away!"

Reframing sex in these ways was not just a way of legitimizing formerly tabooed sexual feelings or behaviors or "rationalizing" what ex-Mormons otherwise knew to be "harmful" but also an act of disenchanting the authority of an institution and the people who represented it, thus combatting its ongoing hold over them. For example, ex-Mormons grew up looking to church leaders as the de facto authority figures on issues of both cosmological and mundane importance; they were paragons of moral virtue, divinely inspired leaders of "the one true church" who spoke with the authority of the heavens. Even after leaving the church, I often heard ex-Mormons talk ambivalently about the church leaders they had known and loved their whole lives. Did these men really set the bar for righteous living, they worried, and were they as ex-Mormons living lives of sinful sexual debauchery?

In reframing sex as natural, ex-Mormons were able to reverse the logic of sin and pathology. In part, this took the form of a backdoor denunciation of church leaders' professed piety. "Do you think they never really masturbate?" one man asked the group. Another answered, "Yeah, I do. I think they're being honest. But only asexuals and psychopaths are able to do that. That's what the church does; it brings up psychopaths through the ranks. They're the ones who reach the top." Another woman interpreted early church leaders' practice of polygamy as an extension of evolutionary theory. Taking multiple wives in "celestial marriage," she suggested, although thought of within the church as a divine mandate (though now suspended), was in fact evidence of church leaders selfishly leveraging their status and promising eternal life to a multitude of women in order to satisfy their own sexual desires.

The idea that Mormonism hides sexual impropriety under a veneer of "righteousness" was thus a powerful way for ex-Mormons to critique the church and call attention to what they saw as its hypocritical and bankrupt moral order. One woman in the group was vividly reminded of this as she tearfully recounted an encounter with her church bishop. Called into his office for an interview, she was asked if she ever masturbated. She remembers flushing red with embarrassment. "Here I was, sitting alone in this old man's office, and he's asking me if I touch myself. I didn't know what to do, so I tell him yeah. Then he asks me how often I do it, where exactly do I touch myself, and what I think about when I'm doing it." It was imperative, he said, for her to fully "atone" for her sins. "In any other situation," she concluded, "an old man asking a kid about sex and masturbation would be a crime! There I was cringing inside, and he was enjoying it!"

Richard's explanations introduced his audience to a way of thinking and conversing about the sexualized body that allowed them to reconceptualize what stepping outside of Mormonism's corporeal and moral ontology meant for them as ex-Mormons. Sexual bodies, objectified, scrutinized, and deconstructed in this way, were thus opened up for thoughtful reflection and critical scrutiny. For them, sexuality was no longer governed by the logic of divine sanctity, with its prohibitions, divisions, and inherent dangers. By gaining more "adequate ideas" of the body's natural functions, instincts, and dispositions (Spinoza 1985), they instead began to construct a secular ontology of life that was not divided against itself, did not require living in fear of individual passions and desires, and effectively expelled the church's authority to morally mediate their sense of self.

In addition to a conceptual reframing of sexuality, the essence of these newly sexualized self-assessments lies in what Heidegger (1977) calls enframing (*gestell*), or an ontological process of "revealing," "opening up," or "bringing forth" new worlds. For Heidegger, the emphasis is not on the particular tool or apparatus used in the process of enframing but rather on how enframing constitutes the conditions of possibility in which a deeper, more real "truth" may be revealed. Gaining sexual knowledge about the body, including a new understanding of its pleasure-inducing parts and the techniques to stoke them, constituted a new plane of awareness for ex-Mormons. The body could now be enlisted in the pursuit of pleasure, as an expression of desire in and through the flesh rather than a lingering source of fear and guilt. "We're really so lucky," another woman at the group meeting proclaimed, commenting on her female sexuality. "Not only is sex amazing when you know what you're doing, but we also get to have multiple orgasms! Who knew!?"

Repossessing the Body

Despite providing an audience of sympathetic people to talk to, there were relatively few "breakthrough moments" in support group meetings that I attended. Those who eventually stopped attending did so not because the group had resolved their issues but because they had found other ways to "move on" or no longer found a benefit in talking about their problems.

According to Breuer and Freud (1893), relief for psychic injuries was not achieved through talk alone. While talk therapy could effectively uncover repressed memories, alleviation of people's symptoms also required the patient to experience an authentic emotional release. True healing came when representational talk and embodied affect worked together: "Each individual hysterical symptom immediately and permanently disappeared when we had succeeded in bringing clearly to light the memory of the event by which it was provoked and in arousing its accompanying affect, and when the patient had described that event in the greatest possible detail and had put the affect into words. Recollection without affect almost invariably produces no result" (6).

For ex-Mormons, talking about sex outside of its former religio-symbolic framework allowed a new way of ordering and mapping the human body, an "opening up" to new ontological horizons. However, real transformation happened when that talk was accompanied by deliberate acts of sexual experimentation, when the pain of sexual guilt could be directly confronted, released, and channeled into personal healing. Posting on an online ex-Mormon message board, an unnamed woman provocatively summed up this progression and many of the themes I've discussed so far in her personal experience of sexual transformation while leaving the church:

> I realized that I am a woman with a body that has sexual desires that I had not been acknowledging. My desires had been masked and shut down through many years of shame. I had no sexual identity of my own; duty sex was on the weekly list of wifely chores and God knew I wanted a gold star next to each finished chore. I had no idea what it looked like to be a sexual being without shame or a submissive, timid approach. Sex was empty and time could always be spent doing more important things like balancing my check book or scheduling next week's events. But now it could be different. I began to approach sex with the intent of finding out how much physical pleasure I could get out of it. I admit, at first it felt selfish, but I eventually was able to give myself permission to lose myself in the pure, clean energy of sexual pleasures. It was uncharted territory that I discovered upon the terrain of my body that I never felt before—I didn't even dare to look. I realized my own desires, once they peeked out from behind the rock they'd been shoved under, had just as much validity as a man's. My body began to sync with my mind and my heart. I realized that pleasure was mine to own and explore; it was not something to hide from myself or something to give the ownership of away to my husband or Church. The damage of the years in the Church was not easily overcome in one night—although once I allowed myself to be curious enough to get lost in pure, personal ecstasy, a whole new world opened up for me. I am beautiful, powerful and I love my feminine beauty—whatever it looks like today. Women's (and men's) sexuality has been owned by the Church and governed by God since the early years in the Church. To find out, through personal bravery, that I actually owned my body was the pivotal point in changing my mindset. I began to build resilience to the shame all around me, especially from those in the Church. I later found that this resilience was the key to arming myself against the cultural stigmas. It was a path I was going alone, that was very clear.[2]

In this passage, the author describes her disaffection from Mormonism in terms of a shift in sexual awareness. She began in a state of alienation, a self that was constituted by its very lack of sexual identity and "masked" desires, unable to conceive of herself as a "sexual being." Sex was "empty" and a waste of time except as a part of fulfilling her sacred duties as a wife and mother. In this prior state, personal fulfillment came through labor that was future-oriented and religiously defined—it was no different than balancing the family checkbook, just another contribution to the endless effort of building a celestial family. Sexual desire was described in explicitly repressed terms—masked, shut down, shoved under a rock, damaging. After leaving the church, she says that sex at first felt selfish. The feelings of shame and guilt came back. But she soon worked through these feelings and was able to "lose" herself in sexual pleasure. This venture into the depths of uncharted territory opened up a "whole new world" waiting to be "discovered." For her, this direct engagement with a long-repressed psychical trauma was therapeutic. It resulted in a joining of mind and body, an overturning of the moral dualism of mind versus body to which she had been so accustomed and a return to a fuller sense of self. The part of her once owned and possessed by the church was reclaimed. She could look at her feminine beauty in the mirror with acceptance and satisfaction. In so doing, she built resilience to other forms of shame and cultural stigmas projected onto her. Sex as embodied practice thereby constituted for her a transformation of a whole mode-of-life outside the church. Her disaffection and distance from the church were realized in the act of "opening up" to her body and "discovering" its sexual pleasures, her mind and body working with one another to release Mormonism's hold over her life.

For many ex-Mormons, it was therefore not enough to just talk about sex differently. Sexual guilt is hard to overcome, and simply talking about it did not alleviate the pain. Instead, the values and ideas that frame sex as pleasurable and natural must first be put into practice. Echoing Freud's emphasis on the therapeutic value of affective release, Kopping notes, "The transformation of ideas cannot occur without the surrender to practice which is inscribed in our bodies and only expressible or retraceable through the sensual encounter with the environment and thus through performative praxis" (2002, 23). I found that this "sensual encounter . . . through performative praxis" occurred on an individual basis among Utah ex-Mormons and took place as collective action, particularly among some ex-Mormons who attended "swinger parties" or lived a "monogamish" lifestyle, a term loosely related to having an open marriage.

At first, I did not understand how people who not long before had lived quite conservative lives could transition to a sexual lifestyle completely at odds with their upbringing. From the church's perspective, this morally aberrant behavior was to be expected of those who drifted from the church. Unleashed from their religious commitments, they fell into temptation. While this explanation may be compelling, I think something else more profound is at work. These activities point not to the inherent moral depravity of ex-Mormons but to a sexual form of communal therapy for those deconverting from the church.

However, while indeed transgressive, this kind of sex was not amoral. In fact, in the anthropological literature, instances of transgressive sex are often discussed as a way of not only challenging moral boundaries but reaffirming them. As Max Gluckman (1963) suggests in reference to the upending of conventional moral hierarchies and categories during "carnival," transgression reinforces the existence of a normative order by ritually reversing it in highly predictable ways. Ex-Mormon swingers did in fact play by a set of rules governing the frequency of encounters, the activities allowed (or not), and the need for transparency with all spouses involved, including the imperative that, at the end of the night, everyone returned to his or her spouse.

Yet for ex-Mormons, transgressive sex was not about temporarily lifting the rules and taboos that Mormonism placed on sex only to reinstate them when the lights came back on. Instead, it was about challenging and changing those rules—and the affect-tinged memories they evoked—directly and spontaneously. It was about two nervous, hesitant sets of couples meeting at a party, getting to know each other first by chatting about the church and the reasons they left, then progressively flirting, touching each other's partner, and heading upstairs.

In casual meet-ups, threesomes, and swinging, sex was brought down from the divine pedestal on which it sat in the church. There, it was a jointly dangerous and hallowed experience, either avoided or not fully embraced. Here, it was made into a tool for bringing about carnal pleasure and rewriting not just the idea of sex or the moral prohibitions attached to it but the affective memories of guilt and shame with which it was intimately bound.

This kind of sex—messy, pleasurable, and unrestrained—transgressively transcended the sacredness of the act, the bodies that partook in it, and the church that once controlled it. As one man explained to me, "In the church, you're taught that sex is this amazing, heavenly experience, like sitting down at a four-star restaurant and having a fifty-dollar steak. And that's fine. But that also gets boring and isn't really how it works. I think sex should be like eating. Sometimes you want to take your time and go to a fancy restaurant to eat that nice steak. But sometimes you just want to go through the drive-through for a nasty, greasy hamburger."

In this way, spouse swapping and the "monogamish" lifestyle allow a "symbolic inversion" (Babcock 1978), a rearticulation and realignment of sex and the people who enjoy it, outside of the normal parameters of fidelity and procreation where God exists. Descriptions like these point to the messiness of sex outside the church, describing the potential to participate in experiences with muddled physical and symbolic boundaries and to productively dismantle sex as an orderly, rule-bound activity. That is, this kind of sex, as immanently eruptive, informal, and fun, directly challenged Mormon conceptions of sex as purposeful, sacred, dangerous, and routine. While choosing a spouse in the church was done with deliberation and much prayerful consideration in order to find that special person to be joined with for "time and eternity," in sex play, ex-Mormon couples were able to experiment with sex as mutable, its pleasures independent of the morally bounded venue in which they first experienced it as church members. Spouses broke off from their celestial partners and found others for a night. No one person was "meant for you"; each offered his or her own assortment of tastes and pleasures to be explored. Sex became explicitly unholy, an unsanctioned exploration of the differences in people's bodies—the way they taste, smell, and move—a pleasure-driven discovery of how each one feels a little different from the others and how a person's own body feels differently with various partners.

All of this is not to say that sex was not a form of physical, psychological, and emotional intimacy for these ex-Mormons. Research on hypersexuality often pathologizes "overactive" libidos as an individual's inappropriately directed attempt to realize lost intimacy. The focus is on the individual, who has lost something and now resorts to aberrant forms of interaction to find it again. But by framing hypersexuality in medicalized or psychologized terms, it too easily equates it with a religiously inspired moralism. Embedded within the logic of addiction, pathology, and excess exists an enduring Victorianesque predisposition toward framing hypersexuality in terms of guilt, shame, and the imperative to control corporeal desires through the individual's application of moral reason—a logic eerily similar to the religious moralism of Mormonism.

However, understanding ex-Mormons' sexuality in these terms misses sexuality's immanent sociality, its ability to bridge difference and division and to resubmerge the individual in the oceanic feeling of being in the world with other people—an experience characteristic of most religious ritual. Religious disenchantment is indeed for ex-Mormons initially an experience of alienation, isolation, and individuation—they've been cut off from their former ontological and social horizons and find themselves alone, "floating" in an existential abyss, fearful of a life and death isolated from the ones they love. Sex, however, has the potential to remedy this particular existential malady. Writing on the subject of eroticism, the philosopher Georges Bataille (1986) suggested that sex has the capacity to temporarily yet profoundly dissolve the boundaries and divisions between the self and others. In the coital act, culminating in orgasm, one's individuated existence ceases for a moment and is submerged in a tidal force of interrelationality. Yet there is a mnemonic component to this as well—a restoration of repressed, traumatic, embodied memory—an experience that, in the language of Lacanian psychoanalysis, equates to a return to the "Real," before ego, identity, and divisions internal to the self and between self and world have been constructed. In sex, participants reach a new state of communality and continuity with each other, and in so doing, they heal the fragmented, self-conflicted sexual subjectivities that they carried with them out of Mormonism.

Fantasizing Freedom

I sat with Marissa, her husband, and several other couples one evening after an ex-Mormon "secular parenting" meeting about how to teach children morals and values outside of religion. At the meeting, participants discussed strategies for parenting outside of a religious environment, concerned with how to effectively "inoculate" their kids against the kind of "fantastical thinking" and irrational thought that leads people to become emotionally and intellectually dependent on the church, including the kinds of sexual repression they felt they had been subjected to. The discussion was supplemented by stories about their own childhoods, their grievances growing up Mormon, and their frustrations with making a life outside the church. At a coffee shop where we all convened after the meeting, Marissa asked if anybody wanted to hear about a sexual fantasy she often had. "Yes, yes, yes!" another woman excitedly answered.

> In the fantasy, I'm bound, gagged, and blindfolded. I'm in my living room, and all of the lights are on, but I can't see anything. I'm dressed in sexy lingerie, but it's been partially ripped off of me. Some of my male friends come in the door while I lay there, but I can't see them. Each of them takes turns spanking me with these leather crops . . . they fondle me and eventually penetrate me. Because I'm blindfolded, I can't see who or what is going to come next. I'm stuck there; I can't move or get away, and so I just let them do whatever they want.

At first, I was distressed at the frankness of her account—I didn't know how to react. But the other women in our circle nodded in agreement as she finished her description, eager to talk about their own fantasies. Each one repeated the same basic components of submission, helplessness, violence, and unidentified men.

Through numerous informal conversations with Marissa before and after that day, I was able to piece together her life history, which began to shed light on the underlying sources of this fantasy. Marissa grew up a highly sexual person in what she calls an extremely devout Mormon family. Even at a very young age, she remembers being curious about her body and trying to examine her vagina in the shower. However, her mother always reprimanded her, telling her that body part was not a place she was allowed to touch. "Sex was not something we talked about in our family. Just mentioning it was dirty and sinful. [My parents] acted as if just learning about sex would lead to immoral behavior." Puberty brought on a heightened sense of self-consciousness as she learned her body was dangerous and potentially sinful; her budding breasts, she was told, risked inciting immoral attention from her childhood friends and could lead them all into sin.

The responsibility she personally bore for other people's sexualities was impressed upon her even further at the age of thirteen when an older boy in the neighborhood, who was soon leaving on a mission, sexually abused her.

Although she told her parents what had happened, they refused to do anything. Without proof to back up her story, they worried that "making a fuss" would perhaps unjustifiably tarnish this young priesthood holder's reputation right before he left to do "the Lord's work." Marissa remembers learning, at that early stage in her life, the sad truth that men often harbored unspeakable desires thinly veiled beneath a veneer of righteousness.

As she grew older, Marissa says she learned to repress her desires so that she could have a "normal" marriage. It worked. She eventually met a man while attending Brigham Young University, married him, and soon after gave birth to three children in quick succession. She began to put on weight and eventually found that sex with her husband had become routine and unsatisfying. "I didn't care anymore. I did a real good job of convincing myself that I just wasn't worth it."

It was only after beginning to question the church at thirty-seven years of age that Marissa began to explore her sexuality again. Yet the guilt remained, leading to reoccurring bouts of depression as she cycled back and forth between periods of activity and abstinence. When I first met Marissa, she said she felt stuck in a state of indecision. She did not attend church any longer but did not feel fully free of it either. She struggled to shake the nagging feeling that somehow sex really was primarily for making babies and pleasing her husband—not for pleasure. Her sexuality in many ways kept her entangled with Mormonism.

Often unacknowledged, much less spoken about, sexual fantasies are often thought to exist in the unconscious recesses of our mind, a product of repressed or sublimated desires brought into conscious awareness when spurred or triggered by a word, image, interaction, or event (Scott 1994). At times bizarre, fantasies allow for a temporary escape from the perceived bonds of sexual restraint in daily mundane existence. Through these fantasies, people are able to reflect on and in some sense unconsciously act out their deepest desires and fears about their bodies and social relationships (Strassberg 1998). As such, sexual fantasies focus the imagination onto the feelings and sensations of the erotic encounter—the physical tastes and textures, the relationships between bodies, and the emotional responses to them—and allow people to come to terms with their tensions, frustrations, and unexpressed desires. Although typically thought to be highly individual, fantasies can also be thought of as products of shared circumstances, experiences, tensions, and conflicts. But what does sexual fantasy do for Marissa? One interpretation might be as follows.

In the fantasy, Marissa imagines herself—in an exaggerated and twisted form—as the repressed and alienated Mormon woman she is struggling to overcome in her daily life. She is in a position of utter loss of self-control, having given herself, her autonomy, and her individuality over to the group of men, the priesthood holders, who stand in for the patriarchal culture that binds her. In their presence, she is made powerless and submissive, gagged and blindfolded, mute and blind. Like her relationships to the men of her youth who lustfully watched her and the one who abused her, she imagines herself in an adversarial relationship with men yet still stripped of the ability to anticipate, reproach, or repel her sexual assailants. The guilt and fear she felt as a woman in the church is here as well in hyperbolic form. She is humiliated in the face of numerous, anonymous, staring eyes—the men of the church watch her in a deceitful confluence of righteous judgment and lustful desire. Yet her bare flesh is exposed to all who would want it, no longer modestly covered by conservative clothing. The guilt of being so exposed manifests in the form of lashes from the leather tassels, her flesh wracked by pain that punishes her for transgressing tabooed moral boundaries yet also perhaps reflecting a masochistic desire to be forcibly drawn out of the endless cycle of self-reflection and recrimination she's been stuck in since leaving the church.

Yet for Marissa, fantasy also functioned as a window into these tensions, a way of negotiating and gaining control over her afflictions. In the fantasy, rather than giving over to the sexual domination she's been subject to her whole life, she gains control over it; she repossesses the body she feels she lost to the church. Such fantasies provide respite from the unending need to uphold an image of Mormon moral uprightness, both to herself and others, the stuff of which "losing one's body" is made of. Her sex is not tied to a single man, and she is not held morally responsible for its expression only within the confines of procreation. In the fantasy, she is able to imagine her sex as desirable for the pleasure it provides, not the babies it produces. She is made erotically accessible to anybody and everybody for moments at a time—not a single man "for time and eternity."

There is similarly something instructive about the fantasy. Her presence in the living room, bound on the ground, brings into stark relief the "reality" of sex, which for so long has been covered over by talk of its "sacredness"—its play of dominance and submission, pain and pleasure. Despite imagining herself bound by her hands and feet, the men do not control her—submissiveness is not what it seems. In the fantasy, her vulnerability is instead made into a tool of seduction. During the time that I knew Marissa, she always came across to me as timid and insecure. In leaving the church, she said she felt utterly confused and unsure about life on the outside, sometimes complaining about feeling "overpowered" in her relationship with her husband. I often cringed when her husband would joke about Mormon women's "naïvety" and "squeamish" attitude toward sex. But in the fantasy, like a good femme fatale, she entraps men by making herself into the extreme version of what she believes they have deceitfully desired all along—a submissive, controlled woman. She appropriates power by provoking and exposing men's latent "unrighteousness" and so effects retribution on them by exposing their own lustful desires.

In the months after this secular parenting meeting, Marissa gradually lost weight and eventually decided to seek a divorce and begin dating other men in the ex-Mormon community. Reflecting on her marriage, she often spoke of her love for her husband as driven primarily by a sense of duty and obligation rather than passion and excitement. She suggested that her deteriorating relationship had been symptomatic of the ongoing transformation she was experiencing after breaking from the church. "When we got married, I didn't know anything else. I thought it was what I was supposed to do. Now I see that life doesn't have to follow one set path." Above all, Marissa sought to escape "God's presence" in the bedroom by exploring sexuality outside of her husband's overpowering symbolic presence as a constant intrusive reminder of God, the church, and the Mormon past that she sought to transcend.

For Marissa, veering from the "one set path" laid down for her by the church was accomplished through sexual fantasy and experimentation. The fantasy was a therapeutic device and imaginary template for reconstructing herself as a woman outside the church. In it, she was able to work through her guilt, fears, desires, and hopes, condensing them into manageable chunks in the erotic fantasy. In her imagination, she was able to come to terms with their meanings and find her means of escape. In talking about fantasy, Marissa accomplishes what Lacan refers to as *la traversée du fantasme* (the traversing of fantasy), in which the subject assumes "a new position with respect to the Other as language and the Other as desire . . . a utopian moment beyond neurosis" (Fink 1996, 72). For Marissa, fantasy therefore constituted a therapeutic reclamation of self, a repositioning of self in relation to the forms of desire and control that long shaped her sexual subjectivity. In Marissa's fantasy, the tensions and ambivalences of her sexual subjectivity were thus made visible and provided an imaginative framework through which she was able to begin repossessing her sexuality and life outside the church.

Feeling the Spirit

I now shift a bit to discuss another form of embodied memory afflicting ex-Mormons. While anthropologists have studied how individuals come to experience the divine through various sensory modalities, including prayer, spiritual possession, or ecstatic worship (Csordas 1994, 2002; Lester 2005; Luhrmann 2005; Luhrmann, Nusbaum, and Thisted 2010), they have not yet asked what happens to such "somatic modes of attention" when people change faiths or lose faith altogether. This issue becomes especially pronounced among ex-Mormons, who are faced with the uncommon task of attempting to forget how to feel in particular spiritually significant ways.

In the LDS Church, belief and belonging are predicated on being sensitive to and getting caught up in experiences of "feeling the spirit." Members describe times in which the spirit overcame them—while reading scriptures, singing hymns, praying, or having a particularly meaningful conversation about the gospel. It is a feeling of warmth, calm, peace, tranquility, being "filled with light," or sometimes urgency and cautionary counsel in the face of danger. Church members must build their testimonies of the church's authenticity, developing trust in its teachings and leadership, by attuning themselves to these feelings and listening to the whispers of "that still small voice" speaking to them throughout the day.

Unexpected manifestations of the spirit are made into a routine practice during fast and testimony meetings, when on the first Sunday of every month, congregants devote the weekly sacrament meeting to sharing their testimonies with each other over the pulpit. Men, women, and children stand behind the podium and give tearful renditions of faith-confirming experiences and their absolute knowledge that "this church is true." "I want my family to know I have a testimony," a man confided one Sunday afternoon to the congregation I occasionally attended. Choking up, he struggled to get the words out as tears streamed down his face. "I shouldn't be crying like this, but when the spirit comes over you, there's nothing you can do."

Central to Mormon understandings of "feeling the spirit" is its ability to overwhelm the person. Thus "feeling the spirit" is effective in bolstering one's testimony in the church only inasmuch as it is experienced as involuntary. One is made passive to the upwelling of the spirit as it consumes, overpowers, and leaves one's memory and mind undeniably marked by its affective force.

Rather than condemning feelings as merely subjective, the church grants emotion a uniquely objective character. Feelings alone have the capacity to reveal the sacred truth of reality as it is experienced in the banality of day-to-day life. Importantly, it is by learning to read these embodied sensations that a syncretic unity is achieved between the community as a whole and the individuals of which it is composed (Riis and Woodhead 2010). The emotional resonance of feeling the spirit forms the intersubjective backbone to church membership and solidifies the church as an emotive authority in individual's lives.

Day-to-day experiences thus become saturated with sacred significance via their ability to provoke an unexpected emotive reaction. As a result, church membership and spiritual knowledge is acquired, and required, not simply through textual or discursive engagement with scriptures and theological principles but also through emotional and affective experiences that become the site and source of spiritual knowledge. Within Mormonism, spiritual knowledge via "feeling the spirit" is, I argue, the equivalent of having a carnal knowledge of God. He consumes, overtakes, and overwhelms people, filling them with his love. In these moments of sensuality, there is indeed a loss of self and a visceral euphoria as the person comes to know God personally and intimately.

Ex-Mormons, however, describe the church's emphasis on "feeling the spirit" as a kind of emotional colonization of its members' hearts and minds. The church co-opts everything they feel, and they are left unable to discern which emotions are their own and which are the church's. As one man put it, "If you feel happy, joyful, peaceful, the church takes that and claims it comes from God. It then sells it back to you, saying that it was the one that gave it to you in the first place and that if you want to continue feeling that way, you have to keep going to church." Your whole life, he says, becomes a game of chasing those good feelings, thinking that you can only get them through the church. "It chains you to itself," he explained. "Not literally, of course, but if you grow up thinking anytime you feel the warm and fuzzies, it comes from God, then what else are you supposed to think?" For ex-Mormons who grew up constantly interrogating thoughts and feelings for traces of these heavenly whispers, any stirrings of the soul after leaving the church became immediately suspect. Emotions, rather than constituting the whisperings of a heavenly father, were now looked at with an ambivalent distrust.

An Encounter with the Spirit

In ex-Mormon support group meetings, participants seemed to create a stark division between themselves and their former faith. Mormonism was depicted as cultish, a religion that brainwashed them into a repressive mind-set. And they, as ex-Mormons, had now "woken up" from or been able to "see through" the deception and now stood on the other side of the rational/irrational divide. The separation between themselves and their former faith seemed complete.

However, I began to question ex-Mormons' ongoing affective attachments to Mormonism as I sat talking one day with Paul, an ex-Mormon man who I came to rely on for insights into the ex-Mormon experience, on his back porch in a suburban Utah Valley neighborhood. I knew Paul to be an intellectually restless, at times stoic, and hyperrationalist thinker. He read broadly across various scientific disciplines, his bookshelves filled with texts on philosophy, psychology, astronomy, and sociology, all of which he accumulated since leaving Mormonism. He claimed that his research was a necessary obsession, vital in his efforts to make up for all the "brain cells [he] lost while in the church." In most of our encounters, Paul avoided speaking too intimately about his life in the church, instead taking a distant third-person voice or talking in vague generalities. I often attempted to engage him about his childhood growing up Mormon in Utah and his experience raising his own family in the faith over the past fifteen years. During these conversations, however, he was typically aloof, analytical, and even surgical in his intellectual deconstruction of Mormonism.

Perhaps this reticence stemmed from Paul's antagonistic relationship to his family, with whom he rarely spoke. They had not "disowned" him for leaving the church but, like most of the Mormons I spoke with, had stridently disapproved of his decision. On most occasions, Paul said, they avoided talking about religion altogether when he was around, a tacit silence that Paul keenly felt as passive-aggressive condemnation.

A week before, however, Paul's brother had sent him an email confronting his apostasy. Paul had printed it out in anticipation of my visit that afternoon. He handed me a copy, then read aloud:

> I want more than anything to shake you until you realize what it is you are doing. I am not sure you are grasping the gravity of your decision and how extremely important this choice is. The consequences will for sure bring you sadness and great suffering at some point. Either when you come to the realization of your mistake, or when you stand before your Maker and have to answer for why you left and led your family and posterity with you. Satan is waging his most fierce war and I am afraid he has deceived you.
>
> Can you really deny the scriptures are true? How can you possibly believe that all the times you have felt the spirit while reading the Book of Mormon means nothing?
>
> The only way you will be able to ever understand and recognize truth again is to "put off the natural man, and yield to the enticings of the Holy Spirit" (Mosiah 3:19). I promise you that if you do this sincerely and with sincere prayer, you can find your way back. I also warn you that if you don't, serious heartache, pain and regret await you. I know you feel the spirit now, as I relay to you these sacred things, testifying to you of their divine truth. Listen to that still small voice, if indeed you can still hear it, and let it guide you back.

Paul initially dismissed the letter, criticizing his brother's attempts to sway him back into the church. After several minutes, once the initial anger wore off, he confessed, "The funny thing is, I used to be that guy at church who would get all weepy giving my testimony of the church's truth, of Satan's war against the saints, and the need for us to hold fast, by faith, to the iron rod that would lead us to the celestial kingdom." He said it was hard when family "did that to you" because even though he no longer believed, he still knew "what it used to feel like." I asked him what it was like to have those feelings come back, to remember who he used to be. "It's a constant battle," he said, growing contemplative and somber. "It's really hard to deal with. I sometimes think to myself, am I just being duped?" Duped by what? I asked hesitantly. "Satan. Is this just Satan duping me, pulling me into the dark?" He looks down into his glass of beer and chuckles nervously. "Then I have another shot and tell myself, that's stupid!" We went inside the house for a drink. Paul seemed to need a break from our discussion. I did too—I had grown self-conscious, concerned that I would soon be interpolated as the agent of Satan, duping him further down the path of darkness.

When we retook our seats outside, I tried to ease the tension from before. I asked him what it was like to feel the spirit, to hear its whispers, as his brother had encouraged him to do. I expected him to reply in scientific, if not explicitly psychological and anthropological terms, as he often did. This time, however, he responded slowly, with a self-conscious chuckle and a wistful pause, and then explained. "It's really good when you're in it, when you can shut everything else out and get that warm, comforting feeling inside." His voice drifted off, and he looked away, growing comfortably nostalgic. For these few moments, he seemed relaxed, the memories and emotions spilling out unimpeded—he took pleasure in the temporary abeyance of his typically analytical disposition. I followed along as the spirit seemed to possess our conversation.

All of a sudden, however, he caught himself—his narrative had drifted too far down this path of long-lost sentiment. He looked up at me sternly, his eyes again staring harshly into mine—a burning intensity had replaced his brief meditative melancholia. "But there's no way I could go back," he blurted. "I would need a lobotomy first." He drew his hand, as if a sharpened blade, across his scalp.

I chuckled at the metaphor. He continued, "Sometimes people get stuck into a way of thinking; no matter what you tell them, they can't get out of it. I have a cousin that works for the Department of Corrections in the prison. He told me how sometimes, when an inmate is going berserk, they have to Taser them. But afterwards, he says, they wake up a totally different person. They're calm, clear-headed, and in control." Paul gestures in the air, as if holding a Taser. "Sometimes I think that's what people need, a good jolt to shock them back into their right minds."

Disenchanting Emotions

What does it mean for ex-Mormons to find these emotions, these experiences of "feeling the spirit," as a threat in their post-Mormon lives? As discussed so far, the intimate, corporeal experience of feeling the spirit burning in one's chest grants a particular aura of truth and authenticity to the church. After leaving the church, however, ex-Mormons find these emotions reconstituted as the embodied focal point of anxiety in the midst of disaffection. Despite their outright rejection of the church's teachings about God and the spirit, at any time, the spirit may still whisper to them, planting seeds of doubt in their intellectual repudiation of Mormonism.

In his essay on "The Uncanny," Freud ([1919] 2003) writes that things considered uncanny (*unheimlich*) are those that arise unexpectedly and lead us back to something that was once very familiar but have since been denied, repressed, or concealed. They are only *unheimlich* now because they were once *heimlich*—that is, capable of "arousing a sense of peaceful pleasure and security." As Freud concluded, "Everything is unheimlich that ought to have remained secret and hidden but has come to light" ([1919] 2003, 517). Importantly, for Freud, the uncanny did not simply evoke feelings of uncertainty or confusion. The fear and terror provoked by the uncanny indicated the return or exposure of a formerly concealed anxiety.

What happened to Paul in our conversation? What did Paul's allusion to lobotomies and shock therapy reveal about the potency of feelings to disrupt his secular disenchantment? While in the church, many ex-Mormons say they passionately fought to keep the weight of the facts and reasons that proved the church was not true under control by seeking out the spirit almost obsessively up until their "shelf broke" and all the questions and doubts came tumbling down. No longer seeking truth in the spirit, they then turned to science as a disembodied source of objective knowledge. However, remembering his experiences of feeling the spirit had perhaps reinstated an all-too-familiar cognitive dissonance in Paul. Perhaps his dispassionate estrangement from Mormonism was not as complete as he thought.

Since Paul's disaffection, which had occurred several years prior to our conversation, he had labored to expel any lingering attachment to the church. In our discussions, he frequently lashed out at church leaders, saying they "stole" thirty years of his life and had become leaders of an "immoral institution" that was "hell-bent" on creating a theocracy. He repeatedly challenged them in our conversations, quoting their speeches from the biannual church conferences held in Salt Lake City and dismissing Mormons' beliefs as backward and naïve. Science, he said, had now replaced mysticism as the guiding principle in his life.

One fears the uncanny, it is argued, because confronting it threatens to reveal one's illicit desires that have been carefully and systematically denied out of fear of castration by a powerful superego. For Paul, the feeling of intimate unity with the spirit had become the unconscionable desire in the now thoroughly rationalized and enlightened world he sought to inhabit, a world in which he was free to make up his own mind rather than heed to the promptings of his heart. Feeling the spirit again threatened to return Paul to the state of confusion, dissonance, and indecision that he had been in before his "shelf broke." It threatened to return Paul to a position of submission to Mormonism, to resubject him to the sense of being inhabited, possessed, and penetrated by a spiritual force that took away his autonomy and freedom.

This allusion to a lobotomy, it seemed to me at the time, was not a hypothetical condition that if met would allow him to return to the church. Rather, it was a fantastical attempt, a symbolic self-procedure, employed in that moment to cull the affective hold the church had over his memories and emotions, even after all these years. All the feelings that his science, his philosophy, and his intellectualization had kept at bay unexpectedly broke through in those brief moments of nostalgic memory, necessitating the fantasy of an actual lobotomy to again wrest control once more. Amid the ambiguity and ambivalence in that moment, Paul was forced to make a choice. He could follow the path back into confusion, or he could appeal to a techno-scientific intervention and fantasize about the relief a lobotomy or shock therapy might grant him. In that moment of dissonance, he decided; he reconceived the emotions that unexpectedly welled up in him into a force that threatened to invade him and thus had to be excised and removed from his body via surgical intervention.

A week later, I came across one of Paul's posts on an online ex-Mormon message board. He said he had been in a conversation with a woman who was gifted with intuition, who had the ability to "feel energy." She worked as a freelance energy healer and had been seeking clients in the ex-Mormon community. Paul responded to her request with scathing indignation.[3]

The emotions Paul experienced during our interview seemed to greatly unnerve him, even scare him. In the wake of Paul's disenchantment from Mormonism, he had turned to a highly intellectualized form of atheism informed by scientific detachment and objectivity. His new perspective worked, for the most part, aside from a brief moment in which its therapeutic effects broke down and more drastic interventions—in the form of lobotomies and shock therapy—became necessary. But now Paul had had time to recover from this brief moment of weakness.

Paul now projected all the angst of our previous encounter onto this woman who could "feel energy." "You think there is 'energy' somewhere *out there*? What are you, a Jedi? You think you can actually control this energy?" he asked. Where was it? How do you find it? he wanted to know. "Isn't that just your mind, your emotions you're feeling? Isn't that just a mood?"

His diatribe then slipped into instruction on enlightened reasoning. People in the church attempt to do essentially the same thing with emotions, he said, and it's dangerous:

> Emotions can make us accept things we've no business accepting. Just because they claim "feeling" of the truth doesn't make it valid. Facts are facts. Feelings are bullshit. Saying you "feel" something and that makes it true, means nothing. Your emotions may be very real to you. They may even be very important, but they come from inside you. My atheism certainly includes all those human concepts and emotions as real things. I just realize that they aren't coming from outside us. We don't have a soul that is separate from our physical bodies. We have as many neurons in our heads as there are stars in the Milky Way. All the feelings and emotions we have are supported by the real, physical construct of the brain.

I couldn't help but feel that he was lecturing not just to his online audience but to himself in our conversation just a few days prior. He was interpolating that part of himself that was tempted by the spirit as an imaginary audience, reinstantiating reason and rationality as the basis of truth. Paul sought to overturn the spiritual logic of "feeling the spirit" by levying a scientifically informed sense of the body. He inverted the sensation from one of being overwhelmed by an *external* divine source to one that is better understood as an *internal* eruption of subjective feelings. By relocating emotions "inside the person" and framing them as a neurophysiological reaction, the relationship between the body, mind, and emotions was reconceived as an immanently material one. That is, the body and its sentiments and perceptions could be reconceived as scientifically verifiable, predictable, and controllable.

Emotion's power to envelope believers within a sacred reality stems from its individual, personal, and corporeal immediacy. In the wake of radical disenchantment, therefore, individual emotions, no matter how vivid, must be reconceived no longer as an undeniable basis of truth but as a continuously suspect and dangerous phenomenon that can be subjected to the sterilizing power of rational thought.

By conceptualizing emotions as stemming from one's own psyche and locating them within the neurological processes of the human brain, ex-Mormons mitigate the power that emotions, and by extension the church, have over them. By turning spirituality into biology, the embodied experience of feeling an emotion (e.g., guilt, levity, joy, or sorrow) can then be understood not as the product of a capricious God but as an immanently internal, private occurrence that can be effectively controlled by employing enlightened reasoning.

A scientifically informed atheism thereby gives ex-Mormons an explanatory framework to apply to their own and each other's emotions. And it is through culling the importance of such emotional experiences that ex-Mormons ultimately sever the links with the Mormon lifeworld they formerly inhabited. It is through reconceptualizing emotions and their expression in the body that ex-Mormons negotiate their subjection to Mormonism's institutional, social, and psychological control, a control that stems not from explicit coercion but from tacit immersion in a sacred reality made intimately real through feelings.

CHAPTER 5

"Living in the Shadow of the Church"

APOSTASY, STIGMA, AND PROJECTIVE FANTASY

The figure of "Korihor" is commonly invoked in the church when discussing ex-Mormons. Described in the Book of Mormon as an atheist, an "anti-Christ" who traveled from city to city preaching against the existence of God and spreading wickedness, Korihor is synonymous with spiritual malfeasance and danger. Driven by disbelief and a rebellious spirit, Korihor encapsulates how many faithful church members see those who leave the church—unruly, wicked, and vengeful. The story of Korihor both stigmatizes those who fall away from the church and demonstrates to church members how such nonreligious figures should be handled.

Scriptures describe the religious leaders of the day growing concerned with the threat Korihor posed to their communities, fearing he might "lead away the hearts of many" and turn the people against the government and the church. They therefore forcibly brought him to Alma, chief judge and high priest, and gave him an opportunity to repent of his sins and proclaim his belief in God. But Korihor refused, instead demanding that Alma show him a sign proving God's existence. As the story goes, Alma immediately wielded his divine powers to strike Korihor dumb and blind, forcing him to wander the streets begging for food from those to whom he once preached his lies and deceptions. But even after suffering this punishment, Korihor's presence reportedly continued to threaten and disturb the church leaders. In a vicious climax to the story, the Book of Mormon describes Korihor, while fumbling his way through the streets, suddenly "run upon and trodden down" by local residents "until he was dead." No unfortunate tragedy, church leaders in the Book of Mormon held up Korihor's demise as a spiritual lesson. "Speedily repent," they warned, "lest the same judgments . . . come unto [you]." Such is the end of him "who perverteth the ways of the Lord" (Alma 30).

In the modern LDS Church, Sunday school classes routinely read these passages and discuss how members can identify Korihors in their own lives, other "possible sources of such false teachings today" (Seminaries 2009, 101–105). Be ever vigilant, they are told, wary of those who seek to spread lies and wickedness wherever they may be found. In particular, friends, family, or other loved ones may, if led astray by false teachings, pose a threat to the church and Mormons' personal faith. Avoiding such fallen figures is therefore of utmost importance. Indeed, during obligatory "temple recommend interviews," church bishops routinely ask members, "Do you support, affiliate with, or agree with any group or individual whose teachings or practices are contrary to or oppose those accepted by the Church of Jesus Christ of Latter-day Saints?" (FairMormon 2018). Securing a temple recommend, and thus being granted access to the temple, requires a firm answer of no.

Antipathy toward apostates and the nonreligious is perhaps as old as religion itself. Accusations of atheism, apostasy, and heresy have long been leveled at those thought to pose a threat to whatever religious ideology was dominant at the time (Wilson 2004). Yet their crime is not just the failure to adhere to the same theological beliefs or engage in the same ritual practices as everyone else. To many religious followers, they represent an existential threat to the religious moral order—the rules, boundaries, principles, and traditions that followers believe underpin who they are, in their very substance, as a people. Predictably, we see that the stigma directed at apostates and the nonreligious becomes especially acute during times of uncertainty and instability, when the collective ego is less self-assured and the group worries that the purity of their way of life is at risk of being polluted. The people described in the Book of Mormon were indeed forever caught up in wars and political conflicts among various factions: the Book of Mormon is essentially one long dramaturge of the ancient people's territorial, ethnic, and religious boundaries and identities continuously collapsing and being recreated, of prophets preaching for unity and obedience and against the evils of sin, corruption, moral decay, and the risk of divine retribution.

Against the background of this sociopolitical turmoil, Korihor would seem to be a trifling concern. He commanded no armies and had no power. Yet somehow he seemed to pose an insidious threat to the Book of Mormon peoples (and by extension, contemporary readers of scripture). Why? No mere scapegoat for people's troubles, Korihor represented an inconspicuous existential threat to the church community that was impossible to engage on the field of battle, where enemies were easily identifiable and readily prepared for through the training of warriors and the production of blades and arrows. Korihor's ideas, more sinister and surreptitious, risked permanently infecting the people like a virus, through intimate contact in neighborhoods and on city streets. He risked turning the church community against itself, instilling rebellion against God, church leaders, and the moral order through argument and persuasion. And worst of all, he was one of them.

We can see much of this same antipathy toward nonbelievers reflected on a national level. In much of the American population's collective imagination, the United States is a country founded on religious teachings and home to an overwhelmingly religious majority, where the idea of "religious freedom" has been ensconced in a constitutional amendment legislating for each and every faith's right to religious expression, unfettered by governmental or civil interference (Chaves 1994). This desire for a flourishing pluralistic landscape of religious diversity is indeed visible in tax incentives for religious organizations, laws protecting religious subjects' rights to freedom of religious practice, and the ubiquity of religious motifs in public, in the form of prayers, imprints of "In God We Trust," and religious holidays (Beneke 2006).

Because the United States has historically been thought of as a religious nation, its model of citizenry and full personhood defined by individuals' incorporation into a religious collective, those outside religion face a unique set of stereotypes (Cragun et al. 2012). The nonreligious person is often stigmatized as antiauthoritarian, amoral, angry, unpredictable, and untrustworthy. When asked who they would least likely vote for in a democratic election, contemporary Americans say they are more likely to disregard differences in race, religion, gender, or sexuality than they are to overlook a candidate's lack of faith in God (Hammer et al. 2012). Americans as a whole seem to harbor more antipathy toward atheists than Muslims, Jews, racial or ethnic minority groups, recent immigrants, and homosexuals, to such an extent that they constitute a new contemporary "other" against which many Americans construct a sense of moral and cultural identity (Edgell, Gerteis, and Hartmann 2006). As sociologist Ryan Cragun (2012) contends, this sentiment all too often results in abounding discrimination against the nonreligious, from tacit shunning to loss of employment or even acts of physical violence.

While previous studies of the nonreligious have addressed instances of secular identity formation (LeDrew 2013; Smith 2010) as well as collective lobbying efforts and identity politics both in the United States and globally (Asad 2003; Kettell 2013), the micropolitics of transitioning out of religion have not been studied in a highly localized and culturally specific context. The locus of my analysis for such processes is important. For ex-Mormons living in Utah, leaving the church is not about organizing against school prayer or lobbying against the use of "In God We Trust" on American currency. Rather, it is a decision made with much more immediate and tangible concerns, one that must be weighed against the harsh criticisms, stigmas, and stereotypes they may receive as "apostates" from friends and family, neighbors, colleagues, and employers. As most soon find, their decision to leave the church in Utah unwillingly pits them against a religious community that dominates political, cultural, and social discourse in their homes and larger communities, a condition that often leads them to be socially isolated and vulnerable—latter-day Korihors left to wander the streets of Mormondom.

Just as Korihor was rendered deaf, dumb, and eventually dead because of his ideas about the nonexistence of god, marginalizing ex-Mormons is about silencing people and ideas that pose existential threats to the contemporary church community. Indeed, within Mormonism, to have knowledge of the church's "truth" and then reject it is, within the cultural logic of Mormonism, wholly inconceivable. As mentioned in chapter 1, in Mormon cosmology, the Outer Darkness is a place infinitely removed from the rest of humanity, reserved for those who commit this unthinkable act of betrayal. Apostates' threat is in this way wholly unique and terrifying. Unlike the threat posed by followers of other religions or even non-Mormon atheists, whose verbal attacks can be summarily dismissed as illogical or uninformed, the apostate was once just like everyone else, a trusted friend or family member, a respected church member who had a faithful testimony of the church, who one day stopped believing. Their disenchantment is therefore distinctly unsettling: it throws the very foundation of the reality on which truth rests into question, and it fundamentally undermines members' ability to trust the authenticity and strength of the faith of those who live around them, rendering confidence in an incorruptible moral order incomplete and unstable. And especially problematic are those apostates who, after leaving the church, go on to live a happy and fulfilling life. Because the plan of salvation is the path to happiness, life without the church is assumed to be decrepit and spiritually empty. But a happy apostate is a threatening reversal of this most basic logic undergirding most Mormons' adamant belief that true fulfillment can only be found in the church. If joy can also be found outside of Mormonism, then maybe Mormonism itself is sufficient but unnecessary.

Such spiritual inquietude compels Mormons to formulate explanations about how and why someone could go from faithful church member to nonbelieving apostate. That is, apostates' sudden loss of belief stimulates a reaction formation, a conceptual reframing couched within a faith-promoting logic that effectively shields members from the possibility that the apostate is right.

In this chapter, I explore this dynamic by discussing the various stigmas and stereotypes circulating within Mormonism about apostasy. I first became aware of these faith-preserving, explanatory narratives about apostasy when discussing my research with faithful church members who would, in the course of conversation, offer up their own explanations of the reasons people "really" leave the church and what happened to them once on the outside. I first review the various reasons offered by these church members and contextualize them within contemporary Mormonism's bid for popular acceptance in mainstream American society, arguing that the stereotypes circulating around apostasy are a part of a cultural defense mechanism for assuaging anxieties associated with entertaining doubt or questioning church teachings. I then describe the effects that these stigmas have on ex-Mormons as they attempt to make a life outside the fold.

Stereotyping Apostasy

When I asked church members why they thought people left Mormonism, they would most often claim that people simply had a lack of faith. However, it was not that apostates *lost* faith. Rather, they were imagined to have "never really had a testimony" in the first place. Anyone who had truly felt the spirit and gained a testimony, they claimed, would not willfully deny it. Their disaffection was simply a part of the process of the "chaff separating from the wheat."

As discussed in a previous chapter, ex-Mormons often told me that church members were acutely aware of the fragility of their testimonies and therefore had to deny the fact that apostates once also had a testimony as a means of spiritual self-preservation. As one ex-Mormon man said, "If they admit that someone can have a testimony and then lose it, it means whatever it is they're basing their testimony on, however secure they think theirs is, it can be potentially destroyed as well." Furthermore, if the loss of testimony is not only imagined as possible but spreading among people around them, they must therefore assume that a force exists that can potentially overpower their own spiritual witness. Imagining apostates as never having had a real testimony mitigates this fear. It reassures members that their own testimonies are impervious. In the same way, denying apostates a testimony pre-emptively and retroactively invalidates apostates' statuses as church members. If they never had a testimony, they never were truly members. And if they were never members, their criticisms are the same as those leveled by non-Mormons from outside the church, illegitimate and uninformed.

I saw an especially acute example of this once when discussing my research with a group of Mormon students in a class I taught at a university in Utah. I attempted to explain that I worked with a group of "ex-Mormons" who *chose* to leave the church. Some did not understand. In the course of the conversation, they kept using the term *excommunicated*. No, I asserted, they weren't shown the door; they decided that the church wasn't true, and that's why they left. In the end, we agreed to disagree. But I realized that their attributing apostasy to excommunication stemmed from an unwillingness to accept that something might be wrong with the church's teachings or its history that would cause someone to lose faith. It was easier to assume the apostate was wrong, confused, guilty, ashamed, and so forth. If true faith could unintentionally wither away, then what was to stop it from happening to them as well? But their assertion that ex-Mormons had been excommunicated had an explicit moral judgment to it as well. I knew, as did they, that people were not excommunicated for failing to attend church on Sundays or for committing some other similarly innocuous mistake. Excommunication was a punitive measure resulting from a serious moral offense, such as infidelity or illicit drug use. In describing ex-Mormons as having been excommunicated, my students thus intentionally created an explanation that held the wayward member, not the church, morally responsible for their disaffection.

In doing so, they rendered the figure of the apostate spiritually innocuous. Imagining the apostate as having been excommunicated foreclosed the need to think about other possible reasons someone might want to leave the church, and their faith and the church's moral culpability thus remained safely unchallenged.

This reactionary logic is taught and perpetuated in church educational materials, where members are told that apostasy stems from a serious sin, not because they have valid questions or concerns about the church's teachings, morals, or leadership. Church publications, such as this one found in the *Ensign* magazine, discuss apostasy as the surface manifestation of a deeper personal failing:

> Apostasy frequently results when a person commits serious sin but does not repent. To silence his conscience or justify his sinful actions, the individual moves away from the truth, looking for imperfections in others or questioning Church doctrine with which he no longer agrees. Conflicts between Church members can also lead to apostasy. Some individuals begin to think the Church is not true when they feel that a leader did not treat them well. They become offended and, without considering what they are losing, they stray from the Church . . . I testify that we can avoid the mists of darkness that lead to personal apostasy by repenting of our sins, overcoming offense, eliminating faultfinding, and following our Church leaders. (Zivic 2009)

I frequently heard Mormons talk about people leaving because of a particular unkind word or criticism from a fellow parishioner, a disagreement with a church leader, or an offense taken to a gospel principle they personally disagreed with. The explanation of having "taken offense" was particularly widespread, and I found that it often offered a means of ascribing to the apostate a deep moral failing couched in the rather innocuous language of being offended. Specifically, those who are offended are believed to be deflecting responsibility for some committed indiscretion that they secretly feel guilty about but resist confessing to, such as an illicit sexual affair, infidelity, pornography addiction, or addiction to drugs and alcohol.

I found that such moral accusations function similarly to the logic of paranoia, in which some hidden force shaping reality is believed to secretly exist just out of view. The absence of a visible causal force does not lessen the probability that it truly exists. People instead become drawn to it, perpetually imagining, describing, and fantasizing about it in increasingly unrealistic terms so as to indirectly draw their attention away from the real cause of their anxiety. As such, the apostate's fantasized failing(s) takes on a life of its own. One ex-Mormon man I spoke to described how once trusted family members, to whom he previously felt emotionally close, quickly got sucked into the hyperbole and conjecture when news of his disaffection spread, resulting in a visceral feeling of helplessness and paranoia of his own: "[It's like] you're standing in the middle of this awful narrative that's being constructed around you that you're powerless to fight against."

This logic not only enables church members to unilaterally position themselves as morally superior to the rogue apostate but also allows them to self-righteously marginalize apostates, claiming that such treatment is just and right, necessary to protect the community's moral integrity, in effect creating a category of absolute otherness into which disbelievers fall. Similarly, it articulates and reinforces the pervasive normative moral order built on strict adherence to church teachings. Stories of apostates typically depict them as stricken with unbearable grief and misery, left to lead pitiful existences, isolated from friends and family. Such stories reinforce Mormonism's moral and social boundaries through a negative depiction of life outside of the church as filled with "darkness, ignorance, doubt, pain, sorrow, grief, mourning, unhappiness; [with] no person to console within the hour of trouble, no arm to lean upon in the day of calamity, no eye to pity when they are forlorn and cast down" (Young 1997, 78–84). In this way, making such "downward comparisons" between believers and nonbelievers allows the community of faithful Mormons to collectively reassert the indefatigable happiness and contentment found only in the church. By intentionally making comparisons to apostates' fantasized lives of destitution outside the church, whatever grievances or frustrations they may harbor in the church are rendered innocuous and trifling.

Stereotypes and stigma about apostates are also an effective method of boundary keeping, as they tacitly reinforce orthodoxy and obedience among the church ranks, serving as cautionary examples meant to discourage others who may start to doubt. James, a forty-year-old man who left the church while serving on his ward bishopric, described his partially unconscious awareness of this dynamic and the way in which disbelief may at any time afflict even the most pious of church members. "Growing up, you hear how apostates are talked about . . . you see how they are treated . . . as if they're these monstrous creatures whose lives are full of loneliness and sadness . . . You really internalize this fear of becoming like them, because I think deep down you realize that everyone around you could turn on you too if you start to step out of line."

The fear of apostates can be understood, in some ways, as a communal defense mechanism stemming from each individual member's tacit awareness that the group he or she is now happily a part of may one day turn on him or her too—that apostates may spread the affliction that has stricken them, putting the community as a whole at risk. "Remember," an apostle of the church once counseled a group of BYU students, "when you see the bitter apostate, you do not see only an absence of light, you see also the presence of darkness. Do not spread disease germs" (Packer 1981). In such a fraught psychosocial environment, learning to avoid apostates becomes paramount not out of an immediate fear of losing life and limb but rather out of a fear that their spiritual affliction may be contagious. James's fears were indeed realized when he left the church. He soon found that his former ward members "avoided [him] like the plague." A model member up until his apostasy, James provoked a mix of anxiety and confusion in those with whom he had once had intimate relationships. At the grocery store, in his neighborhood, and at his son's youth baseball games, he was either outright ignored or only engaged with in curt conversation. "It's almost like they think they'll catch what I have if they're around me too much," he confided.

Having lost the constraining power of religion to "uphold" religious virtues and reason, the disease of apostasy is indeed portrayed as an affliction of moral and spiritual pathology and insanity. From the perspective of the faithful church members, there is in fact a certain madness to apostasy: "Let a man or woman who has received much of the power of God, visions and revelations, turn away from the holy commandments of the Lord, and it seems that their senses are taken from them, their understanding and judgment in righteousness are taken away, they go into darkness, and become like a blind person who gropes by the wall . . . They have become darkened in their minds and everything has become a mystery to them" (Young 1855, 301). Here, amid life's tumultuous seas, the church is allegorized as a ship guiding its passengers to calmer waters. In contrast, members are taught that the apostate is he who foolishly abandons the ship of safety to his own demise. "Why do people apostatize?" the prophet Brigham Young once wrote. He continued, "You know we are on the Old Ship Zion. We are in the midst of the ocean. A storm comes on, and, as sailors say, she labors very hard. I am not going to stay here, says one; I don't believe this is the Ship Zion. But we are in the midst of the ocean. I don't care, I am not going to stay here. Off goes the coat, and he jumps overboard. Will he not be drowned? Yes. So with those who leave this Church. It is the Old Ship Zion, let us stay in it" (Young 1997, 78–84).

From church members' perspectives, apostates have fundamentally lost their bearings and their decisions and actions are incomprehensible, outside the bounds of reason. On the one hand, this effectively puts life in the church on a pedestal, granting to those who adhere to its teachings the promise of moral and rational clarity. On the other hand, by projecting madness onto apostates, Mormonism, a religion often denounced for its own "irrational" and heretical teachings and practices, effectively reverses and channels the stigmas that have historically been attached to it.

In order to maintain these self-preserving explanations, stereotypes, and projections, apostates must therefore be held apart from the church community. Like Korihor, their voices are silenced so as not to disturb the narrative being constructed around them. As a result, ex-Mormons often describe themselves as "living in the shadows" of the church, experiencing everyday moments of exclusion and avoidance. They became people who were talked about but not talked to, at least not when it came to the topic of their decision to leave the church. Although filled with inner turmoil and angst as they felt their faith in the church slip away, ex-Mormons found that their friends and family seemed indifferent to their experiences, treating them as a topic of shame that was best avoided. Trying to explain the real reasons they became disaffected—problems they had with church history, doctrine, or theology—were met with blank stares or outright dismissals. "Whatever you do, just don't talk to your siblings," one woman's father told her when she came out to him about her disaffection. Others were simply no longer invited to family functions, or when they were allowed, they were told to keep quiet about religious topics. "We can still have a relationship; it just won't be about religion," apostates are frequently told. I often heard church members express desire for apostates to "just be quiet about it" or to "keep it private," frowning at those who publicized their apostasy in conversation or discussed it on internet message boards. While faith in the church was to be publically promoted and a cause for collective celebration, as manifested in the thousands of missionaries circling the globe and the millions of dollars spent on church advertising and PR (public relations) campaigns, loss of faith was to be secreted away and "dealt with by individuals and their families," as one church member told me. "[It is] not put in the spotlight. Because, you know, it really isn't something to be proud of."

Gordon and Michael

Stigmas are used to legitimize and reinforce hostilities and distance between groups of people. But stigmas must also be understood for the way in which they express, in disguised fashion, deeper tensions circulating within Mormonism itself. That is, they function as projective fantasies through which unacceptable desires, tendencies, or conflicts that are emerging in the course of life in the church can be expelled and rendered safe.

In psychoanalytic language, projection is the act of transferring one's own thoughts or feelings onto others. Having been socialized into a particular culture, with its associated values, norms, and rules, the superego warns of punishment if the dysfunction is found to be internal (Erikson 1973). In response, the ego redirects those unwelcome thoughts and feelings to an external, more acceptable place, often found in other people. This in effect allows one to become aware of these thoughts and feelings' presence, as we "observe" them in others, without feeling the accompanying distress of knowing that they are in fact our own. Externalizing them further allows for their assessment and critique while safely insulating us from our own dysfunctions (Newman et al. 1997).

Gordon was an intelligent, fussy man in his midforties, a family friend with whom I spoke occasionally over the years when I was learning about Mormonism. Although he took his Mormon faith very seriously, he was always willing to talk about my interest in apostasy. During the time I lived in Utah, our conversations primarily revolved around his relationship with a man named Michael, who had recently left the church.

Gordon and Michael had shared a life in the church starting when they were young boys passing sacrament together, and although they were the same age, Gordon said he had always looked up to Michael as an older brother. However, Michael had recently begun questioning his testimony and then left the church entirely, along with his wife and two children. The news of Michael's apostasy confounded Gordon. He initially held out hope that Michael would have a change of heart and return. But after six months passed, it became clear that Michael's decision was final. Accepting this reality, Gordon said he eventually "cut ties" with Michael, explaining that "he wasn't who I thought he was anymore."

In our conversations, Gordon talked about Michael, a man he once loved as a brother, quite dismissively. He said Michael was being prideful. He accused him of having fallen for the false teachings of the world, of having read too much anti-Mormon literature. Most disparagingly, Gordon accused Michael of having committed moral sins. Michael now routinely drank coffee and alcohol, practices clearly forbidden by Mormonism's Word of Wisdom. And to top it off, Gordon said, growing awkward as he spoke, "He probably had problems with the law of chastity." "I wouldn't be surprised if I found out he had been unfaithful to his wife," Gordon concluded.

Yet despite all this talk *about* him, Gordon had not talked directly to Michael in months. He refused to call or visit and explicitly avoided Michael's attempts to contact him. As far as I knew, Gordon had never asked Michael why he decided to leave the church. In the first few months after Michael's disaffection, Gordon said that he sent Michael occasional emails and text messages. He warned Michael to think about the path he was headed down but concluded, "He didn't want to hear anything I had to say." When Michael stopped responding to those particular messages, Gordon took this as a sign that Michael had "chose that life for good" and gave up hope of mending their relationship.

While Gordon accused Michael of being unreasonably angry at the church, citing the "destruction" he was causing in his own life, it was Gordon's anger toward Michael that stood out to me. When discussing Michael's apostasy, Gordon became erratic and hurried, eventually reaching a point where he had to change the topic. He obviously missed his friend and was hurt by his loss. But during these conversations, I struggled to understand why Gordon harbored such antipathy toward Michael. Gordon often professed that Mormonism, better than other forms of Christianity, he thought, taught its members how to incorporate Christlike qualities of love, humility, and kindness into one's life. But when talking about Michael, I saw a petty, at times bitter side of Gordon that reflected something more unruly at work in his life.

Gordon was what I heard referred to as a "dyed-in-the-wool" Mormon. He had been "born in the covenant," and his entire world, from his profession to his romantic relationships, was defined by the Mormon Church. While I had met older generations of church members who seemed at ease in their faith, responding to my questions about why some people leave Mormonism with a complacent shrug and the suggestion that "it's not for everyone," Gordon was argumentative about the need for Mormons to strictly adhere to church teachings. He complained that there was little that distinguished Mormons from anybody else. Polygamy had once defined the church, he said, but no more: "Most Mormons look and act like everyone else." The church needed to reassert some of the doctrines it had pulled away from over the years. "Listen to what the general authorities talk about; it's no different [than Christianity]." Wouldn't emphasizing some of Mormonism's more lesser-known beliefs scare away some church members? I asked. No, he asserted. "It's fine if some can't handle it. That's what we need." He indeed had a black-and-white kind of morality and defined his church membership as much in terms of loyalty as spirituality. "Lazy" or "rebellious" members should, he said, "either fall in line or get out."

As I talked to Gordon, I saw how his Mormon identity, despite appearing confident and secure, was routinely challenged in ways that reflected broader tensions within Mormon culture. Like many other church members, Gordon took his devotion to "following the counsel" of his priesthood leaders seriously, dutifully accepting whatever "callings" were assigned to him, even when they seemed unimportant, as when he was assigned to work as ward librarian. However, Gordon seemed frustrated with his inability to climb the ranks of church leadership, whether by securing a calling in his ward's bishopric or at the larger stake level. His identification with church leaders' authority, power, and sanctity thus in large part went unrealized, his progress in the church bureaucracy inexplicably stymied and increasingly incongruous with the status he felt he deserved. He sometimes wondered what he could have achieved had he devoted all his seemingly wasted energies to his career instead.

Gordon had also in fact experienced his own crisis of faith several years before. He said he had begun to question church teachings after perusing an "anti-Mormon" website. However, when he broached the subject with his wife, she "freaked out," warning him in no uncertain terms of what would happen if he kept heading down that path. Fearing the repercussions of entertaining his doubts any further, Gordon summarily redevoted himself to a life of faith.

Yet Gordon's family life seemed unfulfilled. He had married when he was twenty-two years old, shortly after returning from his mission in Brazil. But his wife had been his first and only sexual partner, and after they gave birth to four children in the first seven years of their marriage, she became uninterested in sex. His kids occupied most of his time now, and he found little space for his own interests.

Yet despite accusing Michael of sexual improprieties and complaining of the "filth" he often saw on TV and advertised in stores, Gordon at times seemed fascinated by ex-Mormons' sexual practices. In fact, I indirectly provided him an outlet for this curiosity when he once questioned me about the temperature of my marriage, a line of inquiry I found uncomfortable in light of his prior accusations of ex-Mormons as hypersexualized and "unable to control themselves." His curiosity indeed seemed characterized by a fantasy-driven imagining of the kinds of pleasures that awaited those who left the church. "I can't imagine what would happen to me if I didn't have the church," Gordon mused once while talking about Michael's life outside Mormonism. "I'd probably fall into all kinds of sex and drugs . . . probably like Michael is doing."

As I talked to Gordon about his life in the church, I realized that many of his frustrations seemed to reflect broader changes in Mormon culture over the past several decades. As Mormonism became increasingly incorporated into mainstream American culture, it shifted from being a marginalized religious sect to in some sense the very embodiment of American "wholesomeness." Church members in Utah almost unanimously align with the national Republican Party and its platform of social conservatism. Church leaders' rhetoric has also increasingly emphasized Mormonism's congruence with wider Christianity as the quintessential American faith. "Mormons are *Christians*," they frequently say. In the contemporary Mormon Church, the historic divide between the Saints and the gentiles is thus increasingly being overlooked in favor of a more global, pan-ethnic, and ambiguously "Christian" orientation.

In many ways, these trends are part of a larger process of secularization taking place in Utah. Driven by a business-friendly tax code, Utah has experienced tremendous economic growth and cultural diversification over the past several decades. For example, the state now boasts more than half a dozen craft breweries and an increasingly eclectic downtown night scene in Salt Lake City. While this development has in many ways been celebrated by the LDS Church, as it provides jobs and financial investment opportunities for the many church-owned companies operating in the state, it has also accelerated Mormonism's acculturation into mainstream American culture and put the enticements of the world increasingly at church members' fingertips.

The narrative stigmas surrounding apostates are indeed a form of projective fantasy that functions in Mormonism as a means of mitigating anxieties provoked by the church's continuing incorporation into mainstream American society and the conflicts that ensue. The construction of such narratives is key to understanding the logic of apostasy from the viewpoint of faithful members, as it points to a pattern of moral projection taking place between church members and apostates, in which members' own illicit desires and fears are transferred to those who leave.

First, while stigmatizing apostates allows moral boundaries to be reinscribed, there is something more at work. As seen in Gordon's case, I found that stigmatizing apostates was an expression of Mormonism's anxiety over the dissolution of the historical boundaries among Mormonism, Christianity, and America culture that had once provided a sense of distinct collective identity. The apostate, as the embodied symbol of disbelief, has become the negated "other"—a position of alterity long held by the "gentiles," those in the "abominable religions," and the American government and society as a whole—against which Mormon cultural and religious identity is constructed. Gordon's statement "fall in line or get out" demonstrates a neo-orthodox entrenchment in absolute faith and Mormonism's distinctive beliefs, serving as the basis of one form of contemporary Mormon identity emerging in Utah.

Second, the cultural pattern of identifying and circulating rumors about the "real reasons" someone left the church makes the pervasive and underlying fears, anxieties, and salacious desires that are normally not spoken about in the church present and conscious. By being made to embody and openly signify the spiritual, cultural, and social tensions that must remain repressed and silenced in the church, the apostate serves as a cathartic conduit through which these tensions can be appropriately expressed. Gordon's dismissal of apostates as morally corrupt, disobedient, and prideful expresses an underlying need to deny what he shares with them yet cannot admit—his frustration with church leaders, his feelings of wounded pride, his sexual curiosity and lust, and his own repressed doubts and questions about the church. In this environment of ambiguous belonging and sensitivity to doubt, stigmatizing apostates serves as a defense against the appeal of openly expressing these tensions. Likewise, the act of alienating apostates, though seemingly "unChristlike," paradoxically serves as a means of performing one's religious authenticity and faithfulness. The stigmas that are routinely attached to apostates therefore not only construct a moral boundary between members and former members, or believers and nonbelievers, but also protect faithful Mormons from consciously realizing and acting out their own illicit desires and frustrations.

But why must apostates be silenced and shunned? Unlike nonmembers and other "outsiders" who may very well be categorized as "enemies of truth," apostates constitute a unique kind of threat to faithful church members. First, they have the capacity to lurk amid the faithful brethren, looking and sounding just like any other member, requiring ever more strident defense mechanisms aimed at repressing their presence. No doubt influenced by the rash of mass apostasy afflicting the church in Kirtland, Ohio, an early headquarters for the burgeoning religion prior to its exodus to Utah, Joseph Smith once cautioned the faithful to be on guard against defectors in their midst. "Those who have associated with us and made the greatest professions of friendship, have frequently been our greatest enemies and our most determined foes . . . Judas-like, [they] seek the destruction of those who were their greatest benefactors," he counseled. In days of rampant spiritual dereliction, in which the faithless seem many and the faithful seem few, apostasy constitutes the most ambiguous of afflictions to strike a religious community—for every true believer also embodies the potential for intimate betrayal. As Joseph Smith warned, the greatest friends can also make the greatest enemies.

Second, unlike other historical "others," apostates are rendered ever more dangerous because they cannot be fully "othered." There is an ambivalence attached to them. Despite their embodiment of moral absolution, they were once loved family members, friends, and faithful church members, just as Michael was for Gordon. The danger they pose is an uncanny one. For church members like Gordon, there is a disturbing recognition of sameness in the apostate. Apostates, by virtue of their former intimacy and inclusion in Mormonism, force believing church members to face a refracted image of themselves. It was, I suggest, Gordon's very identification with Michael as an "older brother" that made his apostasy traumatic. As a result, the apostate comes to represent the possibility of dissolution from within rather than a more easily remedied and defended against attack from without. The apostate holds a metaphorical mirror up to faithful church members, granting them a glimpse into what their life could one day come to as well. Indeed, the apostate comes to represent the very possibility of madness lurking within the faithful church member; the apostate becomes the symbolic embodiment of the consequences of metaphorically eating from the tree of knowledge of good and evil, as depicted in Genesis, and gaining forbidden knowledge. This is what contemporary church members *know* happened to these erstwhile members yet cannot bring themselves to admit.

In apostates, church members confront an uncanny visage of their own potential for doubt and disaffection and perhaps even desire for sin and disbelief, yet the consequences are too disturbing to consciously entertain. The apostate forces the awareness of an internal foreignness within individuals and the collective body of the church as a whole so that the very thing church members renounce in apostates still circulates within the unconscious undercurrents of Mormonism. When encountering the apostate in reality or the imagination, the distinction between member and nonmember, the sacred safe church and the profane dangerous world, and belief and doubt collapse. And so the apostate must be kept silent, marginal, hidden, and repressed in order for the projection to be successful. From the perspective of faithful church members, the apostate must be made into an ultimate silenced, distanced other, for anything less would be to risk recognizing the "other" in themselves, bringing about an eruption of internal foreignness that would disassemble the boundaries between self and other on which their religious subjectivity rests.

In fact, contemporary Mormonism *needs* apostates. It is through the denigration of apostates in stereotype and stigma that the effects of Mormonism's internal tensions, rising amid its acculturation into mainstream American life, are expiated. Indeed, as Mormonism becomes more fully intertwined with the American public sphere, its sense of self further fragmented by competing allegiances and identifications, it will grow ever more dependent on the need to conjure up projective fantasies about apostates' sins. It is only through this, and by subsequently treating apostates as outsiders, that Mormonism will be able to maintain the illusion that a perfect, harmonious religious society is actually possible. It is in these types of psychosocial maneuvers, Žižek suggests, that ideology performs its "supreme conjuring trick" as it translates the impossibility of social continuity and harmony into an imagined "theft" by a historical "other," thereby effectively "concealing the traumatic fact that social harmony never existed and that it is an inherent impossibility" (1989, 125–127). What social entities like Mormonism fail to realize is that "society is always already divided," its "Symbolic order" already fractured and incomplete. However, by collectively imagining the apostate as a diseased entity, pathologically introducing into the social body the roots of "disintegration and antagonism," the fantasy image of society as a harmonious whole is made possible. And thus the "dream of holistic fulfillment—through the elimination, expulsion or suppression of the Other" is forever maintained (Daly 2004).

Living in the Shadow of the Church

Being is being perceived . . . [We] exist first through and for the gaze of others.

—Pierre Bourdieu

Leaving Mormonism often comes at a steep cost. The church-dominated social climate of Utah ensures that those who leave the church find themselves quickly relegated to the status of second-class citizens. Stereotypes and stigmas about apostasy come to impact every facet of peoples' lives, from relationships at home to their professional work and personal finances.

Ex-Mormons often experience this stigma in terms of a heightened sense of visibility, as if they have now become highly conspicuous objects of moral scrutiny. They find that friends and family begin seeking to confirm their suspicions by looking for telltale signs of sin creeping into their lives. Women reported being frowned at disapprovingly when they wore tank tops or thigh-length shorts. Men sometimes described people who would scan their chest, arms, and legs with their eyes, looking for seamlines that would indicate if they were still wearing garments. Ex-Mormons' home lives are scrutinized as well. "My Mom comes over to my house, and you can just see the anxiety well up in her," one woman described to me. "She gets so nervous. She starts looking around the house, eyeing our coffee maker or the beer bottle in the garbage . . . One day I asked her what was wrong, and she told me she can 'feel that the spirit has left' our home. She said it makes her feel ill."

However, the moral othering of apostates is most acutely felt in the way it often leads to fractured families. Within Mormonism, families are touted as the most important part of one's life. Monday evenings are routinely set aside for Family Home Evening, where family prayer, singing, and fun activities solidify these sacred bonds of kinship. "Families are forever," members of the church often say. In Mormon homes throughout Utah, that phrase is ubiquitous, often found reproduced on plaques, signs, decorative plates, posters, and wall decals. And indeed, that is what membership in the church is about—creating everlasting, eternal family relationships that will last for all eternity. These are not just lofty aspirations; by engaging in certain forms of "temple work," Mormons can effectively "seal" themselves together—husband to wife, parents to children, and so on—"for time and eternity." This emphasis on family, however, is what makes leaving the church so difficult. Ex-Mormons often learn that so-called eternal families can indeed have a finite existence when loved ones choose to disassociate themselves in order to avoid putting the eventual exaltation of the larger family at risk.

Standing in a hotel lobby while waiting for an annual ex-Mormon conference to begin, I met Richard, a tall, partially balding man, who was in a panic about his family. He stood alone, pensively waiting for the opening session to begin, liberally availing himself of the free cocktails. Richard seemed lost. He had just found out about the conference a few hours ago and decided on impulse to attend. And about an hour before that, he had told his wife he was leaving the church. "They're all going crazy trying to figure out why I left," Richard told me, "but I just had to get out of there." His wife had looked at him "like [he] was a stranger." "She told me she felt like she didn't know me anymore. That I wasn't the man she married," he said. She had asked him if he had been cheating on her or was going to start drinking, the imagined transgressions and wild accusations streaming from her panicked mind. Richard had hidden his doubts for almost a year but had feared mentioning anything. "What am I going to do? We've been married for thirty-seven years. I knew I shouldn't have said anything," Richard said. His wife had already threatened divorce. With eyes that shifted between stoic glares and erratic glances around the room, he shared his story in stream-of-consciousness ramblings and repeated monosyllabic stabs of "I-am-just-so-angry." "I don't know what I'll do now," he confessed, beginning to calm as we made our way into the conference's opening address. "I'll have to see what she decides, but it doesn't look good."

Divorce in many cases seems unavoidable for ex-Mormons, as the loss of faith provokes panic in their spouses, the promise of an eternal life together in the celestial kingdom slipping away. A partner's loss of faith is believed to jeopardize the eternal family unit, as husbands may no longer "use their priesthood" in the home and wives are believed to no longer prioritize caring for the family. Stories of broken homes abound on online ex-Mormon message boards and in support group meetings, reflecting the pervasive consequences of disbelief. Jenna told me how, during her divorce proceedings, her ex-husband used her apostasy as "evidence that I was mentally unstable and unsuitable to care for my children." Her husband also frequently told their three small children that their mother "had chosen other priorities in life . . . that I wasn't living gospel anymore," Jenna said, feeling a wedge being driven between her and her children. "He was trying to turn my own kids against me. And I can't tell them anything different because they've already been taught to think people like me are evil. And then I can't get upset at their dad because that will just reinforce the idea that I'm angry and vindictive . . . I'm trapped."

In a similar case, Brian had two small children and a third on the way when his wife packed her bags and went to live with her parents in Seattle. "She told me if I didn't hold the priesthood, she basically didn't want me," he said. In his wife's eyes, he had become "useless." In leaving the church, Brian would no longer be able to preside over his family as a priesthood holder and thus would no longer be able to baptize any of their future children, give them blessings when they fell ill, or do the temple work that would seal them all together. Distraught, Brian went to his mother to ask for guidance and advice on how he could get his wife back. "[But] she said she agreed! I couldn't believe it. I said 'Mom! I'm your son!' But she said she would've done the same thing if my dad had done that to her."

Ex-Mormons found that their positions in their neighborhoods changed as well. In some situations, they were the subject of intense scrutiny, and in others, they were entirely avoided, living in a state of "censored presence." For example, I often heard stories of how former members' waves of hello to neighbors passing in their cars were met with downturned eyes and how chance meetings at the grocery store provoked church members' hasty retreats as they sought to avoid uncomfortable conversations. Once vibrant social relationships dimmed as neighborhood kids no longer stopped by apostate families' homes to play, parents were no longer invited to monthly book club meetings and rounds of golf, and whole families were taken off the neighborhood circuit of rotating barbecues and communal babysitting responsibilities.

Apostates are also at times made into objects of collective pity. Some ex-Mormons find that shortly after leaving the church, they become the subjects of intensive "rescue missions" staged by members of the congregation in an attempt to persuade them to come back to the fold. One woman described it to me this way:

> You become this service project for them. They see it as their duty to help you and bring you back. I know what's going through their heads; I used to do it too when someone in our ward stopped showing up or was having some kind of trouble. Everyone always thinks the worst about the situation, about what happened to you. But they act like all they want to do is love you. It's a funny kind of love, though. The first few months I stopped going to church, members of my ward would "muffin bomb" me every week. I'd come home from doing whatever, and there'd be a basket of muffins or something on my doorstep. Is

that love though? If they think that I've turned to the dark side, and my life really is in shambles, are muffins really going to do anything? "Take back your muffins!" is what I think. I don't need your pity.

This behavior can be stifling and patronizing. In a similar case, Brent's family began to treat him like a charity case in need of intervention. While attending a family reunion with relatives, he quietly avoided discussing church topics, not wanting to "spread the word" about his decision to leave the church. But "when members hang out together, there isn't much else they *do* talk about," so Brent avoided talking to anybody for much of the afternoon. Shortly after the reunion, however, a sister who lived out of state found out that he had left the church. She frantically emailed him, pleading for him to not take his life. She said the Holy Spirit had revealed to her that Brent was suicidal. "It's so condescending," Brent told me. "She thought because I'd left the church I wanted to kill myself, when really the only reason I may have looked like I wanted to kill myself was because I was stuck spending my Saturday afternoon listening to all of them instead of drinking a beer at home!"

The effects of stigma can also jeopardize people's employment and financial security. People employed directly by the LDS Church face the greatest risk. Losing one's testimony, or even being accused of apostasy, can result in immediate dismissal and a loss of benefits and retirement funds. Because religious organizations are exempt from federal laws in the hiring and firing of employees and operate under the guise of "ministerial exception," which gives religious institutions the right to "require that all applicants and employees conform to the religious tenets of [the] organization," discrimination against someone based on his or her loss of faith is legally justified.

However, there are also more tacit forms of employee discrimination based on the stigma of apostasy that have an especially pernicious effect in states like Utah, where a single faith dominates. One man I met named Roger owned a small engineering consulting firm that worked on residential and commercial projects throughout Cache County (an hour north of Salt Lake City). For those whose professions rely on professional reputation and garnering new business through referrals and word of mouth, apostasy often leads to a loss of business. "I was basically run out of town," he said. "All of my contracts [got] pulled when word started to spread that I'd left." Leann faced a similar, though more immediate, form of discrimination. Working as a fourth-grade teacher in a suburb of Salt Lake City when she decided to leave the church, Leann's students' parents began calling her school's principal, demanding their children be reassigned to other classes. In the midst of the financial recession in the mid-2000s, Leann's principal eventually let her go the following year, citing statewide budget cuts. "I know what really happened though," Leann said. Her principal confided to her that parents had been growing concerned that she was being a "negative influence" on their children and that she had become, in her principal's words, a "liability" for the school.

As I discuss in the next chapter, ex-Mormons attempt to respond to these forms of social exclusion (perpetuated by the circulation of stigmas and stereotypes) through collective action. Ex-Mormonism, to whatever extent it can be said to constitute a "social movement," is emerging in direct response to living in such a religious environment, where the choice not to believe begets such forms of sectarian intolerance.

CHAPTER 6

"I'm Apostate, Yes I Am"

THE POLITICS AND PERFORMANCE OF SECULAR IDENTITY

Over the past decade, an amorphous "ex-Mormon" movement has been taking shape across Utah and throughout the United States. In online chat rooms, annual ex-Mormon conferences, and "mass resignation" rallies, ex-Mormons are creating a new form of identity politics to resist the religious institution, community, and ideology of which they were once faithful members. As marginalized and stigmatized "apostates," ex-Mormons are joining together to weather the negative stereotypes projected onto them and even "speak back" to their former faith, staking their claim to a space of social personhood defined by its explicit opposition to or even "transcendence" of religion.

Such developments are not unique to Mormonism and in fact reflect wider trends of secular identity politics and positioning at the national level. Although nonreligious individuals have long existed, the widespread formation of explicitly secular or nonreligious groups has been driven by several factors. First, nonreligious people are demonstrating a growing concern over religion's tendency to foster "exclusionary and divisive in-group mentalities" (Kettell 2013), creating divisions and antagonisms between people of differing faiths and lashing out against those with no "faith" at all. Second, with the rise of the internet, previously isolated individuals have now been able to begin creating and demarcating a space to meet and converse with each other while still inhabiting a religiously dominated society (Cimino and Smith 2011). In response to these developments, nonreligious people in the United States are increasingly adopting a discourse of "group rights" and articulating demands for equal treatment (Taira 2012), issues in which the ex-Mormons in Utah are embroiled.

The ex-Mormon example further evidences wider trends and strategies used by secular groups around the country. Drawing inspiration from the gay rights movement, secular groups in the United States are attempting to "introduce" themselves to the larger American populace, in the hopes that increasing their mutual familiarity will allay the negative stereotypes typically projected onto them. Staging "Out" campaigns and "Reason Rallies" and engaging in other promotional and public outreach work, including writing articles, hosting public talks and debates (broadly disseminated on YouTube), and producing documentary videos and podcasts, these groups are attempting to establish an explicitly "secular" identity under which people can congregate and mobilize. Through these efforts, nonreligious people are not only able to begin raising the visibility of their minority status but also effectively counter stigmatizing public perceptions by articulating their own moral discourse of pluralism and acceptance.

Following my discussion of the various stigmas and stereotypes attached to apostates in the previous chapter, this chapter discusses how ex-Mormons attempt to engage in a politics of alterity as they carefully negotiate their fractious relationships with their former religious community. I discuss how this has unfolded through a micropolitics of nonreligious labeling, a mass resignation march staged in a suburb of Salt Lake City, and a series of "I am an ex-Mormon" videos.

Deciding What to Call Yourself

In the contemporary LDS Church, the proclamation, "I'm a Mormon" has become something of a rallying cry for members who are attempting to reassert their collective identity on a U.S. religious landscape that was once skeptical and even antagonistic to these "peculiar people." As with most religious communities, the ability to publicly identify oneself, to fix a label to your particular set of ideological or group affiliations, and to feel as if that label expresses something essential about your sense of self and place in the world is a powerful component of religious practice and belonging. Former members of the LDS Church, however, lose this moniker and the work that it does in positioning, grounding, and categorizing them as social people.

Part of constructing a new identity in the wake of religious disaffection involves deciding what to call oneself now that "Mormon" is no longer available. Ex-Mormon, apostate, atheist, or secular-humanist are several options. Yet as I came to see, for former members of the LDS Church, each term is seen to carry its own set of cultural baggage or is limited in its ability to define the people who they see themselves becoming. One woman said to me, "I'm not really a Mormon anymore, but I don't know if I'm an atheist. That seems too strong of a word. But I can't go along the rest of my life saying I'm an ex-Mormon either. Can't I just be 'me'?" As Pierre Bourdieu (1984) suggests, social struggles—such as the one between Mormonism and its former members—often take the form of conflict over classification and representation. For newly nonreligious people who live in a world suffused by religious identifications, deciding what to call themselves is therefore not just a matter of being able to affix a label but an exercise in constructing and defining a new sense of nonreligious personhood.

Though the terms *ex-Mormon* and *apostate* are frequently used by both current and former church members, these terms are inherently polysemic and at times highly contentious. There are semantic issues that arise in any identity politics movement, as the labels that are ascribed, adopted, renounced, or embraced involve nuanced tactics of positioning and classification. In the wider United States, using the term *atheist*, for example, a moniker popularly defined by its opposition to religion, has been seen as a mistake by some who argue that it perpetuates the stereotype of atheists as a "cranky sub-culture" (Harris 2007). Similarly, identifying with the term *atheist* or *agnostic* is often avoided, as they are freighted in the American collective conscience with a lack of morality and affront to public order (Edgell, Gerteis, and Hartmann 2006, 230). As Ryan Cragun (2012, 108) notes, nonreligious people's decision to affix a label to themselves is potentially self-defeating, as "self-identification as something beyond 'none' may heighten attention to one's out-group status among those who hear about one's irreligious identity." Others, however, argue that such labels are politically useful as "rallying cries" for the disparate secular communities scattered amid a larger, dominant religious society (Taira 2012).

The people I talked to were keenly aware of the moral stereotypes associated with the various nonreligious labels available to them. When I asked people whether they thought a God existed, they typically responded with either an outright no or some version of "I have no way of knowing whether a God exists or not. Therefore, I can't say definitively one way or the other." Yet they often demurred when I asked if they would call themselves atheists. When I asked one woman, she said that "*atheist* has such a harsh tone to it. I guess I'd rather say I'm an agnostic." To her, the difference between atheist and agnostic had less to do with a difference in definition than a difference in public perception. "When people hear atheist, they think you've got an ax to grind or something," she added. For her, using the term *atheist* implied a decisive and even combative break with the normative religious society from which she was tentatively negotiating her distance. Choosing to label herself an agnostic ameliorated her fears of provoking outright antagonism while effectively distancing herself from being hailed as religious. "When I call myself agnostic, it leaves the question open for people. Especially religious people . . . they get less defensive. It's like they think there's still hope for you!"

Within ex-Mormon circles, there was less of a concern over how a self-ascribed label might affect relationships and generally people were able to adopt a plethora of terms to describe their current nonreligious identity. When I first began attending the various ex-Mormon meetings throughout the state, I would consistently be asked, "So what are you?"—the question making the imperative to identify oneself in these circles not so much a practice of ideological gatekeeping as a reflection of group members' curiosity regarding the diversity of perspectives circulating within the community. During one of my first visits to a local meet-up at a coffee shop in Provo, a group of a dozen or so of us sat on a set of couches sipping our drinks when Christina asked me the question.

CHRISTINA: You're studying Mormonism, huh? I bet that's fun. What are you?

MARSHALL: What do you mean?

RICH: You know, what's your relationship to the church? Were or are you religious?

MARSHALL: Oh. No, I've never been Mormon. I grew up Christian. But I guess you could say now I'm a comfortably apathetic agnostic. Whatever that means.

KYLE: Yeah, I know what you mean. There's a term for that I think—it's an apatheist. At first I didn't know what I was. Someone once told me I'm a pantheist, so that's what I say. I don't believe in a God. It's more about an awareness of the idea of something powerful existing in everything.

MICHELLE: I was like that once. But now it makes more sense for me to say atheist. I have no reason to think God, or any God, exists.

RICH: I think I'm more of an agnostic. If there's something out there, great. If a godlike thing does exist, it surely doesn't care about us down here, at least not the way Mormons think it does. But if there's a heaven of some sort we all get to go to, I'm down with that.

Within these explicitly ex-Mormon circles, deciding on what nonreligious label to use was less a politics of secular/religious positioning than it was a reflection of people's ongoing practice of "trying out" these different identities and nonreligious subjectivities. However, deciding what to call themselves as former church members—that is, how to define and label their explicit relationship to Mormonism outside of these circles—was a different matter. In relationships with friends, family, and neighbors, they chose their labels with care, each choice reflecting a strategic reading and response to particular contexts and situations rather than a representation of their "actual" stance.

Each of the labels—post-Mormon, ex-Mormon, former Mormon, cultural Mormon, and so on—is laden with tacit stereotypes about who and what they were as erstwhile members of the church. For those with "one foot still in the church"—meaning they still regularly associate with active members in their daily lives—using the terms *ex-Mormon* or *former Mormon* can be disadvantageous. "I don't know what I'd call myself now," Craig told me as we discussed all the options. "I guess all of the above given the situation. I would probably avoid using *ex-Mormon* hanging out with church folks. Why give someone else the ability to marginalize you even more?" Craig left the church several years prior to our conversation, yet he was still heavily involved in church life. Craig's wife, children, and extended family were all still members, so Craig often attended baptisms, ward socials, and family events where he was the only nonbeliever. Although he often attended ex-Mormon activities, in church contexts, he describes himself as *inactive*, a term commonly used within Mormonism to denote those who do not participate in but have not severed ties with the church. Craig's decision was indeed strategic and reflected his attempts to negotiate people's understanding of his loss of faith and his ongoing attempts to maintain important connections with the church community. "If I tell them I'm an ex- or post-Mormon or whatever, they'll immediately be suspicious; they'll think I did something wrong or label me an anti-Mormon. So I say inactive. It makes more sense to them. And it makes it easier on my wife. That way, she doesn't have to go through all the 'oh, I'm sorry' conversations when people find out I left." By using the label *inactive*, Craig was able to maintain the illusion that his return to the fold was still a real possibility—he could, ostensibly, be "reactivated" at any time.

Another term, *cultural Mormon*, is often used as a means of softening the boundaries and divisions discursively drawn between apostates and the church. Tom, for example, works in an accounting firm in Utah County and worried about how his coworkers' and employer's perception of his religious status might affect his job. According to Tom, describing himself as a cultural Mormon signals to others that, though he does not believe in the church's theological teachings, he still appreciates and respects his ancestry and upbringing as a Mormon. He recently put this strategy to use when he decided to begin openly drinking coffee at work, advertising his loss of faith. A colleague approached him and directly asked Tom what he was drinking (a rare instance of direct confrontation). "You could tell he was curious and really just concerned. I told him I no longer had a testimony that the church was true, but that I still loved my Mormon friends and family. I don't know if I said I was a cultural Mormon, but that's basically how I described myself." Tom's coworker seemed satisfied with the answer, even asking Tom about how coffee tasted, a conversation that Tom says allowed him to have a "normal" conversation and "let him know I'm really the same guy I was before; I just happen to drink coffee now."

Others are more explicit about their disaffection from the church when conversing with faithful members. While teaching anthropology at a local university in Utah, April, one of my students, no doubt aware of her minority status in a room full of faithful members, self-identified by saying, "I used to be Mormon . . . I've since been enlightened and have transcended the church," while extending her hands into the air and smiling. When I asked her later if she was ever concerned that such pronouncements would antagonize her classmates, she shrugged. "I don't really care. I'm tired of them thinking they own the world, like they know better than everybody else. I'm not going to hide who I am; they're just going to have to learn how to deal with [it]." Such pronouncements, although in this case eliciting eye rolls from classmates, speak against the assumed relationship between current and former members, deftly reversing the hierarchy typically at work in which former members are assumed to have "fallen away."

In conversing with nonmembers—or, as they are colloquially referred to, "never-Mos" (a category in which I was slotted)—some former members said they avoided the labels ex-Mormon, post-Mormon, and former Mormon altogether. Jason told me, for example, "I don't like to label myself as anything with the word 'Mormon' in it. I don't want to be connected to it any more than I already have to. Telling someone you used to be Mormon either leads to lots of questions about the church or they think somehow you're still connected to it." Some former members even find that their public identity as a Mormon has stuck with them despite their private disaffection. James, for example, said that in job interviews he would often be questioned about his education at Brigham Young University, plainly visible on his professional resume. "People just assume I'm Mormon. They see that on there, and they immediately categorize me."

Others appreciate the term *post-Mormon*, as opposed to *ex-Mormon*, for how it still implies a connection to Mormonism, valuing the religion for its personal (rather than interpersonal) significance. As Stacy told me, "Post-Mormon sounds better to me than ex-Mormon. Mormonism was such a huge part of my life for so long. And it still is, really. I was raised Mormon; all my memories are of being in the church. Saying post-Mormon I think does honor to that life . . . but it's still something I eventually have moved past." For Stacy, describing herself as post-Mormon allows her to dually articulate both a lasting connection and an estrangement from Mormonism, reflecting a sense of self with a past she sought to incorporate into her present and future existence.

Unlike post-Mormon or ex-Mormon, *apostate* is a term often thought to be divisive and derogatory. As I discussed in the previous chapter, when used within the church community, the term denotes people who have failed in their spiritual commitments and "turned their back" on the faith or have taken a hostile, antagonistic stance against their religious brethren. Its use tacitly legitimizes and normalizes exclusionary practices and constructs a moral hierarchy in which church members sit at the top and apostates are relegated to the bottom. "Mormons use it when they want to connect all former believers with some grievous sin just to puff themselves up," one woman told me. Another man, a "closeted apostate" as he called himself because he had not yet "opened up" about his disbelief, described sitting one time in Sunday school with his wife as the class discussed the story of Korihor from the Book of Mormon. After hearing people in class vilify apostates they knew as dejected, scornful, and dishonest and as fallen members who believers should be wary of, he finds the term nothing more than a slur.

Despite its negative connotations and its potential to perpetuate damaging stereotypes, the apostate label can also be self-ascribed as a means of preempting its derogatory power when used by church members as a term of derision. I once attended a family barbecue with Judy and Mitch, a young couple I met at a local ex-Mormon meet-up event, that was held in Mitch's parents' backyard. I had been warned on the car ride over to the house that all of Mitch's family would be there and that they were all "TBMs" (true believing Mormons) who were dogmatic in their belief in the church. This was a social situation that caused both Mitch and Judy some trepidation, which we attempted to alleviate by taking shots of dark rum at their house prior to leaving for the barbecue. At the party, Mitch introduced me around to his parents, siblings, and nieces and nephews. While acquainting me with his older brother and sister-in-law, Mitch said, "Meet Marshall. He's our resident anthropologist . . . he's studying the apostates and all of our crazy lives!" Mitch laughed at his joke—as did, to my surprise, his brother and sister-in-law. "I'm sure you're getting a lot of good information for your study," his brother quipped back affably. In effect, Mitch's self-labeling as an apostate in this Mormon-dominated social setting temporarily defused the tension between him and his family members. "It's problematic to do that, I suppose," Mitch later explained to me on the car ride back. "You're basically telling them that it's all right to call people that. But really, they're already thinking it and saying it anyway. So I think in some ways it helps, because it makes being an apostate not so strange and maybe even normal. And that's really what we are."

Some ex-Mormons' hesitancy to use the term *apostate* or general aversion to it as a persistent moniker of religious stigma strikes people like Eli as a passive way of supporting the exact stigma they should be working to overcome. Having left the church two years prior, Eli reflects a growing sentiment I heard expressed by other ex-Mormons attempting to reclaim the label that until then had been unwittingly ascribed to them.

> I think we have to recognize that it's Mormons that attach so much baggage to the word. And that baggage is all tied to their belief that they have the one true faith. If we truly reject that faith and all that comes with it, then the word doesn't mean anything anymore. Or rather, it means whatever we want it to. I personally don't think we should be ashamed of being called apostates. Call me an apostate! That's damn right; I reject all your myths and superstitions! So be it. So you see, I think it's something to be proud of.

Normalizing and even embracing the term *apostate* has thus become among some newly nonreligious people an effective strategy for combatting and overturning the negative stigmas attached to it. Invoking the literal definition of apostate as someone who rejects religion yet otherwise stays "normal" has enabled the term to be appropriated as a "badge of honor" worn proudly by many ex-Mormons aiming to make their rejection of religious dogma an identity to rally under. That such a transformation was underfoot during my fieldwork was made clear to me when a popular ex-Mormon online community began selling T-shirts, thong underwear, beer mugs, and shot glasses stamped in bold letters with the word *Apostate*. Similarly, a song written by Brian, a close friend of mine with a flair for creative rebellion, strategically appropriated the term and used it to achieve a certain degree of consciousness raising. Growing up in the church, he had loved the song "I'm a Mormon," which was a staple in primary classes and the inspiration for the LDS Church's recent ad campaign of the same name. In the song, sung with a plucky sense of resolution, singers rejoice in their peculiarity, their opposition to mainstream values, and their ownership of the name *Mormon*, a label their gentile neighbors historically imposed on "the Saints" in a maligning way.

I'm a Mormon, yes I am!
And if you want to study a Mormon, I'm a living specimen.
Maybe you think I'm just like anybody else you see,
But trust in my word,
you'll quickly observe,
I'm different as can be!

At parties and social gatherings with other ex-Mormons, Brian's song became a hit, with frequent calls for multiple rehearsals so that everyone in the audience could pick up the words and sing along. In it, apostates expressed their own sense of peculiarity, alienation, and excluded collective identity by transforming a song once so loved for its religious inspiration into an anthem of apostatic insurrection.

I'm apostate, yes I am.
After studying the history,
I discovered it's a sham.
Everyone thinks I'm just inclined to disobey,
but maybe I don't believe
the spirit will leave you
just because you're gay.
I'm apostate yes it's true.
And you may think that I'm deluded, but I'm sad to say it's you.
You see now I know the Book of Abraham is just a false translation.
I know we stole Masonic rites and tried to say they're ancient.
Maybe you'd like me to tell you about the women that Joseph screwed,
then you can be apostate too!
I'm apostate, through and through.
And since I broke all my covenants,
I'm sleeping in the nude.

It's not that I'm lazy or offended in some way.
I just don't buy the excuse apologists use
for Indian DNA.
I'm apostate, yes, it's true.
And if that means we can't be friends,
I guess that's what you've got to do.
You see now I am aware of troubling things like Joseph's polyandry.
I get upset when Packer talks; I keep Fawn Brodie handy.
Maybe you'd like a list of the things that prove the Church isn't true,
then you can be apostate too.

That the phrase "I'm apostate" can come to express a sense of collective pride points to a shift in ex-Mormons' conceptions of self and identity outside of the church toward one of group solidarity and collective consciousness. They are no longer simply as marginalized subalterns but authors of their own existence. In the song, the apostate position is strategically appropriated and essentialized as a condition brought about by an abundant knowledge of the church's defects (Joseph Smith's sexual exploits, historical inaccuracies, the lack of Indian DNA, etc.) rather than moral deficiencies, as stereotypes often depict. This idea is further engendered in the song by depicting the apostate position as one void of the personal idiosyncrasies or individual circumstances that church members often point to as "causes" of apostasy. Rather, the song reads as a collective position statement under which apostates can uniformly congregate, united by a common positionality vis-à-vis their marginality from and antagonism with the church. An apostate identity is generated and harnessed as a basis of struggle, effectively creating a foundation of temporary solidarity on which social action can occur.

"Out of the Shadows and into the Light"

The only real way to change the system is to reject it in its entirety. This of course has huge social cost, which many have had to bear. But those cultural costs will lessen with each individual who chooses to publicly refuse to support the organization. And this break, to get through the structures of silence has to be loud and pronounced. It has to come in the form of willful non-participation in events and formal statements of position that are clearly understood as such. But this brashness is not due to the heretics being louts, it is necessary because the system makes it necessary, it is the only way to get out of the trench and make the message heard.

—Ex-Mormon Vanguard

On a hot June afternoon in 2012, several hundred ex-Mormons hiked to a prominent hill overlooking Salt Lake City in what was billed as a "Mass Resignation

March." There, marchers signed a "declaration of independence from Mormonism," mailed in resignation letters to church headquarters, and carried signs that read "Transcend Mormonism," "It's OK to be an atheist," and "Ask me if I'm Mormon." Not all were resigning that day. Many had left the church years ago and were prominent players in Utah's ex-Mormon scene; others had yet to tell their spouses that they no longer believed the church was true, harboring their secret in silence. What they all had in common, though, was that in the eyes of the church, whose headquarters and temple stood prominently in the valley below, they were apostates.

For the ex-Mormons gathered there, the march was a strategic, symbolic act of speaking out against a new form of religious intolerance they felt they were victims of. As an event attended, recorded, and publicized by newspaper reporters and anthropologists, it was a venue through which the frustrations of apostasy could be voiced and a narrative of religious persecution could be generated and dispersed.

The march was billed as a journey "out of the shadows and into the light," and according to marchers, was an attempt to openly embrace people's decisions to leave the church and invert the shame typically attached to apostasy. Through the march, ex-Mormons sought to overturn the stigma and transform themselves, as apostates, from being silent objects of criticism to vocal agents in their own public representations. One woman described her motivation for marching as a desire to undermine the taboos attached to leaving the church and transform the process into something that people could be "open and proud about." For her, being an apostate was an identity that she hoped people could gather

Figure 5.1. Poster displayed at the mass resignation march in Salt Lake City, photo by author

around, feeling strength and support as they saw others like them come out into the open with their disbelief. If they were going to be identified as apostates, it was going to be an identity they controlled.

Ex-Mormons' desire to "make a statement" and their public show of apostasy must be understood within the particular context of Mormonism's rise to prominence on the public stage, a presence ex-Mormons sought to capitalize on. Although only attended by a few hundred marchers, news of the march spread widely across both national and international news outlets, reflecting the media fervor for all things Mormon that existed at the height of the Mormon Moment. Articles covering the march were picked up by papers in major cities across the country—in Chicago; Detroit; Washington, DC; Phoenix—found on Yahoo News and even a front-page spot on the *Huffington Post*'s website (Dobner 2012).

Their identity as Mormons, until now undermined by characterizations of apostates as spiritually and morally deficient, was solidified by the media's presence. It allowed their dissent to transcend the normative representation of "angry apostates"—a category within which vocal criticism of the church is typically cataloged and thus easily dismissed. It instead indexed their cries as coming from a group of people enveloped within a new form of religious identity—that is, as disaffected apostates—who in their disbelief also fell victim to a peculiar form of religious intolerance in need of atonement. Newspaper reporters' presence at the event, particularly the Reuters news service, bestowed a sense of legitimacy on the ex-Mormons' efforts to engage in this unique form of subaltern political expression by showing them first and foremost as "Mormons" with legitimate criticisms and complaints. Headlines hailed them not as de facto outsiders but as disenfranchised and disenchanted *members* of the church: "Mormon Group Quits LDS Church En Masse" and "Mormons Quit Church in Mass Resignation Rite," the headlines proclaimed.

For individual ex-Mormons, the march provided an opportunity to publicly gather around an identity that most had previously been afraid of embracing. I met Roger standing nearby the staging grounds for the march, slathering sunscreen onto his arms and legs, and asked how he was feeling. When I had spoken with him a few days prior, he had not been entirely set on marching. Roger was somebody who, despite not attending church for several years, had still not told his family he no longer believed in the church. He seemed taciturn and reticent, saying that he had been nervous to come to the event, what he described as a mix of "fear and trepidation." Gesturing toward a nearby reporter, he said he worried that his parents might see his face in a picture or video. Perhaps by marching, he suggested, he could break free of the cycle of silence and frustration.

The politics of embracing an apostate identity, for some of the marchers, therefore served as a public reclamation of a sense of self lost in the private sphere of family relationships. For example, Bob became an atheist several years ago, yet in the eyes of friends and family, like Roger, he is as devout a member as ever, as his wife has forbidden him to speak of his disaffection from the church. I originally got to know Bob at biweekly ex-Mormon support group meetings held on Sunday afternoons. He would occasionally show up late, having just gotten out of the church service he attended with his wife. He seemed resigned and embittered about the life he led—I never understood how he stayed with a woman who he complained "kept him in the closet." However, in the march, Bob seemed resolute, unconcerned about the possibility of having someone see his picture in the newspaper. "I kind of hope I will get outed," he said, "then that way it'll all be over." A woman I marched next to lived in constant fear of having her husband "outed" as an apostate to his employers, a turn of events that she felt sure would lead to his swift dismissal. For her, the march was, as she described, her only means of making a statement. "I'm tired of being avoided and ignored. This is my way of saying this is me, and I'm not going away," she told me.

I met a man named Peter as he stood chatting with a reporter from the *Salt Lake Tribune* who was a stark contrast to the trepidation I saw expressed in others. With a smile on his face and a gleam in his eye, he carried a stick with a white button-down collared shirt tied to the end—the same garment, he said, that he wore on his mission several decades ago. On it, black permanent marker scrawled the words, "In honor of our integrity, our reason and freedom, and our peace of mind, our wives, our children, and our friends—both straight and gay." "Life is so much happier now that I've left," he told the reporter. "Instead of thinking in terms of regretting the past and dreading the future, I'm doing much more of living in the present." Like others, he voiced frustration with Mormonism's continued intrusion into his life despite the fact that he had stopped attending church several years ago—missionaries, visiting teachers, and other ward members continued to visit his house, inviting him to church. Resigning that day was both a public declaration of his opposition to the church and a final salute to his life as a Mormon. For Peter, the resignation march was the culmination of his personal journey out of the church—he told the group of several reporters now huddled around him. "It's now complete. I turned in my resignation letter today. I left the church philosophically six years ago, physically two years ago, and now I've left legally."

Embracing an ex-Mormon apostate identity was, for ex-Mormons, a potential source of power and pride around which they could congregate and feel a sense of unity and camaraderie. As previous studies of marginalized communities—whether based on sexual, racial, or religious difference—have suggested, it is often only through a mimetic reappropriation of the stigmatized identity that a change, however slow and incremental, can be made. For ex-Mormons, simply walking away from the church and "moving on," as members of the church frequently admonished them to do, was in many ways not possible. Those who did found themselves quickly isolated. It was only by maintaining an identification with the church as ex-Mormon apostates that they found a voice

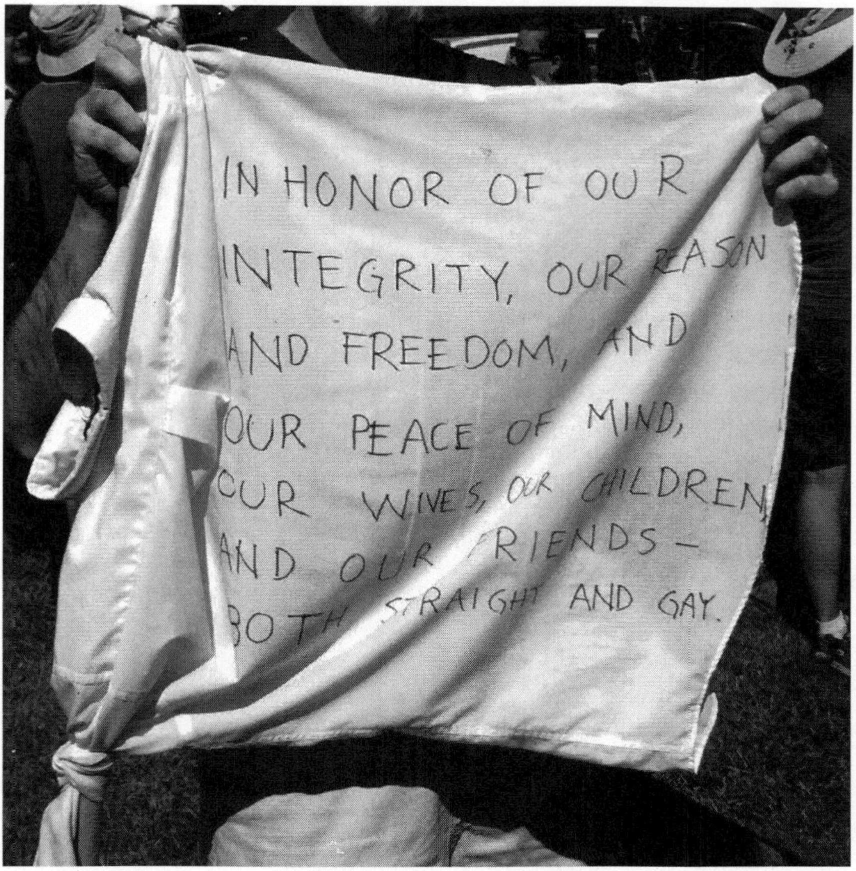

Figure 5.2. Missionary shirt flag carried at mass resignation march in Salt Lake City, photo by author

with which to speak and a locus around which to gather, in contrast to their previous positions of silence and defenselessness.

The march, however, was not just about seeking recognition within the Mormon community. Rather, by rejecting their memberships in one community, ex-Mormons effectively identified with and indexed their unification with a larger, and explicitly pluralistic, U.S. community.

In a speech to the marchers before their ascent to Ensign Peak, Paul, one of the organizers, explicitly drew on the rhetoric and iconography of democratic pluralism to make his case. In a grassy field from which the marchers would soon depart, Paul stood between a pair of American flags blowing in the wind, a few feet from a table on which a "Declaration of Independence from Mormonism" had been signed by hundreds of the marchers, and gave his remarks:

In fundamentalist religions, there are only three states of existence. Those who believe, those who don't yet believe, and those who have stopped believing. For fundamentalists, however, in the end, there will be only one, and everyone will bow before the people who are right, and the heretics and apostates will burn.

No matter how much we try to get along, there is that force that is hanging out there. Our goal today has nothing to do with the church per se. And that's why we're here and not down there. We're here because we reject that paradigm fundamentally, and we reject the idea that we have to fall in one of those three states.

There are literally thousands of people who are supporting us. But there is another group that would love to be here, but they can't. The fact is that the state of apostasy, the state of leaving the church, the state of leaving religion, leaves people in fear of losing custody of their children, losing jobs, losing their careers, losing their families, being ostracized in their communities, their children being locked out, and all sorts of negative ramifications that are happening today, right now. Divorces and destroyed lives, simply on your belief in metaphysics, which is not very understandable to people outside the paradigm.

About one hundred sixty years ago, after the first party of the Saints came into this valley, with their slaves and their polygamist wives, they came up here to this peak a few days later and they blessed the valley. One of the reasons they were on this peak was because just over those mountains, the trappers had set up a community and lived there permanently. And just over those mountains, the Paiutes lived there permanently. This valley, from the get-go, was a three-state valley. It wasn't always the Mormons, and the Mormons didn't always control it.

Now we have a time and a place when those who are pluralistic in their views and their society outnumber those who want the one true path. And I think our goal here is to take it back. But not in a demanding sort of way, but only to say that we're here. And for our brothers and sisters who can't be here because of those ramifications, who are here with us in spirit, who know that they will face that, we're here for them.

Next year, there'll be more of us, and the next year, there'll be even more of us. But the goal is not to conquer the other. The goal is to live together and not believe the worst of each other. Our inspiration is Dan Savage in his "It Gets Better" project, which encourages people to publicly come out of the closet who are homosexuals. Because the studies show that your attitudes about folks has to do with how well you know them, how many homosexuals you know, how many you interact with every day.

We don't want to be offensive; we just won't kowtow to those things. We're not telling people to go out and be proselytizing non-Mormons, but we're talking about living authentically and letting others know we're here and that once you cross through on the other side, there's peace and happiness. That's where we're at, and that's where we want to lead our brothers and sisters.[1]

In Paul's narrative, the goal of ex-Mormons is to restore the valley to a state of pluralistic inclusiveness. He identifies the apostates' plight with the historical precedents of American pluralistic democracy, from which he could articulate both the need for redress and a direction for ex-Mormons to turn as wayward members of the church. Referencing an earlier pluralism in the Utah area, the stark divisions among diverse factions of trappers, Paiutes, and Mormons, his was an appeal to an original state of plurality to which Utah, and the United States, could now ideally return. In doing this, Paul enacted ex-Mormons' identification within the United States as a sacred community that transcended the sectarian and marginalizing politics they had been subject to within Mormonism.

After the march, the internet message boards lit up with discussion—particularly on the *Salt Lake Tribune* website, where the article on the march was said to have received the highest number of discussion posts in the newspaper's history. The debate focused on whether this "public show of a private matter" was newsworthy, with members of the church proudly arguing that a drop of several hundred members was statistically insignificant given the church's fourteen million worldwide members. One poster's remark reflected an anxiety felt by many Mormons, who—despite their criticism of the march as unworthy of news coverage—took the time to read and engage in heated conversation over the matter, saying, "These people leaving the church is SOOOOO not newsworthy. It's not even interesting. These people are sad and pitiful because instead of living their lives, they DEFINE their lives by leaving an organization that they're not compelled to be a part of anyway." For an image-conscious church in the midst of the Mormon Moment, apostates vocally proclaiming their disaffection was an affront to the image it was attempting to construct in the media of members who were happy and satisfied.

The march, its news coverage, and particularly the response it received on the boards revealed a latent insecurity and anxiety within Mormonism over its public image and what it meant to have those who chose to leave the faith be vocal about their decision. If the church was selling itself as full of happy, contented members, this was where ex-Mormons could have the most impact. Responding to one poster's assertion that ex-Mormons were just attention seekers, another poster drew attention to the "field" of attention that both ex-Mormons and Mormons were playing on, replying, "So when the LDS Church builds its temples high up on the hill, builds them larger than all surrounding buildings, and lights them up in bright white lights, that's not drawing attention? Just be honest, you don't have a problem with drawing attention to yourself. You have a problem with people leaving 'your team.'"

For ex-Mormons, it was exactly this sort of shameful secrecy that they were seeking to combat and expose to a wider public. Many articulated the need for and legitimacy of a public demonstration as an inverted form of religious freedom, one that was equated to the rights Mormonism benefited from daily. "A lot of folks make their faith a very public thing, and express their private convictions. Choosing to make your lack of faith public doesn't seem to be very different," one man remarked. The freedom *of* religion must, according to commenters, be extended to those outside the church in the form of freedom *from* religion. "If the LDS Church would leave the rest of us the hell alone, we'd be more than happy to return the favor. However, the LDS Church has inserted themselves into our lives by campaigning against our Civil Rights as American Citizens," someone caustically remarked. In reply to another commenter arguing that the *Salt Lake Tribune* should have followed the church-owned *Deseret News*'s lead by not covering the event, one ex-Mormon wrote, "Your demand then, is that an event critical of the LDS church, staged in the city that is the headquarters of the LDS church, receive no press coverage in that city whatsoever. That would be censorship of the most blatant and restrictive kind and would be completely incompatible with the functioning of democracy in our state." Having a "voice" as an apostate was framed not just in the register of freedom from religion but as necessary in upholding the virtues of a politically democratic and religiously pluralistic state.

By making public what was supposed to be private and by framing apostasy within wider discourses of tolerance and respect for difference, ex-Mormons sought to make Mormonism morally and publically accountable for its treatment of apostates in the wider sphere of public opinion, where Mormonism was still negotiating its own inclusion. By presenting themselves as victims of intolerance at the hands of a hegemonic religious majority, it catapulted the act from one of isolated internal significance to one with a much larger importance on the American political stage of minority rights and pluralistic inclusion.

"I Am an Ex-Mormon"

The LDS Church's entrance into the American public's imagination in the twenty-first century was marked most notably, perhaps, not by the attention drawn to it through Republican Mitt Romney's presidential campaign but by the hundreds of average faces that appeared on billboards, television, and internet ads across the country as part of the "I'm a Mormon" PR (public relations) campaign. During the so-called Mormon Moment, the PR campaign was a deliberate attempt by a newly empowered church public relations department to construct an image of the average Mormon as different from the stereotype of straight-laced, upper-middle-class, and dominantly white members epitomized by the well-dressed missionary figures that often appeared on people's doorsteps. Instead, the ads sought to normalize the public image of the church by profiling its members' racial, ethnic, and cultural diversity, their inherently rational faith based on family values and integrity, and their membership in a church community that valued personal expression. On YouTube and the church website Mormon.org, viewers could watch dozens of professionally produced profiles of members describing their personal interests, hobbies, professions, faith, and family life with the words "I am a Mormon" tagged at the end.

While the "I'm a Mormon" campaign sought to normalize Mormons in the pantheon of American religious pluralism, in 2010, another series of videos began appearing on the internet under the label "I Am an Ex-Mormon." Filmed and produced by a group of ex-Mormons, these videos sought to capitalize on Mormonism's mainstream success by publicizing the stories of those disaffected from the church. Parodying the format of the church's videos, the video series depicted average members telling their "exit stories," narratives of religious disaffection and loss of faith.

The videos, accompanied on the "I Am an Ex-Mormon" website by longer written versions of people's exit stories, followed a format loosely similar to religious conversion narratives or even Mormonism's own practice of "bearing testimony." In these narratives, the apostate recounted his or her previous life in the church community; the emergence of social, theological, or psychological tension between him- or herself and the religion; a period of profound doubt and questioning; and finally the experience of "breaking free" from the church and "converting" to a new, largely secular worldview. As others have written (Payne 2009; Avance 2013), such "deconversion narratives," "exit stories," or "apostimonies" as they were colloquially referred to in Utah, are common among religious apostates. However, in these studies, the exit story is interpreted either as an analytical window into how the psychological and emotional process of deconversion correlates with the typical conversion experience or as a dramatic narrative performed by apostates to gain entry into a "subculture" of apostates (just as "conversion narratives" are used by the newly converted to signal their identification with the church body).

Yet what is not taken into account is how exit stories are instead a constitutive element of an ongoing politics of identity making for those transitioning into the social category of nonbeliever. While exit stories do to some extent mediate the boundaries between religious and formerly religious communities, in the "I Am an Ex-Mormon" videos, the primary audience was not groups of ex-Mormons to whom the speaker was seeking entry. Rather, through such narratives, ex-Mormons sought to "speak back" to the church they had left but with which they were nevertheless still intertwined. They attempted to draw attention to their plight as a stigmatized minority and to challenge the stigmatizing stereotypes they were often subjected to. The telling of exit stories or deconversion narratives should therefore be understood as a strategic counterhegemonic discourse rather than simply a reflection of the psychological or social transformations ex-Mormons were experiencing. They are an attempt by ex-Mormons to strategically inhabit their new social positions on the margins of Mormonism and to discursively challenge the stereotypes they feel leveled at them in everyday life. This requires the use of several distinct rhetorical strategies.

Establishing credibility as a once "true believing Mormon" is important if the subsequent criticisms or complaints against the church are to be taken seriously. At the outset of several clips, the speaker is seen standing in front of the Salt Lake and Provo temples, narrating his or her story of disaffection and disbelief while flanked by the towering spires of the temples in the background. In one video, a man paces silently in front of the Provo Temple's gates in an uncanny visual juxtaposition of the now nonbelieving apostate and the most sacred of Mormon iconography. Describing his once full-hearted dedication to the church as a temple worker and Sunday school teacher, he describes Mormonism as being "at the very core of [his] identity" and "influenc[ing] everything [he] did." Common in exit narratives, this intimate identification with the former religion is a rhetorical strategy employed in order to deflect accusations that those who leave are spiritually lazy or institutionally uninvolved. Another ex-Mormon similarly explained, highlighting his status as a "dyed-in-the-wool" Mormon, "I am a sixth-generation member of the LDS Church. My family was always active in the church . . . I served a mission for the church completely convinced that the church was 'true.' I knew that I was helping to build the kingdom of God on earth and bring people into it."

Once the former religious identification is established, however, several of the videos sought to draw attention to the symbolic violence committed against those who question or lose faith. That those who question religious dogmatism can be socially ostracized and maligned strikes many ex-Mormons as a contemporary form of social injustice committed against nonreligious minorities. Jim, an ex-Mormon man I knew who had traveled throughout the United States, once marveled to me at the unique "backwardness" of Utah as an enclave of religious bigotry in the country. Looking around the room at a local ex-Mormon atheist meeting, he explained to me, "We all come here because we feel oppressed by religion. It's weird because we live in a country where that doesn't happen, but here it is, happening to us." I wanted to question whether he considered places in the Midwest or Deep South—where Pentecostal, Baptist, and Evangelical strands of Christianity prevail—as similarly oppressive but nevertheless understood his point. Perhaps nowhere else in the United States other than Utah do strict categorical divides between current and former members come with such punitive consequences for those who stop believing. Ex-Mormons therefore seek to draw attention to these repercussions as a means of demonstrating the ways in which they have been collectively and categorically oppressed by a dominant religious majority. Accentuating this condition of "living in the shadows," as apostates from the church often described it, one anonymous man's video was filmed at night, a bright street lamp shining behind his head, effectively shrouding his face in darkness, out of fear that his family would find out about his disbelief.

> Hi, we're standing here in beautiful rural Utah, in the United States of America, land of the free, home of the brave, peak of the Information Age. Where

thoughts are shared with impunity and celebration. And I'm afraid to say what I truly feel. There's this tyranny of thought that we're trapped within, that tells us what we're supposed to believe, what we can believe, what we can say, and to whom we can say it.

I've been told that it's OK if I have doubts, it's OK if I don't believe everything that Joseph Smith [taught]. But I was also told that I must not tell that to anybody else. Some of these people that I talk to, we have to talk in hushed voices, because were afraid of anybody overhearing us. . . .

I know a gal who decided because of the church's position in Proposition 8, she stopped going to church; she just could not handle it anymore. And her kids are not allowed to play at some of her neighbors' houses, simply because she had a problem with bigotry against gays. Her children are ostracized in this community.

When you go to church and you hear how bad those people who leave all are, and how those people are sinners, it makes you silent. And those people who intellectually can't handle it are stuck. They can't express what they feel, and they're afraid to lose their family, they're afraid to lose their job, they're afraid to be ostracized from the community. They're afraid what will happen to their children if they just come out and say no I can't believe it any more. So they stay. They stay silent. They're afraid to say anything.

And there are many who are like this. The Mormon Church teaches that it's right. That it has the answer to anything. And that if you question it . . . you are seen as an enemy; you are cast aside. It shuts you up. It keeps you quiet. It keeps you going and playing the game that you don't want to. And there's a lot of people who are trapped in that same scenario. My heart goes out to them. We're stuck. We don't know where to go. We don't know where to turn to.

This is a problem that's becoming greater and greater in areas that are predominantly LDS. You cannot come out as a nonbeliever without risking losing everything. I think that the church is doing more damage to itself than they know. I can't tell you my name. I don't want to lose my family. But I'm an ex-Mormon.

The fear of voicing doubt or dissension is driven by stereotypes of ex-Mormons, which presume that those who leave have committed some grievous sin or have fallen into spiritual apathy and thus must be avoided. Ex-Mormons therefore also used these videos as an opportunity to describe their disenchantment, to counter the gossip circulating about why people leave, and to provide explanations for their loss of faith. As Nick says in his video, the notion of having a testimony based on personal feelings seemed increasingly unsubstantiated and lacking "objective" proof:

As I began to study church history and church doctrine and scriptures seriously, for the first time in my life, I began to have more and more questions

> about it . . . for the first time, I let myself think, what am I really basing this on? And I realized I was really basing it on subjective experience. You're always taught to read the Book of Mormon and pray about it, and if you get a good feeling, that means it's true. And I began to really consider for the first time, does that really mean it's true? Doesn't a Muslim praying in Mecca have the same feeling and use it to confirm their faith? I decided that even if that feeling is from the Holy Ghost, that subjective feeling isn't good enough. Because no matter how powerful it is, no matter how much it feels external, it's still subjective and it still could be self-delusion and wishful thinking.

For others like Alex, the obligation to "know the church is true," the very foundation of every faithful member's testimony, precipitated his personal experience of disenchantment. Standing in front of the Salt Lake Temple, Alex told his story:

> I suppose my story starts around seven years old when I was at Sunday school. My mom was the substitute that day. She gave a lesson on giving your testimony. She wrote the first line of what we were supposed to say on the board. "I know the church is true." As her son, she called on me to say it, and I refused. I knew I didn't know the church was true. I didn't have such knowledge that I was aware. And I wouldn't lie; that's not how I was raised. And everyone else seemed to know, they always said they knew the church was true in their testimonies every fast Sunday. People would ask me how my testimony was going, and I would say fine. But I didn't actually know if I had one.

Not "knowing" the church is true, or otherwise having a weak testimony is a frequent occurrence in the church. Alex described reaching out to his bishop for help. Yet the disappointment he felt at realizing there was little the church could provide for those who questioned prefigured his total collapse of faith: "I told him I was having problems believing. And he told me what everyone else had told me. That I should do Moroni's challenge. I knew this didn't make any sense, I knew there was only one answer you could get. It was biased from the start. You either knew the church was true. You got that feeling. Or nothing happened, and then you were supposed to do it until you die, I suppose."

"Moroni's challenge" is an appeal found in scripture to those pondering the truth of the Book of Mormon. The seeker of truth is told to "ponder in [his or her] heart" and ask God about the truth with "a sincere heart, with real intent." At that time, God would "manifest the truth of it . . . by the power of the Holy Ghost." His lack of testimony, Alex exclaims, is not based on a lack of spiritual fortitude or motivation but an inherent fallacy in Mormon logic. The challenge only accepts responses that affirm its assumptions. His loss of faith therefore revealed more about Mormonism's own impotency in handling those who question and doubt, he asserted, than it did about his own deficiencies as a believer.

Constructing an ex-Mormon identity also at times means identifying moral hypocrisy within Mormonism. In such a way, ex-Mormons attempt to reverse the stigma of nonbelief and position themselves as having transcended Mormonism and achieved a moral high ground outside of the church.

In her video, Eva stands in a forest, silhouetted against the white snow layered in the background. Eva always wanted to live the perfect Mormon life that her parents taught her to pursue. "I've always admired my parents. Their love for me and their love for their beliefs always impressed me, and I wanted to be like them. So I tried my best to do everything we were taught to do in church. I listened to the prophets, I even served a mission. When I came home from that mission, I snagged myself the perfect Mormon boy, and he was just what my family wanted from me." However, two years into her marriage, Eva describes her husband's research into church history and decision to leave the church, a turn of events that left her "devastated." Turning to her parents, bishop, and stake president for advice, she was counseled to divorce her husband. It was a decision, she says in the video, that seemed antithetical to the stated mission of the church. "I thought that I was doing the right thing, that I was following my belief and my faith," Eva explains. "Looking back, this church that had told me that family was first had [instead] ripped mine to pieces." Shortly after her divorce, Eva also left the church and, despite the turmoil the church's teachings had put her through, reconnected with her husband.

Similarly, Mormonism bills itself as a bastion of family values, touting a theology that proudly boasts the ability to grant families an eternal existence together after death. Those who leave the church are therefore believed to be jeopardizing their eternal families and are thought to live in temporal disarray as well, as they no longer have the guiding, steady hand of the priesthood to lead them. In the "I Am an Ex-Mormon" videos, several ex-Mormons attempted to counter this hegemonic discourse of the family within Mormonism while undermining the stereotype that ex-Mormons were invariably living in "bad families." For example, Kerri describes how Mormonism's teachings on "eternal families" affected her relationship to her children.

> My innate feelings are that I love my children so much, that I am bonded to them so much, that I'm not going to lose them. Yet this doctrine, these ordinances, make it so that I'm separated from them if we don't all obey . . . This doctrine is about the cruelest thing that can be foisted on a human brain. Your love for your family is being used against you to keep you in line, to keep you obeying. You know, as a little kid I feared that, I feared losing my parents, having to go to the lowest kingdom and be without them forever. That is cruel and

> unusual punishment, that is fear programming; I do not think that a loving celestial parent would use fear programming to maintain membership in its church.
>
> When you're always in fear of losing them, you kind of put up a little shield over your heart. "Well, what if I lose them?" I don't want it to rip my heart out completely. So you put a shield there. And you don't bond with your kids the way you're supposed to. Then you're always yelling at them because you want them to be good so they will stay with you forever.
>
> Well, guess what? Now that I'm not part of this church, I can just love my children as deeply and fully as I wanted to. And when they make mistakes, I hug them, I cuddle them, and I don't scold them. We talk through it, we bring wisdom in, and share enlightenment. And I don't just say "You're not going to get to the temple if you do this" or "You're not going to get to be with me forever if you don't do this." That's all irrelevant. And I was so happy to be able to realize that and take the shield down and to love my children deeply and properly the way I always wanted to.

Ex-Mormons also sought to counter stereotypes of the dysfunctional ex-Mormon family by "normalizing" the appearance of ex-Mormon families and displaying the same "traditional values" found in church teachings. "Hi, we're the Leavitts." Sean's smiling face greets the viewer. "We're the typical Utah family. We have fun together. We do a lot of activities together," Sean's wife, Stacy, explains as the camera pans over their family of four playing boccie ball and climbing trees in the backyard. The image turns to the family sitting side by side on a couch.

> SEAN: We were a bit nervous when we decided to talk to our kids about leaving the church. We weren't sure how they were going to react. We were kind of afraid they'd be really upset. But they took it really well. They were worried whether we were still going to do stuff as a family still or, you know, how things were going to go. We just assured them that we were still a family and still going to do stuff as a family.
>
> SEAN AND STACY'S SON: When my parents told us that we were leaving the church, we had the option to stay or leave or go to a different religion. They left the choice up to me, so I thought that was really cool.
>
> SEAN: It's cost us a couple of friendships, but we've gained a lot more friendships with people who really want to be our friends because of who we are and not because of what organization we belong to. And I count myself really, really lucky. We're all together, and we're a lot more together than we've ever been.

Micah similarly emphasized his enduring appreciation for "traditional family values" when he was a Mormon and now as an ex-Mormon. In his video, he fluidly transitions from a story of growing up Mormon to describing the continued vibrancy of his marriage.

> Growing up in a large family, when we would go on vacation, my parents would put us all in bright colored T-shirts, bright neons or greens, or we'd have neon-pink hats, for example. It made it really easy for them to keep track of us, because there were ten of us. We'd get a lot of looks when we were out east or in New York or wherever we were going. Now I have my own family; we have three kids, [and] my wife and I are coming up on our ten year anniversary actually. And we really are best friends. We often turn down invites for guys' nights out or girls' nights out because we'd rather be together.

Religion is often heralded as not just a purveyor of religious truths but a source of personal fulfillment and happiness. Religious apostates, in contrast, are often stereotyped as combative, bitter, or vengeful. The video campaign, however, complicated these divisive assumptions by describing a life outside religion as one in which the nonreligious are able to realize their full potential without being circumscribed by religious dogma. "Leaving the church has been the best thing I've ever done with my life. I've never been happier, I've never been more fulfilled. I've never felt more satisfied, more hopeful, optimistic, and positive about life in general," one woman describes. Another suggests that losing her faith has allowed a side of herself long hidden to shine through. "The best thing that has happened is I feel like I'm living in tune with myself, that I'm being honest with myself." The benefits of personal transformation and discovery following apostasy were the subject of many people's exit stories. Mike, for example, who in his video opened up about his disaffection to his family for the first time, focused on how in his disbelief he has become more open to and better at empathizing with other people.

> One thing that I've gained is I feel a lot more comfortable when I am talking with people. I feel like when I'm having a conversation with somebody, I don't need to worry about spinning the conversation to some gospel direction in an attempt to try and convert the other person. I feel like I can have a meaningful conversation with the other person without a hidden agenda. I find that I'm more respectful of other people's beliefs, and as a nonbeliever I'm less judgmental of other people. Everyone that knows me knows that I constantly seek after the truth and that I try to be a better person every day. And I want you to know that that's still how I live my life.

Similarly, Micah described his apostasy as a transformation to a much more hope-filled mode of existence, in which the dour cynicism of Mormon teachings concerning "the world" have been shed, allowing for him to embrace an ethics of inclusivity.

> Often you hear in the LDS Church about how you should bring all the good that you have, if you're not a member, for example, and see if they can add to it. Leaving Mormonism, I kind of took that same approach. I took the good that I got from Mormonism and still have that in my life today and have found so many other things that have expanded my view and enjoyment of life. In leaving Mormonism, it was like my eyes were opened. I see a lot more hope in the world than I did before. That there doesn't need to be an apocalypse. There doesn't need to be a World War Three that ushers us into some millennium for example. I think with science and technology as it is, the more advanced we get as a society, the more we expand our family circles and we can start thinking about us as a global society . . . My religion now is my integrity and follows the evidence where it leads me and to live life to the fullest.

In addition to appearing on the "I Am an Ex-Mormon" website, the videos were also available for viewing on a dedicated YouTube channel. There, in the comments section under each video, the identity politics of ex-Mormonism waged on, with self-identified Mormons and ex-Mormons vigorously criticizing and praising the videos, respectively. Those identifying as ex-Mormon praised the courage it took for the people in the videos to talk about their experiences or wrote their own confessions of doubt and disillusionment, perpetuating the creation of a "class" of ex-Mormons. However, self-identified church members lambasted ex-Mormons as full of lies and doing the work of "anti-Mormons" who were intent on "destroying the church." The politics of adopting an ex-Mormon identity were revealed to be a social process fraught with religious sectarianism and bigotry toward those speaking out against the church. Some commenters, for example, attempted to discount the very legitimacy of an ex-Mormon identity—that is, an identity based on a personal decision to denounce and oppose one's former religion—by accusing those who adopt it as secretly having been excommunicated for having led a life of sin: "'Ex-mormon' [*sic*]? . . . HA Oh please! . . . If you left the church which [*sic*] means you are less activity [*sic*] in the church not ex mormon. . . . if ex mormon that means you are excommunicated from the church for wrong doing against God's wills and no longer a member of that church . . . You are judging the LDS church and other churches . . . you know that? . . . Only God knows which church is true." Another stated, "Plain and simple. This guy had a breakdown in his life and snapped. He now lies to himself and others. He obviously had sin in his life that he couldn't cope with and give up. So he snapped. He is foolish and has a lot to learn, if he ever chooses to learn again. He needs to wise up!"

Others simply dismiss ex-Mormons as unqualified to have a voice on religious matters—including their own experiences of losing faith in the church—by virtue of the fact that they no longer identify with the religion. As one commenter replied, "You clearly are not saved by the blood of Jesus Christ. So shut up."

Such responses are familiar to ex-Mormons. As they find out, becoming an ex-Mormon is equivalent in the eyes of many church members to aligning oneself with Satan, the very embodiment of nonbelief: "The truth is that the LDS church REALLY is Christ's true church. That is the real truth. Anti-Mormons don't like truth, just as Satan didn't like it when Moses wouldn't worship him. What did Satan do? He ranted upon the earth. What is another way of saying that? Satan threw a temper tantrum when Moses wouldn't worship him . . . Anti-Mormons don't like truth, because anti-Mormons have the same contentious spirit that the devil himself does. That's the real truth. The LDS church IS TRUE!"

When I talked to my ex-Mormon friends in Utah who had filmed their own videos, their primary concern was not to "embarrass the church," as church members often claimed. Rather, I came to see these videos, these exit stories, as heartfelt pleas for respect and understanding from a church community that was often antagonistically at odds and dismissive of ex-Mormons' very personhood as nonbelievers. They were struggling to figure out what it meant to no longer be Mormon while also attempting to inhabit this ambiguous and marginalized zone of ex-Mormonism. They sought to do this, primarily, by reaching out to loved ones and trying to explain what it meant for them to no longer be members of the church. One of my close friends in Utah, Nathan, said he hesitated before deciding to film his video. He was concerned that his family might misunderstand him, that they might see it as an act of hostility. Yet he wanted to be heard; he wanted his family and every other ex-Mormons' family to "see who we really are, not who they think we are." Sitting in the lobby of a hotel in downtown Salt Lake City during the intermission of an annual Exmormon Foundation conference, with his characteristic straightforward, gentle demeanor, Nathan told his story.

> One of the things that's been important to me throughout my life is my family. I really love them. I was always brought up with beliefs that were just fine by me. In fact, I loved them. And then I started to learn some information that was different than that . . . This was fine except that my parents or siblings, their beliefs didn't change when mine did. My decision to leave the church has not always been easy for my family to deal with, and yet it's a reflection of my sincere belief that a person should have integrity. Their actions should match their words. My name is Nathan, and I'm an ex-Mormon.

"Is 'Ex' All We Are?"

As can be seen, ex-Mormonism in many ways defines itself in its collective opposition to Mormonism. It is an identity of ultimate alterity, a positionality sustained and fostered by a constant antagonism to the former faith. However, defining a sense of collective and personal identity strictly in terms of what you are not is inherently precarious. It requires reifying representations of the other that are not always stable and that, among ex-Mormons, came to be a source of internal division (as not everyone agreed what this thing called Mormonism was, how they were wronged by it, or what they should do about it). At a more existential level, *ex*-Mormonism is, as a collective grouping or nonreligious identity, only made possible inasmuch as it maintains its opposition to Mormonism. Ex-Mormonism can never stand on its own. In order to be an *ex*-Mormon, Mormonism must be continuously reengaged with, talked about, and rejected. Disidentification from Mormonism is thus predicated on a persistent identification with it. For ex-Mormons, then, collectively rejecting the church was both empowering and debilitating, as it necessitated a recursive reinvigoration of the thing they were trying to escape.

One ex-Mormon I knew, Jake, understood quite well how ex-Mormons' ambivalent relationship to the church was a central component of its continued vitality as a distinct social grouping. He explained this by saying that there is a cycle of growth and dissolution that the ex-Mormon community goes through that reflects the unsustainable nature of maintaining an "ex" positionality. "We're part of the second generation of ex-Mormons, and there's clearly a third generation cropping up now." Every few years, this happens, he says, describing it as a process of crystallization and fragmentation. He worries that the circle of friends he is currently a part of now might not be around for much longer. His group of friends "crystallized" together two years ago when he and his wife began attending ex-Mormon support group meetings when they were "fresh out of the church." But now he worries that his group of friends is beginning to fragment, individuals' personalities and idiosyncratic interests pulling apart the solidity they once felt in the early years of their disaffection and the shared anger they held toward the church. "We all are so different from each other," he says. "When you first leave the church, it is easy to make friends because you can just get together and talk about how bad the church is. But after the anger subsides, people tend to break back up and stratify again."

It seemed that this was a pervasive structural vulnerability within ex-Mormonism. Anger and its emotional correlate fear, once abated, no longer serve as the intersubjective nucleus around which groups could "crystallize." Joan told me of a book club she and a group of her friends used to be a part of called the "Infidel Women." She says they typically read "hard-hitting, edgy books," feminist works, and books on science and philosophy that questioned the foundations of religion and "gave [them] a way to intellectually rage against the church." After six or seven months, however, it dwindled away. "We were really passionate at first. But after a while, there was nobody to fight against, so we kind of lost interest." She said that once they all realized "there's no big bad monster in the closet," they slowly lost interest and the group dwindled away.

I witnessed a similar case at an ex-Mormon atheist book club meeting I once attended. While discussing Bertrand Russell's "Why I Am Not a Christian," one of the participants briefly interjected into the heated conversation about how Russell's criticisms of Christianity coincided so well with how they all felt about Mormonism. "It's OK that we get together like this to complain about the church," he said, "but we need to think about what brings us together other than our rejection of the church or religion. What does it mean for us to be atheists beyond our contempt for religion?" His words, however, were quickly drowned out by the ensuing fervent conversation. He fell silent, his exhortation having fallen on deaf ears. Indeed, at times it seemed there was no ready answer for such questions. For ex-Mormons in the midst of distancing themselves from their former faith, creating and gathering around an identity defined solely by its opposition to religion was all they really had. And sometimes, that was enough.

CHAPTER 7

Religious (Dis)Identification

ACQUIESCENCE AND ANGER ON THE EDGE OF MORMONISM

The study of nonreligious, secular, and atheist groups in the United States has been rather scant, despite growing numbers of religious "nones" on the U.S. religious landscape (Lee and Bullivant 2010, 26). When I began my research on religious apostasy and disenchantment in 2012, there were only several, mostly edited, volumes dedicated to "apostasy" or "religious disaffiliation/exiting" (Babinski 2003; Bromley 1988; Bromley 1998; Wilson 1994; Winell 2006; Wright 1987). Part of the problem, as I have found in my research, is identifying who or what specifically is the object of study. To isolate a social collective as belonging to a clearly defined "group" with a consistent "identity" is problematic not only because these "groups" are largely amorphous, informal, and de-centralized but also because they are internally heterogeneous with largely porous social boundaries across which "members" frequently traverse. Another difficulty is that labels such as nonbeliever, nonreligious, secular, atheist, agnostic, humanist, skeptic, apostate, and so on are nondescript and overlap with nonexclusive ideological boundaries.

Although the people I spoke with would contend that the church on a "factual" basis was not "true" in the way they once thought it was, there was little consistency in what that meant for how they related to Mormonism in their present circumstances as, for lack of a better word, "nonbelievers." The people I spoke with ran the gamut from sympathetic admirers of Mormonism's strength and fortitude as a religious movement to outright iconoclasts bent on "disproving" Mormonism, variously viewing religion as a matter of individual consciousness that should be respected, a corrupt moral institution that should be dismantled, a social organization that although fictitious should be tolerated for its ability to bring "good" into the world, and a natural byproduct of human development that modern humans have evolved past the need for.

While in the previous chapter I discussed people's strategic reappropriation of the apostate label and the creation of a distinct "ex-Mormon" identity, I now seek to complicate these categories. What I present here is a way of thinking deeper, and in more nuanced terms, about the categories of "apostate" or "nonreligious" and the positionalities they are assumed to inhabit vis-à-vis their relationship to religion. If we are to understand the effects of secularization in its local, historically contingent, and culturally specific iterations, we must attend to the various outcomes the experience of a loss of belief can take, aiming for less categorization and more contextualization, and be sensitive to the multiple, often contradictory identifications that prevail amid "nonbelievers."

To these ends, this chapter explores and compares two case studies of "nonbelievers" in Utah—one a "middle-way Mormon" and the other an "angry ex-Mormon"—as a method of discussing the various ways in which religion is variously (dis)identified with in the wake of disbelief. My aim, however, is not to impose another set of conceptual or cultural categories but rather to present two cases that reflect the diversity within the category of Mormon "nonbelievers." It therefore seeks to address a set of questions stemming from the rise of apostasy in Utah, including: How is the loss of belief circumscribed or intersected by ethnic and cultural identities? And how does (dis)identification with religion inform people's beliefs and behaviors as "nonbelievers" and their relationship with their former faith? What my comparison of middle-way and ex-Mormons illustrates is how nonbelief can lead to widely divergent attempts to maintain or sever ongoing attachments to a former faith, can blur boundaries between believers and nonbelievers, or can passionately insist on those boundaries' reification.

I begin by discussing the phenomenon of "middle-way Mormonism" through a case study of a man who was, to whatever extent the word is useful here, a "leader" in this community. Among middle-way Mormons, the boundaries between belief and disbelief are productively blurred as its proponents seek to focus on their primary goal of maintaining a cultural identification with Mormonism. This identification with Mormonism, despite the absence of belief, reveals itself as an emergent form of nonbelieving melancholia in the contemporary church. What is lost in religious disbelief is nevertheless held on to through new forms of religious belonging. I then juxtapose middle-way Mormons' cultural identification with the manner in which ex-Mormons disidentify with Mormonism using "anger" and "craziness" to performatively inscribe boundaries between themselves and their former church. Finally, I describe how ex-Mormons further perform and reinscribe these boundaries with Mormonism by sharing "exit stories" and engaging in a practice I describe as "policing disbelief."

Melancholic Middle-Way Mormonism

When I first met Josh at a dinner party, he struck me as a walking contradiction. Through a mouthful of toothpick-skewered pork appetizers, he told me, "I'm a vegetarian that sometimes eats meat." And in regards to his Mormonism,

Josh describes himself, with equally self-satisfied contradiction, as a "religious humanist with atheist tendencies."

He believes that, in all probability, God does not exist, and he's fluent in the historical and doctrinal issues with the church. Yet he studies religion with passion and conviction, even finding the "power of worship" at times personally gratifying. "I like to say I'm a religious pragmatist," he says, a phrase he is fond of using as a point of pontification in conversations with the other "middle-way Mormons" in his social circle.[1]

Despite his "nonbelief," Josh never describes himself as an ex-Mormon. Rather, he prefers the terms *cultural Mormon* and *middle-way Mormon*. For those like Josh, "ex-Mormon" reflects an ideology of secular intolerance, a scouring dismissal of religious belief and practice that is too antagonistic in its relationship to the church and too black and white in its notions of spirituality and rationality. It reinforces the very barriers and boundaries that they are trying to overcome.

As a member of the church, Josh enjoyed "using the priesthood" in his daily life, the communal intimacy of leading family prayer, and the familial economy of care he oversaw by giving blessings to his wife and children. Reading the scriptures daily allowed for quiet reflection, while singing hymns at church ritually entered him into a state of collective effervescence.

Like other middle-way Mormons, Josh cherishes his Mormon heritage and looks back with fondness on his life in the church. Losing his faith in Mormonism's truth claims, its theology, mythology, and cosmology, did not mean he lost faith in Mormonism as a set of social relationships and cultural practices and a symbolic ordering of the temporal world. He sought to hold on to these elements. "I have too much to lose by walking away," he said. "Why can't being a Mormon mean something bigger than how people typically think of it, even bigger than the church itself? I think that's possible. And if I'm right, that means people won't have to risk losing everything just because all the other stuff turned out not to be true." So despite experiencing his own crisis of faith in the "one true church" several years prior, Josh would proudly proclaim "I am a Mormon" from time to time when we discussed the complexity of his disbelief, stubbornly holding onto the identity, the way of life, that was at risk of slipping away.

Indeed, as I came to appreciate, while Josh disavowed the theological tenets of his faith, he was striving to hold onto his cultural heritage. "These are my people. That's why I poke fun at them so much," he once chided. Rather than outright rejecting the religion, Josh maintains a cultural identification with Mormonism that complicates an understanding of *loss of religious faith* as an inevitable path to *loss of religious identity*. Instead, middle-way Mormons like Josh actively promote the blurring of boundaries between members and former members through imaginatively repositioning faith as a sufficient, though not necessary, component of church membership.

For example, part of Josh's brand of middle-way Mormonism is his belief in the existence of a multitude of ways of "being Mormon" that do not require a literal belief in religious truth claims. I was once unwittingly made complicit in this imaginative redefinition of "Mormonism" when, at a middle-way Mormon barbecue, Josh enthusiastically introduced me to a group of friends as someone "researching the plurality of Mormon identities"—what Josh and other middle-wayers proudly refer to as "Big Tent Mormonism." "Anybody is welcome here," Josh proclaimed, looking around at the mass of people celebrating their spiritual diversity, "no matter what you believe." This imaginary community of Big Tent Mormonism allowed Josh to conceive of a mode of religious personhood and belonging big enough to encompass an almost infinite diversity of Mormon believers and nonbelievers, with no one put at risk of being excluded and no one at risk of losing the communal embrace of the church.

While Josh is indeed aware of the "harmful effects" of religion when defined in its institutional and ideological dimensions and despite his atheism, he says religion can in fact be harnessed as a "force for good." "Mormonism has so much potential," Josh quipped one morning as we took our seats at a Sunday morning sacrament meeting we attended together. As we sat together, I noticed that there seemed to be an affective longing in Josh to tap back into Mormonism's unrealized potential, a potential that he said had been spoiled by Mormonism's insistence on a dogmatic allegiance to absolute belief at the expense of religion's inherent ability to bring people together by bridging social divisions and uniting them under a common identity and purpose. "The church is in a slow state of collapse," he whispered to me as we sat amid his fellow parishioners in the crowded pews. "Look around; no one really wants to be here. It's all so rigid and unfulfilling." Yet as the piano began to play that morning and the congregation started to sing, I saw Josh stand with alacrity, his baritone voice ringing out in unison with the congregation, wholeheartedly joining the emergent symphonic sociality of the hymn. Later that morning, as we walked back to his car in the parking lot, Josh reflected on that potential some more with equal parts melancholy and hopefulness. "All we need to do is take what's good about the church," he said, "and let go of all the rest."

This sentiment informed much of Josh's activities during the time I knew him. Along with a group of other middle-way Mormons, Josh had begun to put this vision of religious redemption to work. For Josh, the ideal form of religious practice was one in which church members, while intellectually aware that the church is not literally "true," act as if the actual "truth" of the church did not matter. This perspective would grant them the ability to participate in the church's sacred rituals and relationships and glean whatever benefits may come without experiencing cognitive dissonance when its "truth claims" do not hold up to critical scrutiny. Reflecting on what this might look like, Josh described for me a church of enlightened patrons free to mix intellectual and spiritual pursuits and allegiances under one "big tent Mormon" roof. "I imagine a church community," he said, "where at one moment we can discuss science and evolution, deconstruct religion with philosophy and rationality, then in the next moment sing hymns and read scriptures for all that they can teach us about love and grace and redemption."

It seemed as if Josh and middle-wayers in general were imaginatively seeking a purer form of Mormon authenticity not through promoting stricter forms of orthodoxy—as is the institutional church's current tactic—but through glorifying heterodoxy. Indeed, according to Josh, a discordant understanding of scripture and theology, rather than undermining people's religious identifications, could be a means of restoring and strengthening a more primary identification with Mormonism, in more essential terms, as *Volk* ("a people").

So despite his ostensible atheism, Josh's identification with Mormonism seemed genuine. Josh considered it his personal duty to bring about a restoration of the church from within, to salvage what was best about Mormonism and discard the rest, a feat he said he could achieve only if he further entwined himself in the church and maintained his appearance as an active, faithful member. "That's why it's so important for me to stay on good terms with everybody in my ward. They need to think I'm one of them," he says when talking about his plans to bring about an internal transformation of the church. "Otherwise I'd never be able to talk to them about all this stuff." In a sense, Josh was seeking to collapse the boundaries of being or not being "one of them" as conditional upon adhering to a set of orthodox beliefs. "See, what you have to do is make them start asking questions, make them start critically thinking, without activating all of their defenses. You can only do this if you speak their language and are able to get underneath their radar."

Josh's relationship to religion is therefore not one of antipathy but productive, empathetic identification. Rather than arguing with church members directly, Josh said he aims to give them the "intellectual tools" to "dig themselves out," seeing himself as a savior of sorts, preaching the gospel of the "middle-way." "I think I can heal people by educating them," he said, referring to his participation in Sunday school classes where he attempts to "get people to start thinking" by creatively interpreting scripture without being overtly heretical. He also produces an online blog and podcast in which he discusses Mormon scripture, theology, history, and culture in a way that will "challenge people" while still maintaining the semblance of being "faith friendly." As such, he acts the part of a messianic Christ or Joseph Smith figure, ready to usher his people into a "healthier" appreciation of their Mormonism that focuses on the stories, values, and community that make it great and not the "mindless obedience" to the lessons and leadership who currently dominate it. He slyly told me, when he talked about the impact of his group on the church, that the ultimate goal of his work was to function as an "agent of disintegration" to the institutional church while also providing a viable "substitute" for Mormons to flock to after it crumbles. Yet Josh rather seemed to enjoy his status as "one of them." He sustained a mode of existence that ambiguously straddled the boundaries of the church, for he could dress the part of a Mormon, sing hymns, and spiritually reflect on scripture stories, all the while telling himself that he was "helping" these other naïve Mormons. He could then return home, take off his garments, and drink a beer on his back porch while critically debating the existence of God.

For the middle-way movement as a whole, maintaining such identifications actively mitigated the various experiences of loss that arose in the wake of disbelief. Unlike ex-Mormons, middle-way Mormons sought ways to "make it work," to stay engaged with Mormonism *despite* their nonbelief, to blur and shift the typical boundaries constructed between what it meant to be a believer or nonbeliever. Middle-way Mormonism, it seems, arose in response to people's inability, or unwillingness, to "let go of the church all the way" and sustained the imaginary presence of Mormonism in their everyday lives, despite their actual loss of belief in it as a "true" religion.

Middle-way Mormons were in fact actively working to create a parallel church, one in which the ideals of heterodoxy, inclusivity, and a nostalgic reclamation of Mormonism in its most basic form could be achieved. Unlike ex-Mormons, who met together primarily through informal social networks and in online spaces, middle-way Mormons hosted quasi sacrament meetings, during which participants could give their own versions of a "testimony" in support of whatever belief or value they held and congregants could join together to sing Mormon hymns. While attending one of these meetings, held at a Protestant church that the middle-wayers had rented out, I sat next to a man in his early forties attending with his young son. The man clasped his son's hand as they sang hymns together, his face pensive and intent. As we filed out of the pews after the makeshift benediction (consisting of announcements for other middle-way activities going on and an invitation for people to attend the next meeting in a few months), he stopped me to say hello. As we got to talking, he described the "cloud" he had been living in over the past several months since he began losing his faith, a deep sense of despair that left him despondent and sad. "It's so strange being here," he said, "but this is exactly what I needed. I feel like a weight has been lifted off of me." Although his wife was still a believing member of the church, he said he was unable to attend sacrament meetings with her. He said he "couldn't bring [himself] to go anymore once [he] saw through the charade." "I missed all this though," he confessed, looking around the room at the hundreds of people milling about. "I really did. I thought I'd lost it all forever. Maybe I'll reach a point someday where I don't need this kind of stuff anymore. But for now it's really all that's keeping me together."

As I have discussed in previous chapters, leaving the church brings with it the loss of a sense of community and collective purpose. Middle-wayers know this, and rather than leave Mormonism altogether, rejecting their faith and the church community as a whole, they choose to stay engaged with Mormonism as a means of retaining a sense of collective and personal identity. By articulating their allegiance to the "benefits" of religion, Mormonism was neither negated nor denied. Rather, it was strategically reappropriated and deployed as an essential form of identity that mitigated the threat of fragmentation and dislocation Mormons might experience should they "cut ties" completely.

Further, criticizing and disavowing the institutional church and its doctrines while simultaneously identifying with the "Mormon people" enables middle-way Mormons to create a collective (and even messianic) sense of purpose for themselves. This is illustrated in one woman's comment on an online message board dedicated to middle-way Mormonism, when she says, "We have a duty to hold onto our church membership as long as possible . . . Our families and friends need us . . . this is the burden we have to bear on behalf of those who are still victims of intellectual and spiritual repression in the church. We are their only hope." Such seemingly contradictory positionalities and motivations are in fact not contradictory at all. As Georg Simmel writes, "One might even say that obedience and opposition are merely two sides or links of one human attitude which fundamentally is quite consistent" (1950, 193). Only by maintaining some semblance of relations of obedience can the possibility of coordinated, purpose-driven opposition be fully sustained.

Related to this, I also found that the "middle-way Mormon" groups in which Josh circulated stayed engaged with Mormonism, despite their personal nonbelief, partly because it maintained the sense of power and satisfaction at possessing certain secret knowledge unshared with the larger community. For example, during a conversation at a middle-way barbecue, Drew began talking disparagingly about the historical circumstances of Joseph Smith's practice of polygamy. His wife, Pauline, after taking a quick glance around her, nudged him with her elbow and whispered in his ear, pointing toward a woman standing nearby in earshot of Drew's voice. Looking over his shoulder, Drew cringed, dropped his voice, and said that he would "keep it down." I looked at Pauline inquisitively, unsure what the problem was. "She doesn't know about all that," Pauline whispered to me with a giggle. "She's still a believer, and we don't want to burst her bubble too soon." This pleasure of secret keeping is in fact quite central to religious groups (like Mormonism) who maintain a set of teachings and ritual practices held apart from the wider populace. In Mormonism, church members feel themselves in possession of religious "truths"—found in scripture and ensconced in sacred temple rituals—which set their sacred community apart from the larger non-Mormon world. However, many middle-way Mormons, after losing their faith by reading about Mormonism's other "secrets" hidden in its historical past, feel that they were "duped" by church authorities who "kept the real truth hidden." In effect, they lost the feeling of control and satisfaction that their sacred knowledge had once afforded them—the pleasure of keeping secrets had turned against them. Now, instead of simply abandoning the church community amid their personal disbelief, they have created a "shadow church" parallel with Mormonism, within which their shared knowledge of "Mormonism's dirty secrets" grants them a comparable sense of electness. Like Pauline, they seemed to take pleasure in being the ones who would shoulder the burden of this knowledge on behalf of the larger church community who "couldn't handle it." And in some sense, they usurped the paternalistic position of being "the ones who know."

While such acts could be interpreted as promoting the respectful tolerance of people's diverse beliefs, in line with Josh's promotion of "Big Tent Mormonism," they also promoted what I sometimes heard described as a kind of tyranny of tolerance, in which those who engaged in critical discussion or argument were marginalized from the "big tent." Many of the people who eventually became self-described "ex-Mormons" indeed began their journey out of the church through the middle-way groups. This was where their disbelief matured and strengthened. However, once it did and they became more vociferously critical of Mormonism and religion in general, they found themselves occluded from conversation (especially in internet forums where moderators would often revoke people's access to the sites). "Respect" for people's beliefs took precedence over open and honest discussion about Mormonism's problems. The middle way, despite advocating for tolerance and pluralism, had become in some cases dogmatic itself. The continued vitality of middle-way Mormonism depended on the strategic ideal of Mormonism not being disrupted.

Finally, by maintaining a marginalized position vis-à-vis the church, yet insistently inserting themselves into its signifying universe, middle-way Mormons like Josh were also able to create for themselves a renewed sense of individual purpose and power, to become the messianic saviors of a fallen church, much like Joseph Smith aimed to do more than a hundred and fifty years ago. For example, despite Josh's nonbelief, he put a tremendous amount of thought and study into understanding how Mormonism operated and the potential benefits it could bring to people if "used correctly." By calling for a new form of Mormonism defined by tolerance and inclusion of heterodox beliefs, with an emphasis on Mormon ethnicity divorced from religious dogmatism, Josh and his middle-way compatriots were able to clothe themselves in a superordinate authority above and beyond that of the institutional church and thereby appeal to the increasing numbers of spiritually disillusioned and disenfranchised people in the church. He was able to wield a form of cultural capital increasingly valuable and sought within contemporary Mormonism—the ability to explain why life in the LDS Church had lost its luster while providing hope and encouragement to those discouraged by doubt and confusion, as seen on various internet blogs where middle-way writers like Josh touted ways to "make it work"—that is, how to maintain church membership while also questioning the veracity of its religious truth claims.

While in some sense this reflects a creative adaptation to the struggle of maintaining ties to a church community increasingly entrenching itself in unquestioning orthodoxy, the mutability of middle-way Mormons' personas and positionalities at times frustrated me. It was not that they resisted some sort of facile categorization of belief and belonging that I was after. Rather, for those who organized and directed much of the middle-way activities and events, their enigmatic stance on issues of belief and belonging seemed to betray an attempt to capitalize on their ability to straddle, traverse, and blur boundaries between insider and outsider, current and former member, believer and nonbeliever. Indeed, in the various online communities, blogs, podcasts, barbecues, book clubs, and conferences in which middle-way Mormonism's "shadow church" has taken shape, various "leaders" of the movement—like Josh—have achieved a highly localized celebrity status. With their own partisan factions and devoted followers, some even garnish wages from their work in the form of donations, membership fees, and fundraising drives from a cadre of followers happy to pay a new form of "tithing" to their newfound quasi-religious community. Touting the middle way has become, in many cases, the lucrative way.

Josh and the phenomenon of "middle-way Mormonism" reveal key dimensions about the contemporary transformation of Mormonism and the concomitant creation of ostensibly "nonbelieving" people in the United States who have maintained a productively empathetic relationship and identification with religion. But let me now turn to another form of nonbelief, which has resulted in a more explicitly antagonistic relationship to religion.

Angry Ex-Mormons

While middle-way Mormons seek to maintain an aura of faithful membership as they work toward reconciliation and transformation from within, "ex-Mormons" are up to something quite different. While middle-way Mormons are conciliatory, their goal to bring about an internal metamorphosis of the church, many ex-Mormons are vocally hostile, seeking the dissolution and dismantling of a church they deem morally bankrupt and patently false. Among faithful church members and even middle-way Mormons, such a stance has bestowed on ex-Mormons the designation of being "angry." The terms *angry* apostate, *angry* atheist, and *angry* ex-Mormon, pervasively used and circulated within Mormonism, characterize people's alterity to religion as one defined primarily by animosity and acrimony. Indeed, even in wider American religious discourse, so-called new atheists are often dismissed as vengefully vitriolic against religion, their diatribes against the perils of religiosity arraigned for their illiberal intolerance of people's faith and spirituality. But what does being angry at religion signify? How does this affectively marked stance reveal deeper processes of disidentification from religion?

Anger, as I want to discuss it here, reflects and reveals a micropolitics of boundary making that ex-Mormons are attempting to navigate as nonbelievers. Boundaries, for ex-Mormons, are not something to be blurred or traversed, as they are for middle-way Mormons. Rather, ex-Mormons are at pains to identify, construct, and police the affective, moral, and social boundaries between themselves and their former faith in the hopes of effectively insulating themselves from its pernicious influence.

Lori's Craziness

I met Lori at a biweekly "recovery from Mormonism" support group meeting. She attended sessions off and on throughout the time I was in Utah, showing up flustered and agitated, greeting other participants with short, curt hellos. She at first avoided eye contact when people spoke to her. But when it became her turn to speak, she pensively locked eyes, as if desperate to convey her thoughts through the intensity of her glare. I grew to know Lori's story through these meetings and visits to her house, where we would sit together talking, sipping gin and tonics, her stories growing increasingly animated the more we drank.

Since she had stopped believing in the church a year and a half prior, Lori said she felt like she was going crazy. Often, when I would arrive at her house in the evenings to catch up with her in-between support group sessions, I would go unnoticed for the first half hour. Usually, she had just arrived home from work and would scurry around the house, entrapped in her own world, while her husband offered me a drink and something to eat. This otherwise aloof demeanor, however, only thinly veiled the "craziness" broiling underneath. Soon she would pour a drink and let loose with her frustrations with the church. Lori was an example of the "angry ex-Mormon" that my Mormon friends often spoke dismissively about. But as I came to appreciate, Lori's "craziness" and anger were reflections of her particular subjectivity as a nonbelieving ex-Mormon woman stuck in a hegemonic Mormon world.

As I grew to know Lori, her anger seemed to stem from a panoply of feelings of betrayal, insecurity, and vulnerability and a persistent sense of being inexorably entangled in Mormonism. She said she felt angry, frustrated, and trapped by the church. "I'm just done. I'm done with it all. Everywhere I go and everything I do, it's about the church. And I haven't had a testimony in over a year!" Lori's ongoing entanglement with Mormonism stemmed primarily from her husband's employment with the church. Jared worked in the church's public relations office, where employees were told that they were the frontline defenders of the increasingly globalized church's "public image to the world." However, a crucial component of his employment was that he and his family maintain their "temple-worthy" status in the church. Should anyone find out he or his wife had "become apostate," the church could quickly dismiss him, permanently revoking his pension and benefits.

Jared's employment with the church put them in a precarious financial situation, necessitating a careful management of their public identities. "I have to be careful," Lori said. "If they find out I'm an *apostate*, they [the church] could get suspicious of him, and he could end up fired, and I'd be the one to blame . . . No one would ever suspect him. Look at him; he's too cute to be an apostate. Me, on the other hand, ha! They could probably see it in my eyes." This meant Lori had to maintain a carefully managed existence, presenting an illusion of faithful membership to her friends, neighbors, coworkers, and family that hid the anger she felt, lest someone be able to peer beneath her faithful veneer and see the disbelief inside.

The church, she said, manufactured consent and passivity among its members by emphasizing uniformity in all aspects of church membership, including personal dress, hair style, and conversation topics and speech patterns, all of which she was obliged to incorporate into her daily demeanor as the wife of a church employee. "As soon as you start to show in whatever little way that you're not conforming to the rules or breaking the mold in how you think or act, you're going to get called out." Out of fear that her husband's job would be jeopardized should her nonbelief be discovered, Lori even continued to wear her temple garments daily lest someone see she was not wearing them and begin to ask questions. "I hate these things," she said, pulling down on the T-shirt portion she wore under her regular shirt and bra. "I can't even dress how I want . . . I can literally feel the church gripping my body everywhere I go."

Maintaining a facade of being the "good Mormon wife" while at the same time harboring internal discontent with the church left her feeling repressed, fragmented, and invaded. "I feel like I'm living two lives," she complained; the toll of living "inauthentically" increasingly bothered her. Trapped by the need to embody and perform a religious identity that she resented, Lori felt increasingly stifled by the need to tacitly accept Mormonism's hegemonic control over and *intrusion into* her life. At times, she would unexpectedly erupt in manic outbursts that revealed this derision for the church and its leaders—"You know what that fucker bishop said to me last week?" she asked rhetorically, referring to their ward bishop. In a private interview with him the week before, which Lori was obliged to attend, the bishop had suggested that she be more active in their ward, questioning her "commitment to the gospel" and warning her about what might happen to her children if she did not strengthen her testimony. Lori was incensed at his presumptuousness. "He can question my testimony; who cares? But don't tell me how to raise my kids!"

Much of Lori's anger indeed revolved around the church's continued intrusion into her family life. Various "visiting" and "home" teachers—women and men in the church assigned to visit other ward members at their homes—frequently stopped by her home, uninvited, to "offer inspiration" in the form of prayers and scripture lessons. Other neighbors kept inviting her children to youth activities with the ward, where Lori knew "they're just going to try and brainwash them."

Lori saw such advances as an immediate threat to her family and worried about the effect it would have on her children. Like other ex-Mormons I talked to, she now understood Mormonism to be a repressive, hypocritical, and destructive religion, with professed "values" and "morals" that ultimately caused more harm than good. Indeed, ever since her disaffection, Lori had increasingly scoffed at the lessons taught in Sunday school classes. "Everything we're taught is meant to keep us enslaved to the church," she reasoned. In particular, Lori found the lessons on "honesty," "virtue," and "obedience" infuriating. Honesty, she said, was only valued as long as it worked in the church's favor. Virtue was about teaching little girls to feel shame in their bodies and to repress their sexualities. And obedience meant to never question your male priesthood leaders' authority, whether he was your prophet, your bishop, or your husband. Indeed, whenever I saw Lori talk about the church's "values," she became visibly disturbed and vindictive against the church, trying with the force of her anger to verbally and physically purge herself of its lasting influence over her. "That's what makes it all so fucking ridiculous," she explained to me one night at her house. "Everyone's constantly hammering away at how we all need to live more righteously and how the world's this big, bad, sinful place. But they're all hypocrites. I can't believe I ever listened to that shit . . . That's why we need to get away. I can't let my kids grow up with that getting inside their heads."

Lori had indeed learned the duplicitous nature of church values early in life. As a young girl, Lori was sexually abused by her childhood bishop's son, who lived down the street. In contrast to the often emotionally charged erraticism I saw at her house, at the support group meeting, she was composed and sober while recounting this story of abuse, temporarily disassociating from this traumatic ordeal. "There was a group of us who played basketball together every day after school," she began. "That day, though, it was just the two of us. His parents weren't home yet, so we went in his house, and he made me touch him." After returning home, she told her parents about the abuse but was ignored. And despite pleading and crying with her parents to believe her, they repeatedly accused her of lying, running interference for the bishop's son so as to avoid any unseemly public embarrassment for their priesthood leader. "I was told to keep quiet, to not make up stories that weren't true. They said he was preparing to go on a mission and that I had better think twice before I accused someone like him of doing something like that. Because, you know, it would have ruined his chances of being a missionary." Lori had felt betrayed by her parents, by her church, and by its teachings of virtue, honesty, and obedience. To the church and her parents, maintaining the young man's appearance of "virtue" was more important than her experience of being sexually violated. In learning that "honesty" was conditional and "obedience" trumped justice, her violation at the hands of the boy was matched by her violation at the hands of a moral order that refused to acknowledge her suffering. They had effectively allowed her personal moral and sexual boundaries to be transgressed, undermined, and dismissed.

In psychological terms, anger is an emotional response to a threat levied against, or an outright violation of, personal boundaries. Emotions like anger should also be understood for their intersubjective dimensions. As a clearly recognizable and patterned emotive expression, anger is effective at explicitly reestablishing, marking, and policing social boundaries through sheer affective force. As such, anger emerges as an emotion-based form of cultural practice used by social actors to engage with and bring about change in their relationships with others and the world around them.

Ex-Mormons are often accused of being angry due to the way they are perceived to be trying to "embarrass the church" by drawing untoward attention to the troubling parts of its history or by criticizing its peculiar beliefs and practices. And as I suggested earlier, within Mormonism, anger has become a stereotyped attribute of ex-Mormons' vengefulness. After her disaffection, and despite the threat of her husband being fired, Lori indeed repeatedly looked for ways to retaliate against the church, to "express" her anger. For instance, she began working with a group of other ex-Mormons, creating an online Wiki devoted to encyclopedically documenting the church's historical fallacies, lies, and cover-ups. And she anonymously "trolled" Mormon websites and online message boards, posting vitriolic diatribes against the church, attempting to provoke believers' defensive reactions. However, each of these outlets required her to remain hidden, anonymous, and faceless. And despite having these emotional "outlets," her anger continued to grow as Mormonism's intrusion into her life went on unabated. In the last few weeks that I was in contact with Lori, she said her mother-in-law had become increasingly critical of her erratic behavior, calling into question her roles as a wife and mother, and their bishop had ominously called Jared into his office, threatening to not give him a "temple recommend," effectively putting his employment in jeopardy. Expressing anonymous anger online did nothing to quell her feelings of enduring violation at home and in her everyday life.

However, Lori eventually said she "couldn't take it anymore." She stopped attending church altogether and made her misgivings with the church more public on Facebook for her friends and family to see, posting humorously insulting jokes and cartoons about Mormonism on her personal "wall." Though rumors started to circulate that she had "turned apostate," Lori was undeterred. "I don't care what people think. I'm so pissed," she said. "I can't stand it anymore. It's my life, and I'm going to do what I want."

Lori began to give into her anger, letting the craziness boiling within her take over her outward appearance and demeanor. Over several weeks, I watched her appearance transform as she dyed her hair a harsh platinum blonde, shaving it on the sides and back, and began wearing intensely colored lipstick and eyeliner with increasingly deeper cut blouses that prominently displayed her cleavage. She also said she had recently "told off" her bishop, fiercely yelling at him one day when he knocked on her front door. "I let him have it. I'm not holding back anymore. I want people to know how angry I am. They deserve it," she said. She had also moved out of the house, a temporary separation between her and her husband in order to give them both "time to breathe." During one of the last support group sessions I saw her at, she explained what she had been going through to the group.

> The way I've been dressing and looking, I'm trying to be this outrageous statement in a way, just in being seen. I'm tired of being marginalized. I'm tired of when people find out that I've left the church, suddenly my opinion doesn't matter anymore. It's my little "fuck you" statement. And in fact I realized, part of my motivation for moving out of the house is *I felt so torn*. I figure now if I go public with who I am, then it's like "oh the crazy wife that was just you know *bucking for separation anyway*," so how can they [the church, her husband's employers] blame him if it's his crazy wife who's going to divorce him anyway because he's just living with this crazy woman. And frankly that's what I've been, is the crazy woman. So he's gotten a lot of sympathy I think and a *very wide berth* from some of the church leaders. Because I found that *setting boundaries* and doing it a healthy way didn't work, *I let out my crazy and that worked.*

Lori did seem "better." A few weeks later, she moved back in with her husband and seemed more at peace with herself and her life. Yet Lori was indeed an "angry ex-Mormon," even becoming the very personification of anger in the last few weeks that I knew her. However, her anger was more than a vindictive and unjustified emotional reaction, as church members implied in their use of the phrase "angry ex-Mormon" or "angry apostate." Instead, anger was an expression of her frustration at being unable to erect respectful boundaries between herself and the wider religious culture of which she was a part—a religious culture that had violated, abused, and made her vulnerable throughout her life. Embracing her anger and craziness allowed for her to rewrite the dimensions of her own existence, pulling together the pieces of herself once torn apart by the need to "act the part" of a good Mormon wife and even reclaiming those parts taken away from her as an abused child. Anger, when fully embodied, personified, and performed, allowed Lori to begin inscribing and policing new boundaries around her, effectively carving out a space of *autonomous* alterity for her life. Finally, anger was a purifying emotion for Lori, allowing her to effectively expurgate the church from her home, her relationships, and her life by signaling to those around her that she was no longer open to their influence—no longer open to hearing whatever the bishop had to say and the lessons the visiting teachers had to give and no longer held hostage by the possibility of being branded an apostate. The issue of becoming "angry" in the context of ex-Mormonism therefore points less to individual person's isolated emotional reactions than to a pervasive social transformation of relations between believing and nonbelieving people and communities. And indeed, this transformation of social and moral boundaries is exactly what Lori achieved as she became the "angry ex-Mormon." At the last support group meeting I saw her at, she smiled and triumphantly proclaimed, "No one knocks on my door anymore to ask why I wasn't at church!"

Policing Disbelief

Moral, social, and ideological boundaries are also marked and negotiated collectively. At ex-Mormon gatherings, parties, conferences, and support group meetings, the first question a newcomer would most likely be asked was some version of "So what's your story?" or "When did you leave the church?"

I became aware of this as I saw two of my friends who had not previously known each other meet for the first time at a party. "So when did you find out it was all a lie?" Brian pointedly asked. Chris laughed, giving a perfunctory and scripted answer about "studying his way out of the church." As Chris was talking, however, Brian only seemed half-interested in hearing Chris's story. Brian had heard the requisite answer and only responded, "You're lucky. You figured it out pretty early. I was stuck in it for over thirty years." Conversation then seamlessly turned to talk of sports, music, and each other's taste in alcohol.

This obligatory exchanging of "exit stories" among ex-Mormons was not just a convenient conversation starter. I eventually came to think of them as an obligatory discursive ritual by which people communicated their disidentification from Mormonism. In these types of conversations, participants were expected to give their "exit story," a narrative chronicling their disaffection from the faith, their "awakening" from the "deep sleep" Mormonism had put them in. Informed by the logic of enlightenment rationalism, existential freedom, and individual sovereignty, such talk framed Mormonism as a debilitating and constraining religious mind-set and church community that had to be utterly and wholly rejected. People described the church as something that had "brainwashed" or "blinded" them. Those who had left the church were understood to now "see things as they really are."

These interactive rituals were a way for ex-Mormons to stake intergroup boundaries and maintain individual and group security. This in part stemmed from the need for people entering and circulating within the community to clarify their absolute separation from the church, because aside from the occasional visible tattoo or low-cut blouse, everyone still "looked Mormon." As with the discussion between Brian and Chris, questions like "When did you figure out it was all a lie?" began a conversation in which each party obligingly divested themselves of a Mormon identity. As a discursive ritual, these exchanges temporarily disenchanted the social space people inhabited and enforced an obligatory logic of secular rationality.

Obliging others to tell their stories indeed serves as an explicit means of marking group boundaries and auditing those who are entering into the space of ex-Mormonism. But as with any social or ideological boundaries, they are constructed not only to signify those who stand within their borders but also to exclude those who may prove a threat to the group's health and vitality.

For example, during one ex-Mormon get-together held at a local coffee shop, a quiet, meek woman named Shawnee introduced herself to the table I was sitting at. As this was the first time any of us had ever seen Shawnee at an ex-Mormon function, Nathan, a longtime member of the group, began the discursive ritual of asking her when she "left the church." Shawnee responded by saying that she "stopped attending" several months after she began to question Joseph Smith's practice of polygamy. Nathan immediately took notice of her word choice and asked, "What do you mean 'stopped attending'?" Then without waiting for a response from Shawnee, he pressed further, unleashing a torrent of questions: "Do you still believe in the church? . . . Who do you think Joseph Smith was? . . . What about God, do you still believe in him?" His persistence unsettled Shawnee. She looked around nervously, not knowing how to respond to what now amounted to an interrogation of her disbelief. I later found out from a friend of Shawnee's that she was "fresh out of the church" and was not sure where she stood on the questions Nathan had asked her. Although she no longer wanted to be a Mormon, she had not settled on whether she believed in God or not. She still maintained some semblance of "belief" in something, and Nathan immediately sniffed this out, sensing a threat to the acerbically secular space he and others in the group had created. No one was surprised when Shawnee did not return to the next week's meeting. The ritual had worked.

Such forms of boundary keeping proactively avert the introduction of ideas and beliefs thought to be harmful to the secular life ex-Mormons were attempting to build outside of the church. But it also at times reifies a normative mode of ex-Mormon personhood defined not by the absence of religion but explicit antagonism toward anything resembling religious belief. Cheryl, for example, usually avoided ex-Mormon gatherings. Though she no longer believed the church was true, she felt like the ex-Mormons she knew were always "angry," just like church members insisted they were, always "picking fights with people" or "fighting the church." "It makes it hard to really be yourself around them," she confessed. "I don't always agree with what everybody else thinks." However, when her husband, who was actively involved in the community, pleaded with her, she sometimes attended. But at those times, she seemed cautious and reserved, hesitant to engage anybody in conversation. All of their friends were also ex-Mormons, so avoiding talk of the church proved nearly impossible. "One way or another, we always get stuck talking about the church," Cheryl said with a sigh.

I sat next to Cheryl once at her house during a "board game night" that she and her husband organized for the community. Kathy, a soft-spoken woman who was avowedly atheist and also virulently antagonistic toward Mormonism, sat next to us. I told Kathy that later in the week I would be attending an "energy healing" session with a Mormon woman who practiced various forms of "spiritual healing." Without questioning why I might be participating in such an event, Kathy immediately dismissed the idea of "energy" as silly. I looked over to Cheryl, who I knew was interested in various forms of reiki. She at first hesitated but then confidently retorted, "I think it exists." Explaining herself, Cheryl asked, "Haven't you ever passed by someone on the street and you just feel something about them? . . . or, when you go into a restaurant with a piano playing, and there's dim lighting, and you just feel different? I think that that's energy."

Knowing that Cheryl struggled to connect with people and groups outside the church, I saw her insistence on the presence of a thing called energy as an attempt to affirm the existence of a tacit empathetic connection with her environment that transcended the limits of her empirical senses. But Kathy read her defense of "energy" as a latent form of religious belief from her life in the church and became immediately argumentative. "Isn't that just what you could call mood?" she challenged. "You're just picking up on unconscious clues about a person or place because of some psychological disposition or personal experience you have," Kathy explained. Though Cheryl made an attempt at compromise, saying "I think we're just using two different words to describe the same thing," Kathy dismissively retorted by asking Cheryl, "Why don't you just call it mood then? . . . do you think that you can actually sense this energy, like 'the force' in Star Wars?"

What is at issue is not merely the semantics of *energy* or *mood*. Rather, it seems there is an ontological distinction being negotiated that speaks to the ongoing relationship to Mormonism that must be collectively negotiated among members of the ex-Mormon community. Here, Cheryl is appealing to a somewhat mystical, implicit, tacit, and at times undefinable palpation to a person, event, or place. According to Kathy, however, any concession to a metaphysical reality smacks of superstitious spirituality and should be stridently disavowed.

According to Cheryl, such interactions evidence the "angry ex-Mormon" at work. However, as I came to appreciate, this insistence on a hyperempirical rationalism is at times a crucial component of the politics of boundary keeping in the ex-Mormon crowd. In effect, it was aimed at enforcing equality in people's interactions with each other, a way of fostering relations of political impartiality within their group, which were widely felt to have been lacking in Mormonism. Specifically, in the church, a politics of feeling was often at work in which a person facing a question or problem could attest to having received personal "confirmation" or "revelation" from the spirit that authoritatively stipulated the course of action that was to be taken. However, while two people—potentially a husband and wife or two people in church leadership positions—could both "receive revelation" on a particular matter, whoever held a higher position of authority in the church—the most senior male priesthood holder—took precedence. For Kathy, and other ex-Mormons like her, challenging the idea that one can "feel energy" was therefore in some sense an attempt to curb this hierarchical and partisan system of decision-making. Specifically, it was an attempt to level and democratize people's status in personal interactions, to bring it back down to a "worldly" level, which disallowed claims of access to a higher power. "Everyone is equal here," I would often hear at community gatherings or on online message boards. "You can say whatever you want, and people will listen to you." So while Cheryl was attempting to overcome ontological boundaries through appeals to an interconnecting energy, from Kathy's perspective, Cheryl's affirmation of a thing called energy threatened to reintroduce divisions between those who could and those who could not "feel" energy or the spirit. For Kathy, the absence of energy allowed for decision-making to be based on the inherent logic or rationality of someone's stance, not the force with which he or she "felt" it to be "true."

As I have described in this chapter, the category of "nonbeliever" is internally heterogeneous. Not all who stop believing become publicly visible "apostates," either out of necessity—as with Lori—or by choice—as with Josh. Likewise, many of those who otherwise stay in contact with Mormonism, even maintaining an image of "faithful member," are not necessarily still "believers." As seen in Josh's case, contemporary Mormon identities in many ways transcend issues of belief and faith and perhaps even religion altogether. Despite the inherent ambiguity of the nonbeliever category, many nonbelievers are in fact at pains to delineate boundaries between themselves and the church. This process of boundary inscription, as I have discussed, takes place externally through the use of emotional performances (Lori) and internally through the use of discursive rituals (exit stories).

Rather than an exception to the rule, these crosscutting identifications define an ever-growing portion of contemporary church membership. While LDS church leaders may assume that the church body is largely homogeneous in their beliefs and affiliations, I believe the Mormonism of the future will increasingly be characterized by such ambiguous identifications and ambivalent positionalities.

Conclusion

"PASTORAL APOLOGETICS" AND THE FUTURE OF MORMONISM

Mormonism's crisis of apostasy continues. In the time since my research, several additional public demonstrations of mass resignation have taken place on the doorstep of the church's world headquarters in Salt Lake City (Miet 2014). And multiple relatively high-ranking church members, including one-time bishops and stake presidents, have become disaffected, drawing attention to the matter of apostasy through newspaper interviews and articles, describing in detail the reasons for their losses of faith (Colvin 2014). Much to the dismay of church leaders, religious disenchantment within Mormonism is far from a private, personal matter.

In response to this threat to its public persona and the solidity of its membership, the church has recently begun to respond to the tide of disaffection. To begin with, in 2013, just after the end of my ethnographic research, the church began publishing a series of informational essays on its main website, addressing a number of the historical issues underlying many (if not most) people's disaffection. The explicit goal is to promote a more "open" and "honest" discussion of Mormonism's past in light of the internet's ability to undermine church-sponsored repression of disconcerting historical information. Marking the formal shift in church strategy, church historian Elder Snow remarked, "I think in the past there was a tendency to keep a lot of the records closed or at least not give access to information. But the world has changed in the last generation—with the access to information on the Internet, we can't continue that pattern; I think we need to continue to be more open" (Bennett and Pike 2013). As such, it seems as if Mormonism's hand has now been forced, its dogmatic institutional authority and unilateral control of information made to acquiesce and adapt to the ideological and technological transformations sweeping the globe.

To some extent, this admission of fallibility and shift toward more institutional and historical transparency is a welcome sign from a typically unresponsive institution seemingly complacent in its unquestioned authority. Many ex-Mormons, long-since disaffected, herald this as a step in the right direction, even if the essays continue to obfuscate facts or ultimately draw faith-promoting conclusions. In writing and publicly publishing essays on the past abuses against black people, the prevalence of polygamy in the early church, and the multiple contrasting stories of Joseph Smith's "first vision," among other topics, the church is at least tacitly acknowledging that such issues are, in fact, issues that have collectively contributed to if not directly caused the rash of apostasy, which can no longer be conveniently ignored in the hope that the average member will not notice. Furthermore, it implicitly validates the reasons ex-Mormons give for having lost their faith, tacitly addressing the stigmas attached to ex-Mormons, which too often paint their apostasy as stemming from either spiritual apathy or moral depravity. The church has indeed seemed to take notice of apostasy as a broader issue afflicting its religious community rather than just a matter of a few isolated individuals getting "offended."

That an institutional and cultural shift is perhaps under way is evidenced by increased calls coming from within the faithful membership for a reconceptualization of the role of belief, faith, and even God's personality to allow for a "softer," more sensitive way of dealing with doubt and questioning in the congregation. In contrast to the combative and dismissive tone of polemical apologetics fostered by various Mormon apologists groups such as FAIR (Foundation for Apologetic Information and Research) and the BYU-affiliated FARMS (Foundation for Ancient Research and Mormon Studies), some church leaders and scholars are now calling for a "pastoral apologetics" characterized by a more tolerant, nonjudgmental, and even empathetic response to doubters, attempting to communicate the "spiritual and moral benefits" of Mormonism rather than argue with its evidentiary logic (Payne 2013). In this vein, Mormon professor of comparative literature Terryl Givens is spearheading an internal transformation of Mormon spirituality that celebrates people's individuality, affirms their doubts, and articulates a conception of God who is filled with empathy and commiserates in members' struggles and pains—who is, in essence, a "God who weeps" (Givens 2012).[1]

While such developments perhaps point to an era of increased tolerance and respect for doubting, questioning, and challenging once unquestioned religious truths on Mormonism's horizons, for most of the ex-Mormons who have departed, or are currently in the process of departing, from the LDS Church, it does not matter. Their lives have already been torn asunder by the discovery of a too-long strategically repressed history, the stigmas that have been too callously ascribed to them, and a religious culture too ardently dismissive of doubt and dissent.

Though living in the shadow of the church, apostates' unique positionalities and subjectivities, when paid attention to ethnographically, shine light onto a religious world obscured by church leaders' rhetoric and public relations departments' advertising. How does such public posturing reconcile with the fact that its religious teachings and church culture have created an environment in which those who dissent from religious truth claims are routinely subjected to stigmas and slander, ostracized from their families and neighborhoods, and made to feel alienated and alone while facing the collapse of their whole lifeworld with no one to turn to for empathy or understanding? When pressed to answer for such inequities, church officials and average members profess that one must not focus on "a few individuals" who perpetuate such hostilities, drawing a conceptual divide between these individuals and "church culture" on the one hand and the sacred purity of "the gospel," which must remain untarnished and uncritiqued, on the other. However, if any meaningful change is going to come, the church must recognize the extent to which its teachings, institutional practices, ritual traditions, and divinely authorized pronouncements have themselves created and continue to perpetuate a culture of intolerance and bigotry toward former believers.

So if a pastoral apologetics is to be fully realized in the church, it must involve a critical self-reflexive assessment of Mormonism's own complicity in fueling the rash of disaffection from the faith and seek an empathy-driven understanding and respect for people's experiences leaving the church. This means accounting for the fact that Mormonism's apostates were not uninterested, apathetic, or uninvolved church members who lost the motivation or willpower to maintain their faith. Rather, the church must recognize that they were in fact one-time faithful adherents, whose earnest search for truth and "further light and knowledge" led them to an inevitable confrontation with the contradictions and falsities of Mormonism's past.

However, beyond recognizing the legitimacy of their former membership and current grievances, pastoral apologetics must also understand that apostates' anger, depression, sexual experimentation, atheism, and attempts to create an ex-Mormon movement are neither examples of a pathology of losing faith nor evidence of rancorous "anti-Mormonism." Instead, as I have attempted to show, these behaviors must be recognized as a by-product of, and reasonable response to, the combination of a lifetime of church membership and a litany of social and psychological traumas inflicted on them as apostates. Mormonism as a whole must begin seeing its apostates not as spiritual turncoats and religious others who must be marginalized and purged from the church body but rather as close friends, family members, and neighbors with whom relationships of mutual trust, respect, and congeniality can still be fostered. If Mormonism truly seeks meaningful incorporation into a global world, one filled with a plurality of people and ideas distinct from its own, it must first learn to respect difference and diversity at home. Presenting an outward public image of acceptance and diversity cannot come at the cost of fostering and perpetuating internal strife and discord.

A central goal of this book has thus also been to make sense of apostasy and apostates as inextricable products of a constellation of historical, social, and cultural transformations taking place *within* contemporary Mormonism. Spiritual, emotional, and psychological suffering, though obscured by the spectacle of the Mormon Moment and its admiration, if not outright glorification, of Mormonism as modern America's religious darling, must be understood in more in-depth terms than the inevitable byproducts of secularization or the consequences of a world fallen into godless disbelief.

Apostasy is a symptom of Mormonism's ongoing transformation as it seeks incorporation into mainstream America and a global religious landscape. Through apostates, we catch a glimpse of the inner mechanizations and transformations at work in the contemporary church—a church struggling to define itself amid its increasing acculturation to mainstream American society, striving to hold onto a sacred past despite it being beset by scandal and plagued by internal contradiction, and being made vulnerable, insecure, and anxious in the face of the receding cultural and religious boundaries by which its sense of distinction, peculiarity, and ascendancy have so long been secured. When paying attention to people's experiences of disillusionment as they discover previously unknown aspects of church history on the internet, we see the conflicts that arise in the midst of a religious tradition attempting to adapt its historical identity to an ever-changing collective sense of self, a process that inevitably involves a litany of defensive reactions, shifting conceptualizations of religious authority, and carefully managed mea culpas. Through all of this, the triadic relationship among religiosity, historical memory, and secular modernity is laid bare.

Finally, beyond its critique and assessment of Mormonism, I hope that this book can complicate the conceptual categories, identities, and processes through which social science has hitherto attempted to understand the tenor and transformations wrought by secularization in the United States. What I hope to have ultimately demonstrated is the extent to which the conceptual categories of nonreligious, nonbeliever, secular humanist, agnostic, atheist, apostate, and so on in the United States can only be understood by attending to processes of intimate, subjective transformation.

There are two dimensions to this. First, the psychological, emotional, and existential trauma of religious disenchantment must be seen as the intersubjective psychosocial foundation for a rising class of nonreligious people in the United States. That is, if we are to make sense of emerging forms of secular sociality, ideology, and institutional practices—whether in the form of changing laws, marriage and family practices, political agendas, arts and music, or intellectual aspirations—we must first attend to the processes of religious disenchantment and disillusionment through which a nonreligious, secular citizenry has risen. Secularization, and the concomitant formation of the ideological principles of secularism, is not driven solely by the circulation and evolution of abstract ideas or by the disembodied mechanizations of social, economic, political, and legal institutions. Rather, it also takes shape through experiences of personal crises of faith, the collapse of subjective lifeworlds, the paradoxical confluences of feelings of alienation and nostalgia, attempts at coping with a tragic sense of loss through personal exploration (and experimentation), and the formation of explicitly nonreligious socialities and identities while inhabiting places suffused with religion. Second, any attempt to describe the formation of contemporary secular subjectivities must take into account the various forms of intersecting religious (dis)identifications and the lasting feelings of embodied religious inhabitation at work within ostensibly "secular" populations. That is, we must never lose sight of the extent to which religion—as cultural identity, moral system, embodied habitus, and so on—constitutes an ever-present antagonist against which, and through which, notions of the secular emerge and take shape.

In conclusion, I hope that the descriptions, arguments, or insights I have been able to articulate can ultimately contribute to a more ethnographically sensitive appraisal of these overlapping issues of secularization, apostasy, and disenchantment. For it is only by rehumanizing our discussions and debates over religious (dis)belief that the antagonism between competing factions of believers and nonbelievers in our contemporary society can be overcome.

Notes

CHAPTER 1 — AMBIVALENT PASTS

1. While simply being in a café was not improper, "members" of the group met there with some ambivalence. To be caught attending an atheist gathering, or drinking coffee, would be in direct violation of the BYU honor code (as well as the LDS's Word of Wisdom, the scriptural prohibition against consuming "hot drinks") and therefore put them at risk of official censure or expulsion from school. Yet, being a café that primarily served coffee and tea, it was largely avoided by faculty, staff, and students of BYU and therefore afforded a certain modicum of privacy. Nonetheless, I found that relatively few group members, erring on the safe side, ever actually purchased a "hot drink."

2. Ex-Mormons often told me that in the church, the mere mention of sensitive topics could provoke swift censure. As a disclaimer, I make no expert claims as to the accuracy of Mormonism's written history, the coherency of its scriptures, or the value of its religious truth claims. A host of historians, religious scholars, and churchgoers have already long debated these matters and will continue to do so in far more detail than I am capable of here. Rather, I aim to provide an ethnohistorical retelling of Mormonism's past and the developments and transformations in faith, memory, and history that have fueled the so-called mass apostasy as I saw it unfold and impact members of the church in Utah. My primary goal is to investigate how apostasy has erupted as a particular cultural phenomenon within the contemporary church and, in doing so, point to the historical, cultural, and religious underpinnings of that eruption.

3. As I discuss further in the sections that follow, in some sense, the whole of Mormonism can in fact be framed as a threefold identification with the restorative powers of memory. The institutional church's entire agenda is to engage in a historical reclamation and restoration of a forgotten, celestial premortal existence, made possible through Joseph Smith's act of archaeological recollection when he unearthed long lost scriptures documenting a churchly people's ancient history. Individuals are expected to "awaken memories of the immortal soul" through careful study of these scriptures and the historical events in the church's past through which they emerged.

4. Key studies of the history of Mormonism include Richard Bushman's *Joseph Smith: Rough Stone Rolling* (2007) and *Building the Kingdom: A History of Mormons in America*

(2001); Terryl Givens's *By the Hand of Mormon: The American Scripture that Launched a New World Religion* (2003) and *People of Paradox: A History of Mormon Culture* (2012); Jan Shipps's *Mormonism: The Story of a New Religious Tradition* (1987); Matthew Bowman's *The Mormon People: The Making of an American Faith* (2012); and Leonard Arrington and Davis Bitton's *The Mormon Experience: A History of the Latter-day Saints* (1992).

5. Though discussed as beliefs held by the first generations of Mormons, all of the principles discussed here continue to exist in LDS canon.

6. Although I do not directly address the golden spike, the symbolic significance of its phallic intrusion and its impact on contemporary forms of apostasy within Mormonism are alluded to below.

7. For more on this topic, see Flanders (1974). See also Quinn (1992).

8. In Packer's demand for history to be "properly written or properly taught," he is essentially calling for a cultural form of secondary revision, a function of the psyche in which internally derived (though seemingly incoherent) unconscious fantasies or desires are rendered palatable to the conscious mind through a process of censorship and narrative revision.

9. For detailed discussion of the Hoffman Forgeries and the Salamander Letter, see Linda Sillitoe and Allen Roberts's *Salamander: The Story of the Mormon Forgery Murders* (Salt Lake City: Signature Books, 2006); Steven Naifeh and Gregory White Smith's *The Mormon Murders: A True Story of Forgery, Deceit, and Death* (New York: St. Martin's Griffin, 2005); and Grant Palmer's *My Years in the Church Education System, 1967–2001* (Salt Lake City: Signature Books, 2010).

CHAPTER 2 — "DIGGING TOO DEEP"

1. Žižek has argued that the "very elevation of something into impossibility as a means of postponing or avoiding encountering it" is an expression of ideology in one of its most virulent forms (Žižek and Daly 2004). Ideology in this case becomes an "impossible dream" in which the desire is not necessarily to overcome impossibility but rather to sustain the impossibility in an acceptable way. This in a more basic form is what Lacan identifies as the true object of desire—not to obtain that which is desired but to sustain the pleasure of desire itself.

2. The theological tenet that God and "man" share a similar substance and being has been firmly and repeatedly asserted by "prophets of God" throughout the church's history.

3. Such instances of public denials function for many believing church members as what Žižek refers to as a "Hitchcockian blot" that disrupts the habitual reality in which we previously, and comfortably, lived. Žižek describes this as an incongruous "stain" in an otherwise idyllic or undifferentiated field of view, whereby "what we actually see becomes nothing but a deceptive surface beneath which swarms an undergrowth of perverse and obscene implications, the domain of what is prohibited" and signals the immanence of an inescapable "chaos world or shadow world" (Žižek 2010, 140).

4. An anonymous author posted this on ExMormon.org in April 2012.

5. In Deleuzian parlance, such structures allow for unmediated "lines of flight" into an essentially "deterritorialized" terrain of the church's past.

6. The issues of (1) when Joseph Smith's vision first took place, (2) how many personages were seen, (3) who they were claimed to be, (4) what they said, and (5) when verbal and written accounts of the vision were created are all hotly contested in Mormon studies and LDS Church historical literature. I do not intend here to rehash or wade into that controversy but

rather to point to the ways in which such empirical uncertainty, ambiguity, and flux not only has been the focal point of intellectual debate but also ultimately has constituted a prime source of confusion and consternation among the laity who wade into it.

7. "Joseph Smith would put the seer stone into a hat and put his face in the hat, drawing it closely around his face to exclude the light. In the darkness, the spiritual light would shine. A piece of something resembling parchment would appear, followed by the writing. One character at a time would appear, and under each was the interpretation in English. Brother Joseph would read off the English to Oliver Cowdery, who was his principal scribe, and when it was written down and repeated to Brother Joseph to see if it was correct, then it would disappear, and another character with the interpretation would appear" (Whitmer 1887, 12).

8. The wording of this text was changed in 2006 from "the principal ancestors" to "among the ancestors" in response to several critical scholarly publications drawing attention to the lack of genealogical or DNA evidence linking contemporary Native Americans to ancient peoples from the Middle East (Murphy 2002; Southerton 2004), the ultimate effect of which drew further attention to the mutability of scriptures and so-called gospel truths.

LDS faithful had long celebrated this piece of scripture because it ostensibly pointed to an empirical foundation for Mormonism as descendants of an ancient civilization with ancestral claims to the American continent. In particular, church leaders promoted the idea of a blood link between contemporary Native American populations and Book of Mormon peoples. For example, Apostle Spencer W. Kimball, speaking at the 1959 General Conference stated, "Millions of you have blood relatively unmixed with Gentiles. Columbus called you 'Indians,' thinking he had reached the East Indies." This unambiguous language was continued throughout the twentieth century, as seen in a 1995 talk from a general authority named Ted Brewerton, who reaffirmed that "many migratory groups came to the Americas, but none was as important as the three mentioned in the Book of Mormon. The blood of these people flows in the veins of the Blackfoot and the Blood Indians of Alberta, Canada; in the Navajo and the Apache of the American Southwest; the Inca of western South America; the Aztec of Mexico; the Maya of Guatemala; and in other native American groups in the Western Hemisphere and the Pacific islands."

9. After receiving scores of such letters, the Smithsonian Institution was prompted to issue a formal statement in 1998 that in unequivocal language denied the validity of these claims. "The Smithsonian Institution has never used the Book of Mormon in any way as a scientific guide. Smithsonian archeologists see no direct connection between the archeology of the New World and the subject matter of the book" (National Museum of Natural History 1982).

10. In the original printed edition of the Book of Mormon, Joseph Smith is quoted as saying that he "wrote" the Book of Mormon. Subsequent editions were modified to say he "translated" it.

11. The witnesses in fact said that they saw the plates with their "spiritual eyes" after much cajoling by Joseph Smith.

12. In the Book of Mormon, Lehi is depicted as an ancient Israelite prophet who led his family out of Jerusalem and into the "promised land" of the Americas via sailing a ship across the Pacific Ocean.

CHAPTER 4 — "I LOST MY BODY TO THE CHURCH"

1. The concept of self in most anthropological writing is discussed as a discursive formation; self exists primarily as self-representation through either narrative enactment or performative invention. The literature on apostasy and deconversion has similarly

focused on analyzing people's narrative descriptions of losing faith rather than the experiential dynamics of that transformation. When the issue of memory is invoked, it is only to critique the validity of apostate narratives. The act of remembering is discussed as a dubious source of information for what "actually happened" in apostates' lives. The theoretical turn to affect in anthropology has in fact opened up a different intellectual space for understanding memory. Affect, understood as a precognitive, amorphous, physiological "experience," instead points to an implicit, nonrepresentational form of embodied remembering that resists the categorical, event-specific narrative form of memory privileged elsewhere. Such is the kind of memory I'm pointing to here.

2. Posted in a private Facebook group.

3. Psychoanalytic theory suggests that a reaction formation emerges in response to anxiety-producing or unacceptable emotions. The subject responds to the threatening situation by exaggerating the directly opposing tendency in an effort to conceal its persistent yet subconscious existence. In a clinical setting, a reaction formation would be suspected where exaggeration, compulsiveness, or inflexibility are observed. As a type of reactive formation in a phobia, Freud (quoted in Hall 1999) argued, "The person wants what he fears. He is not afraid of the object; he is afraid of the wish for the object. The reactive fear prevents the dreaded wish from being fulfilled."

CHAPTER 6 — "I'M APOSTATE, YES I AM"

1. Speech recorded by author.

CHAPTER 7 — RELIGIOUS (DIS)IDENTIFICATION

1. The term *middle-way Mormon* nominally refers to those who have relinquished a literal belief in Mormonism's religious teachings while still holding onto its community and cultural heritage. The "middle way" has become necessary, according to Josh, because traditional ways of being Mormon have become untenable—given the easy access to faith-challenging knowledge about the church—and at times even harmful. While outright renunciation of their Mormon heritage is unthinkable, middle-wayers actively seek solutions to this contemporary predicament of faith versus culture.

CONCLUSION

1. Alongside this, various Mormon academics, apologists, and commentators have begun referring to the root of Mormonism's apostasy problem as stemming not from problems in its doctrine, its leadership, or its sacred history but from a Mormon culture (distinct from "the gospel") that is to be blamed for members' "unrealistic expectations" about the church's past and the unseemly intolerance of doubt and dissent. "If only everyone could focus on the gospel and not on culture," these voices proclaim, "there would be no problems." This is essentially an attempt to displace Mormonism's problems onto an imaginary "culture" that is distinct from "the gospel." However, in attempting to articulate a blameless and pure "gospel" devoid of responsibility, these voices willfully ignore (by constructing this false binary) the extent to which "the gospel" is nothing but a set of social and cultural relations revolving around the church institution, leadership, history, scriptures, theology, and membership.

References

Abu-Lughod, Lila. 1989. "Zones of Theory in the Anthropology of the Arab World." *Annual Review of Anthropology* 18:267–304.

Ahearn, Laura. 2010. "Agency and Language." In *Handbook of Pragmatics*, edited by J. Verschueren and J. Östman, 28–48. Amsterdam: John Benjamins.

Albrecht, Stan, and Marie Cornwall. 1998. "Life Events and Religious Change." In *Latter-day Saint Social Life: Social Research on the LDS Church and Its Members*, edited by J. Duke, 231–252. Provo: Brigham Young University.

Albrecht, Stan, Marie Cornwall, and Perry Cunningham. 1988. "Religious Leave-Taking: Disengagement and Disaffiliation among Mormons." In *Falling from the Faith: Causes and Consequences of Religious Apostasy*, edited by D. Bromley, 62–80. Newbury Park: Sage.

Allen, James, and Glen Leonard. (1976) 1992. *The Story of the Latter-day Saints*. Salt Lake City: Deseret.

Althusser, Louis. 1971. *Lenin and Philosophy and Other Essays*. New York: Verso.

Anderson, Robert D. 1999. *Inside the Mind of Joseph Smith: Psychobiography and the Book of Mormon*. Salt Lake City: Signature Books.

———. 2003. "Constraint and Freedom in Icelandic Conversions." In *The Anthropology of Religious Conversion*, edited by A. Buckser and S. Glazier, 123–132. Lanham: Rowman and Littlefield.

Anonymous. 2008. "My Exit Story." Posted on PostMormon.org, November 23, 2008.

Arrington, Leonard J., and Davis Bitton. (1979) 1992. *The Mormon Experience: A History of the Latter-day Saints*. Chicago: University of Illinois Press.

Asad, Talal. 1993. *Genealogies of Religion: Discipline and Reasons of Power in Christianity and Islam*. Baltimore: Johns Hopkins University Press.

———. 2003. *Formations of the Secular: Christianity, Islam, Modernity*. Palo Alto: Stanford University Press.

Asay, Carlos. 1981. "Opposition to the Work of God." *Ensign* 11:67–68.

Assmann, Jan, and Rodney Livingstone. 2005. *Religion and Cultural Memory: Ten Studies*. Redwood City: Stanford University Press.

Austin-Broos, Diane. 2003. "The Anthropology of Conversion: An Introduction." In *The Anthropology of Conversion*, edited by A. Buckser, and S. Glazier, 1–15. Lanham: Rowman and Littlefield.

Avance, Rosemary. 2013. "Seeing the Light: Mormon Conversion and Deconversion Narratives in Off- and Online Worlds." *Journal of Media and Religion* 12 (1): 16–24.

Babcock, Barbara, ed. 1978. *The Reversible World: Symbolic Inversion in Art and Society*. Ithaca: Cornell University Press.

Babinski, Edward, ed. 2003. *Leaving the Fold: Testimonies of Former Fundamentalists*. Amherst: Prometheus Books.

Bagley, Will. 2004. *Blood of the Prophets: Brigham Young and the Massacre at Mountain Meadows*. Norman: University of Oklahoma Press.

Bahr, Howard, and Stan Albrecht. 1989. "Strangers Once More: Patterns of Disaffiliation from Mormonism." *Journal for the Scientific Study of Religion: Social Science Perspectives* 28:180–200.

Baker, Joseph, and Buster Smith. 2015. *American Secularism: Cultural Contours of Nonreligious Belief Systems*. New York: New York University Press.

Barbour, John. 1994. *Versions of Deconversion: Autobiography and the Loss of Faith*. Charlottesville: University of Virginia Press.

Barker, Eileen. 1998. "Standing at the Cross-Roads: The Politics of Marginal Heresy in 'Subversive Organizations.'" In *The Politics of Religious Apostasy: The Role of Apostates in the Transformation of Religious Movements*, edited by D. Bromley, 75–94. Santa Barbara: Praeger.

Barsalou, Lawrence, Aron Barbey, W. Kyle Simmons, and Ava Santos. 2005. "Embodiment in Religious Knowledge." *Journal of Cognition and Culture* 5 (1–2): 14–57.

Bataille, Georges. 1986. *Eroticism: Death and Sensuality*. San Francisco: City Lights.

Beck, Aaron. 1997. "The Past and the Future of Cognitive Therapy." *Journal of Psychotherapy Practice and Research* 6 (4): 276–284.

Beck, Martha. 2006. *Leaving the Saints: How I Lost the Mormons and Found My Faith*. New York: Broadway Books.

Bednar, David A. 2001. "Ye Are the Temple of God." LDS Church General Conference, Salt Lake City. https://www.lds.org/ensign/2001/09/ye-are-the-temple-of-god?lang=eng.

Bellah, Robert. 1970. *Beyond Belief: Essays on Religion in a Post-traditionalist World*. Berkeley: University of California Press.

Beneke, Chris. 2006. *Beyond Toleration: The Religious Origins of American Pluralism*. Oxford: Oxford University Press.

Bennett, Jane. 2001. *The Enchantment of Modern Life: Attachments, Crossings, and Ethics*. Princeton: Princeton University Press.

Berger, Peter. 1980. *Heretical Imperative: Contemporary Possibilities of Religious Affirmation*. New York: Doubleday.

———. 1996. "The Secularism in Retreat." *National Interest* 16 (46): 3–12.

———. 1999. *The Desecularization of the World: Resurgent Religion and World Politics*. Grand Rapids: William B. Eerdmans.

Biehl, Joao. 2005. *Vita: Life in a Zone of Social Abandonment*. Berkeley: University of California Press.

Boas, Franz. 1914. "Mythology and Folk-Tales of the North American Indians." *Journal of American Folklore* 27 (106): 374–410.

Bourdieu, Pierre. 1990. *The Logic of Practice*. Stanford: Stanford University Press.

Bowen, John. 2010. "Secularism: Conceptual Genealogy or Political Dilemma?" *Comparative Studies in Society and History* 52 (3): 680–694.

Bowman, Matthew. 2012a. *The Mormon People: The Making of an American Faith*. New York: Random House.

———. 2012b. "What Mitt Romney Did to Mormonism." Patheos. Posted December 2, 2012. http://www.patheos.com/Mormon/What-Mitt-Romney-Did-Matthew-Bowman-12-03-2012.html.

Breuer, Josef, and Sigmund Freud. (1893) 2000. *Studies on Hysteria*. New York: Basic Books.

Brewerton, Ted E. 1995. "The Book of Mormon: A Sacred Ancient Record." *Ensign* 25 (11). https://www.lds.org/ensign/1995/11/the-book-of-mormon-a-sacred-ancient-record?lang=eng.

Brimhall, George. 1920, July. "The Brigham Young University," *Improvement Era* 23 (9).

Brinkerhoff, Merlin, and Marlene Mackie. 1993. "Casting Off the Bonds of Organized Religion: A Religious-Careers Approach to the Study of Apostasy." *Review of Religious Research* 34 (3): 235–357.

Brodie, Fawn. (1945) 1971. *No Man Knows My History: The Life of Joseph Smith*. New York: Knopf.

Bromley, David, ed. 1988. *Falling from the Faith: Causes and Consequences of Religious Apostasy*. Newbury Park: Sage.

———. 1998. *The Politics of Religious Apostasy: The Role of Apostates in the Transformation of Religious Movements*. Santa Barbara: Praeger.

Brooks, Juanita. (1950) 1991. *The Mountain Meadows Massacre*. Norman: University of Oklahoma Press.

Bruce, Steve. 2002. *God Is Dead: Secularization in the West*. Hoboken: Wiley-Blackwell.

Bryant, Seth, Henri Gooren, Rick Phillips, and David Stewart Jr. 2014. "Conversion and Retention in Mormonism." In *Oxford Handbook of Religious Conversion*, edited by L. Rambo and C. Farhadian, 756–786. Oxford: Oxford University Press.

Buckser, Andrew, and Stephen Glazier, eds. 2003. *The Anthropology of Religious Conversion*. Lanham: Rowman and Littlefield.

Bushman, Claudia, and Richard Bushman. 2001. *Building the Kingdom: A History of Mormons in America*. Oxford: Oxford University Press.

Bushman, Richard. 2007. *Joseph Smith: Rough Stone Rolling*. New York: Vintage Books.

Campbell, David, John Green, and J. Quin Monson. 2014. *Seeking the Promised Land: Mormons and American Politics*. Cambridge: Cambridge University Press.

Cannell, Fenella. 2010. "The Anthropology of Secularism." *Annual Review of Anthropology* 39:85–100.

———. 2013a. "The Blood of Abraham: Mormon Redemptive Physicality and American Idioms of Kinship." *Journal of the Royal Anthropological Institute* 19 (1): 77–94.

———. 2013b. "The Re-enchantment of Kinship." In *Vital Relations: Modernity and the Persistent Life of Kinship*, edited by F. Cannell and S. McKinnon, 217–240. Santa Fe: Society for Advanced Research Press.

Capps, Lisa, and Elinor Ochs. 2002. "Cultivating Prayer." In *The Language of Turn and Sequence*, edited by C. Ford, B. Fox, and S. Thompson, 39–55. Oxford: Oxford University Press.

Carter, Lewis F. 1998. "Carriers of Tales: On Assessing Credibility of Apostate and Other Outsider Accounts of Religious Practices." In *The Politics of Religious Apostasy: The Role of Apostates in the Transformation of Religious Movements*, edited by D. Bromley, 221–238. Santa Barbara: Praeger.

Caruth, Cathy, ed. 1995. *Trauma: Explorations in Memory*. Baltimore: Johns Hopkins University Press.

Casanova, Jose. 1994. *Public Religions in the Modern World*. Chicago: University of Chicago Press.

Chaves, Mark. 1994. "Secularization as Declining Religious Authority." *Social Forces* 72 (3): 749–774.

Christiano, Kevin, William Swatos Jr., and Peter Kivisto. 1985. *Sociology of Religion: Contemporary Developments*. Lanham: Altamira.

Church Education System. 1975. "In the House of the Lord." *New Era* 4 (5): 20.

———. 2000a. *Book of Mormon Student Study Guide*. Salt Lake City: Church of Jesus Christ of Latter-day Saints.

———. 2000b. "Our Premortal Life." In *Doctrines of the Gospel Student Manual*, 13–15. Salt Lake City: Church of Jesus Christ of Latter-day Saints. https://www.lds.org/manual/doctrines-of-the-gospel-student-manual/chapter-6-our-premortal-life?lang=eng.

———. 2001. *Gospel Doctrine Teacher's Manual*. 5th ed. Salt Lake City: Church of Jesus Christ of Latter-day Saints.

———. 2003. *Church History in the Fullness of Times Student Manual*. Salt Lake City: Church of Jesus Christ of Latter-day Saints.

———. 2004. "Lesson 1: The Message of the Restoration of the Gospel of Jesus Christ." In *Preach My Gospel: A Guide to Missionary Service*, 31–46. Salt Lake City: Church of Jesus Christ of Latter-day Saints.

———. 2018. "Guide to the Scriptures, 'Apostasy.'" The Church of Jesus Christ of Latter-day Saints. https://www.lds.org/scriptures/gs/apostasy.

Church of Jesus Christ of Latter-day Saints. 2011. *Teachings of Presidents of the Church: Joseph Smith*. Salt Lake City: Church of Jesus Christ of Latter-day Saints.

Church News. 1996. "Counsel from the Prophet: Pres. Hinckley Addresses 22,000 at Conference in Northern Utah." *Deseret News*, April 27, 1996. http://www.ldschurchnewsarchive.com/articles/28119/Counsel-from-the-prophet--Pres-Hinckley-addresses-22000-at-conference-in-northern-Utah.html.

Cimino, Richard, and Christopher Smith. 2011. "The New Atheism and the Formation of the Imagined Secularist Community." *Journal of Media and Religion* 10 (1): 24–38.

Colvin, Gina. 2014. "A Former Bishop's Doctrinal Dilemmas." *KiwiMormon* (blog). http://www.patheos.com/blogs/kiwimormon/2014/02/a-former-bishops-doctrinal-dilemmas/.

Comaroff, Jean, and John Comaroff. 1991. *Of Revelation and Revolution, Volume 1*. Chicago: University of Chicago Press.

Cottee, Simon. 2015. *Apostates: When Muslims Leave Islam*. London: C. Hurst.

Cragun, Ryan, and Joseph Hammer. 2012. "On the Receiving End: Discrimination toward the Non-religious." *Journal of Contemporary Religion* 27 (1): 105–127.

Cragun, Ryan, Patrick Henry, Casey Homan, and Joseph Hammer. 2012. "Whom Do People Dislike More: Atheists or Cultists?" *Interdisciplinary Journal of Research on Religion* 8 (9): 1–19.

Crapanzano, Vincent. 1992. *Hermes' Dilemma and Hamlet's Desire: On the Epistemology of Interpretation*. Cambridge: Harvard University Press.

Csordas, Thomas. 1994. *The Sacred Self: A Cultural Phenomenology of Charismatic Healing*. Berkeley: University of California Press.

———. 2002. *Body/Meaning/Healing*. Basingstoke: Palgrave Macmillan.

Daly, Glyn. 2004. "The Constitutive Madness of Being." *Lacan Dot Com* (blog). http://www.lacan.com/zizek-daly.htm.

Davies, Douglas. 2000. *The Mormon Culture of Salvation*. Farnham: Ashgate.

Dobner, Jennifer. 2005. "Pres. Hinckley Answers Myriad Questions about the LDS Church." Associated Press. http://www.deseretnews.com/article/635171604/Pres-Hinckley-answers-myriad-questions-about-the-LDS-Church.html?pg=all./m/.

———. 2012. "Mormons Quit Church in Mass Resignation Ceremony." Reuters. https://www.reuters.com/article/us-usa-utah-mormons/mormons-quit-church-in-mass-resignation-ceremony-idUSBRE86000N20120701.

Dolar, Mladen. 1991. "'I Shall Be with You on Your Wedding-Night': Lacan and the Uncanny." *October* 58 (Autumn): 13.

Duffy, John-Charles. 2005. "The New Missionary Discussions and the Future of Correlation." *Sunstone* 138:28–46.

Dumont, Louis. 1981. *Homo Hierarchicus: The Caste System and its Implications*. Chicago: University of Chicago Press.

Durkheim, Emile. (1915) 1995. *The Elementary Forms of Religious Life*. New York: Free Press.

Edgell, Penny, Joseph Gerteis, and Douglas Hartmann. 2006. "Atheists as 'Other': Moral Boundaries and Cultural Membership in American Society." *American Sociological Review* 71 (2): 211–234.

Epstein, Greg. 2010. *Good without God: What a Billion Nonreligious People Do Believe*. New York: HarperCollins.

Erikson, Erik. 1973. *Childhood and Society*. New York: W. W. Norton.

Evans-Pritchard, E. E. 1937. *Witchcraft, Oracles and Magic among the Azande*. Oxford: Oxford University Press.

FairMormon. 2018. "Questions: What Are the Worthiness Requirements to Enter a Mormon Temple?" https://www.fairmormon.org/answers/Question:_What_are_the_worthiness_requirements_to_enter_a_Mormon_temple%3F.

Farman, Abou. 2013. "Speculative Matter: Secular Bodies, Minds and Persons." *Cultural Anthropology* 28 (4): 737–759.

Fink, Bruce. 1997. *The Lacanian Subject: Between Language and Jouissance*. Princeton: Princeton University Press.

Flake, Kathleen. 2003. "Re-placing Memory: Latter-day Saint Use of Historical Monuments and Narrative in the Early Twentieth Century." *Religion and American Culture* 13:69–110.

Flanders, Robert. 1974. "Some Reflections on the New Mormon History." *Dialogue: A Journal of Mormon Thought* 9 (Spring): 34–41.

Foucault, Michel. 1970. *The Order of Things: An Archaeology of the Human Sciences*. New York: Pantheon Books.

Frankl, Viktor. (1946) 2006. *Man's Search for Meaning*. Boston: Beacon.

Freud, Sigmund. (1919) 2003. *The Uncanny*. London: Penguin.

———. (1937) 1987. *On Psychopathology*. North Brunswick: Middlesex.

Gee, John, William Hamblin, and Daniel Peterson. 2006. "And I Saw the Stars: The Book of Abraham and Ancient Geocentric Astronomy." In *Astronomy, Papyrus, and Covenant*, edited by J. Gee, B. and Hauglid, 161. Provo: Brigham Young University.

Geertz, Clifford. 1973. *The Interpretation of Cultures*. New York: Basic Books.

Giddens, Anthony. 1991. *Modernity and Self-Identity: Self and Society in the Late Modern Age*. Cambridge: Polity.

Givens, Terryl. 2003. *By the Hand of Mormon: The American Scripture that Launched a New World Religion*. Oxford: Oxford University Press.

———. 2012. *People of Paradox: A History of Mormon Culture*. Oxford: Oxford University Press.

Gluckman, Max. 1963. *Order and Rebellion in Tribal Africa*. London: Cohen and West.

Goldstein, Kurt. 1940. *Human Nature in the Light of Psychopathology*. Cambridge: Harvard University Press.

Gooren, Henri. 2008. "The Mormons of the World: The Meaning of LDS Membership in Central America." In *Revisiting Thomas F. O'Dea's The Mormons: Contemporary Perspectives*, edited by C. Jacobson, J. Hoffman, and T. Heaton, 362–388. Salt Lake City: University of Utah Press.

———. 2010. *Religious Conversion and Disaffiliation: Tracing Patterns of Change in Faith Practices*. Basingstoke: Palgrave Macmillan.

Gordon, Sarah, and Jan Shipps. 2011. "A New Mormon Moment." *New York Times*, July 4, 2011. http://www.nytimes.com/roomfordebate/2011/07/04/are-republicans-ready-now-for-a-mormon-president/a-new-mormon-moment.

Gregory, Stanford W., and Jerry M. Lewis. 1988. "Symbols of Collective Memory: The Social Process of Memorializing May 4, 1970, at Kent State University." *Symbolic Interaction* 11 (2): 213–233.

Grossman, Cathy. 2002. "Charting the Unchurched in America." *USA Today*, March 7, 2002.

Habermas, Jurgen. 1985. *The Theory of Communicative Action, Volume 1: Reason and the Rationalization of Society*. Boston: Beacon.

Halbwachs, Maurice. 1992. *On Collective Memory*. Chicago: University of Chicago Press.

Hall, Calvin S. 1999. *A Primer of Freudian Psychology*. New York: Plume.

Hallowell, A. Irving. 1967. *Culture and Experience*. New York: Schocken Books.

Hammarberg, Melvyn. 2013. *The Mormon Quest for Glory: The Religious World of the Latter-day Saints*. Oxford: Oxford University Press.

Hammer, Joseph, Ryan Cragun, Karen Hwang, and Jesse Smith. 2012. "Forms, Frequency, and Correlates of Perceived Anti-atheist Discrimination." *Secularism and Nonreligious* 1:43–67.

Harding, Susan. 1987. "Convicted by the Holy Spirit: The Rhetoric of Fundamental Baptist Conversion." *American Ethnologist* 14 (1): 167–181.

Hardy, Grant. 2012. "The Blessing of Conversation." Patheos. Posted December 6, 2012. http://www.patheos.com/Mormon/Blessing-Conversation-Grant-Hardy-12-07-2012.html.

Heelas, Paul. 1996. *The New Age Movement: The Celebration of the Self and the Sacralization of Modernity*. Hoboken: Blackwell.

Heidegger, Martin. (1927) 2008. *Being and Time*. New York: Harper Perennial.

———. 1977. *The Question Concerning Technology and Other Essays*. New York: Harper Perennial.

Hinckley, Bryant S. 1949. *Sermons and Missionary Services of Melvin J. Ballard*. Salt Lake City: Deseret.

Hinckley, Gordon B. 1996. "Be Ye Clean." LDS Church General Conference, Salt Lake City. https://www.lds.org/general-conference/1996/04/be-ye-clean?lang=eng.

———. 2002. "The Marvelous Foundation of Our Faith." LDS General Conference, Salt Lake City. Church of Jesus Christ of Latter-day Saints.

———. 2010. "The Family: A Proclamation to the World," *Ensign* 40 (11): 129.

———. 2016. *Teachings of Presidents of the Church: Gordon B. Hinckley*. Salt Lake City: The Church of Jesus Christ of Latter-day Saints.

Hirschkind, Charles. 2006. *The Ethical Soundscape: Cassette Sermons and Islamic Counterpublics*. New York: Columbia University Press.

———. 2011. "Is There a Secular Body?" *Cultural Anthropology* 26 (4): 633–647.

Hobsbawm, Eric, and Terence Ranger. 1992. *The Invention of Tradition*. Cambridge: Cambridge University Press.

Hodgson, Dorothy. 2005. *The Church of Women: Gendered Encounters between Maasai and Missionaries*. Bloomington: Indiana University Press.

Holland, Dorothy, and Kevin Leander. 2004. "Ethnographic Studies of Positioning and Subjectivity: An Introduction." *Ethos* 32 (2): 127–139.

Holland, Jeffrey. 1998. "Personal Purity." LDS Church General Conference, Salt Lake City. https://www.lds.org/general-conference/1998/10/personal-purity?lang=eng.

Horowitz, Jason. 2012. "The Genesis of a Church's Stand on Race." *Washington Post*. http://www.washingtonpost.com/politics/the-genesis-of-a-churchs-stand-on-race/2012/02/22/gIQAQZXyfR_story.html.

Hubert, Henri, and Marcel Mauss. 1981. *Sacrifice: Its Nature and Function*. Chicago: University of Chicago Press.

Husserl, Edmund. (1936) 1970. *The Crisis of European Sciences and Transcendental Phenomenology: An Introduction to Phenomenological Philosophy*. Evanston: Northwestern University Press.

Jackson, Michael. 1996. *Things as They Are: New Directions in Phenomenological Anthropology*. Bloomington: Indiana University Press.

Jacobs, Janet. 1989. *Divine Disenchantment: Deconverting from New Religions*. Bloomington: Indiana University Press.

James, Williams. 1902. *The Varieties of Religious Experience*. Harlow: Longmans, Green.

Jameson, Frederic. 1991. *Postmodernism, or, the Cultural Logic of Late Capitalism*. London: Verso.

Joffe-Walt, Chana. 2005. "Shunned Ex-Mormons Form Own Communities." National Public Radio (NPR). Posted October 21, 2005. http://www.npr.org/templates/story/story.php?storyId=4968585.

Johnson, Daniel. 1998. "Apostates Who Never Were: The Social Construction of Absque Facto Apostate Narratives." In *The Politics of Religious Apostasy: The Role of Apostates in the Transformation of Religious Movements*, edited by D. Bromley, 115–138. Santa Barbara: Praeger.

Keane, Webb. 2007. *Christian Moderns: Freedom and Fetish in the Mission Encounter*. Berkeley: University of California Press.

Kettell, Stephen. 2013. "Faithless: The Politics of New Atheism." *Sociology of Religion* 2:61–72.

Kierkegaard, Søren. 1940. *The Present Age and of the Difference between a Genius and an Apostle*. New York: Harper Torchbooks.

———. (1943) 1981. *The Concept of Dread*. Princeton: Princeton University Press.

Kimball, Spencer W. 1959. "To You . . . Our Kinsmen." LDS General Conference report, October 1959, 57–62.

Kirn, Walter. 2011. "The Mormon Moment." *Newsweek*, June 5, 2011. http://www.newsweek.com/mormon-moment-67951.

Knowlton, David. 2005. "How Many Members Are There Really? Two Censuses and the Meaning of LDS Membership in Chile and Mexico." *Dialogue: A Journal of Mormon Thought* 38 (2): 53–78.

Kopping, Klaus-Peter. 1998. "Bodies in the Field: Sexual Taboos, Self-Revelation and the Limits of Reflexivity in Anthropological Fieldwork (and Writing)." *Anthropological Journal of European Cultures* 7 (1): 7–26.

Kosmin, Barry, and Ariela Keysar. 2008. "American Religious Identification Survey." Trinity College. http://www.americanreligionsurvey-aris.org/reports/ARIS_Report_2008.pdf.

Lacan, Jacques. 2006. *Écrits: The First Complete Edition in English*. Translated by Bruce Fink. New York: W. W. Norton.

Laing, R. D. 1965. *The Divided Self: An Existential Study in Sanity and Madness*. London: Penguin.

Landy, Joshua, and Michael Saler, eds. 2009. *The Re-enchantment of the World: Secular Magic in a Rational Age*. Palo Alto: Stanford University Press.

Larry King Live. 1998. "Interview with Gordon Hinckley." CNN. Aired August 9, 1998. http://transcripts.cnn.com/TRANSCRIPTS/0412/26/lkl.01.html.

Lavery, Dennis, dir. 2009. *In the Shadow of the Temple*. Portland: Pepita Productions, Inc. DVD.

LDS Church First Presidency. 2016. "For the Strength of Youth." Salt Lake City: Church of Jesus Christ of Latter-day Saints. https://www.lds.org/youth/for-the-strength-of-youth/sexual-purity?lang=eng.

LDS Media Library. 2014. "Scriptures Legacy." Salt Lake City: Church of Jesus Christ of Latter-day Saints. https://www.lds.org/media-library/video/2014-04-004-scriptures-legacy?lang=eng.

Leder, Drew. 1990. *The Absent Body*. Chicago: University of Chicago Press.

LeDrew, Stephen. 2013. "Discovering Atheism: Heterogeneity in Trajectories to Atheist Identity and Activism." *Sociology of Religion* 74 (4): 431–453.

Lee, Lois, and Stephen Bullivant. 2010. "Where Do Atheists Come From?" *New Scientist*, March 3, 2010. https://www.newscientist.com/article/mg20527506-100-where-do-atheists-come-from/.

Lester, Rebecca. 2005. *Jesus in Our Wombs: Embodying Modernity in a Mexican Convent*. Berkeley: University of California Press.

Lloyd, Alfred. 1907. *The Will to Doubt*. Ann Arbor: University of Michigan Press.

Luckmann, Thomas. 1967. *The Invisible Religion: The Problem of Religion in Modern Society*. London: Macmillan.

Ludlow, Daniel. 1992. *Encyclopedia of Mormonism*. London: Macmillan.

Luhrmann, Tanya. 2005. "The Art of Hearing God: Absorption, Dissociation, and Contemporary American Spirituality." *Spiritus: A Journal of Christian Spirituality* 5 (2): 133–157.

———. 2012. *When God Talks Back: Understanding the American Evangelical Relationship with God*. New York: Alfred A. Knopf.

Luhrmann, Tanya, Howard Nusbaum, and Ronald Thisted. 2010. "The Absorption Hypothesis: Learning to Hear God in Evangelical Christianity." *American Anthropologist* 112 (1): 66–78.

Luttrell, Wendy. 2000. "'Good Enough' Methods for Ethnographic Research." *Harvard Educational Review* 70 (4): 499–524.

Lythgoe, Dennis. 1968. "The Changing Image of Mormonism." *Dialogue: A Journal of Mormon Thought* 3 (4): 47.

Madsen, Truman G. 1980. *Defender of the Faith: The B. H. Roberts Story*. Salt Lake City: Bookcraft.

Maffly-Kipp, Laurie. 2012. "The Long Approach to the Mormon Moment." *Religion and Politics: Fit for Polite Company*. St. Louis: Washington University.

Mahmood, Saba. 2005. *Politics of Piety: The Islamic Revival and the Feminist Subject*. Durham: Duke University Press.

Malinowski, Bronislaw. (1948) 2002. *Magic, Science and Religion and Other Essays*. Glencoe: Free Press.

Manning, Christel. 2015. *Losing Our Religion: How Unaffiliated Parents Are Raising Their Children*. New York: New York University Press.

Martin, David. 2005. *On Secularization: Toward a Revised General Theory*. Farnham: Ashgate.

Mason, Patrick. 2012. "The Mormon Moment, in Context." *Flame, The Magazine of Claremont Graduate University* 13 (1): 20–23.

Mauss, Armand. 1994. *The Angel and the Beehive: The Mormon Struggle with Assimilation*. Chicago: University of Illinois Press.

———. 1998. "Apostasy and the Management of Spoiled Identity." In *The Politics of Religious Apostasy: The Role of Apostates in the Transformation of Religious Movements*, edited by D. Bromley, 51–74. Santa Barbara: Praeger.

Mauss, Marcel. (1902) 2001. *A General Theory of Magic*. Abingdon: Routledge.

Maxwell, Neal A. 1994. *Lord, Increase Our Faith*. Salt Lake City: Bookcraft.

May, Rollo. 1977. *The Meaning of Anxiety*. New York: Ronald Press.

McConkie, Bruce R. 1984. "The Caravan Moves On." LDS Church General Conference, October 1984, Salt Lake City. https://www.lds.org/general-conference/1984/10/the-caravan-moves-on?lang=eng.

Meister, Chad. *The Oxford Handbook of Religious Diversity*. Oxford: Oxford University Press.

Merleau-Ponty, Maurice. (1962) 2002. *Phenomenology of Perception*. New York: Humanities Press.

Miet, Hannah. 2014. "When the Saints Go Marching Out." *Newsweek*. http://www.newsweek.com/2014/01/31/when-saints-go-marching-out-245158.html.

Minkowski, Eugene. 1970. *Lived Time: Phenomenological and Psychopathological Studies*. Evanston: Northwestern University Press.

Morin, Brad, and Chris Morin. 2004. *Suddenly Strangers: Surrendering Gods and Heroes*. Chula Vista: Aventine.

Mormon Newsroom. 2018. "Mormons and Education: An Overview." http://www.mormonnewsroom.org/article/mormons-and-education-an-overview.

Murphy, Thomas. 2002. "Lamanite Genesis, Genealogy, and Genetics." In *American Apocrypha: Essays on the Book of Mormon*, edited by D. Vogel and B. Metcalfe, 47–77. Salt Lake City: Signature Books.

National Museum of Natural History. 1982. "Statement Regarding the Book of Mormon." Washington, D.C.: Smithsonian Institution. http://www.csnradio.com/tema/links/SmithsonianLetter.pdf.

Navaro-Yashin, Yael. 2002. *Faces of the State: Secularism and Public Life in Turkey*. Princeton: Princeton University Press.

Nelson, Afton. 2018. "Six Tips for Successful Scripture Study." Salt Lake City: Church of Jesus Christ of Latter-day Saints. https://www.lds.org/youth/article/print?lang=eng&url=/youth/article/six-tips-for-successful-scripture-study.

Nelson, Russel M. 1986. "Truth—and More," *Ensign*, January 1986, 69.

Newell, Linda, and Valeen Avery. (1984) 1994. *Mormon Enigma: Emma Hale Smith*. Chicago: University of Illinois Press.

Newman, Leonard, Kimberly Duff, and Roy Baumeister. 1997. "A New Look at Defensive Projection: Thought Suppression, Accessibility, and Biased Person Perception." *Journal of Personality and Social Psychology* 72 (5): 980–1001.

Nietzsche, Friedrich. (1882) 2001. *The Gay Science*. New York: Cambridge University Press.
Nora, Pierre, ed. 1996. *Realms of Memory: Rethinking the French Past*. Vol. 1, Conflicts and Divisions. New York: Columbia University Press.
Norris, Pippa, and Ronald Inglehart. 2004. *Sacred and Secular: Religion and Politics Worldwide*. New York: Cambridge University Press.
Oaks, Dallin H. 1971. "Talk of the Month: Standards of Dress and Grooming." *New Era*.
———. 2008. "Testimony." LDS Church General Conference. Church of Jesus Christ of Latter-day Saints. https://www.lds.org/general-conference/2008/04/testimony?lang=eng.
Ochs, Elinor, and Lisa Capps. 1996. "Narrating the Self." *Annual Review of Anthropology* 25:19–43.
Ortner, Sherry. 2005. "Subjectivity and Cultural Critique." *Anthropological Theory* 5 (1): 31–52.
Ostling, Richard, and Joan Ostling. 2007. *Mormon America: The Power and the Promise*. New York: HarperCollins.
Packer, Boyd. 1981. "The Mantle Is Far, Far Greater Than the Intellect," *BYU Studies* 21 (3): 259–271.
Palmer, Grant. 2002. *An Insider's View of Mormon Origins*. Salt Lake City: Signature Books.
Payne, Seth. 2013. "Ex-Mormon Narratives and Pastoral Apologetics." *Dialogue: A Journal of Mormon Thought* 46 (4): 32.
Peacock, James, and Dorothy Holland. 1993. "The Narrated Self: Life Stories in Process." *Ethos* 21 (4): 367–383.
Petersen, Mark E. 1954. "Race Problems as They Affect the Church." Address delivered at the Convention of Teachers of Religion on the College Level, Brigham Young University, August 27, 1954.
Pew Research Center. 2012. "'Nones' on the Rise." Posted October 9, 2012. http://www.pewforum.org/2012/10/09/nones-on-the-rise/.
Phillips, Rick. 2004. "Can Rising Rates of Church Participation Be a Consequence of Secularization?" *Sociology of Religion* 65 (2): 139–153.
Phillips, Rick, and Ryan T. Cragun. 2013. "Mormon Religiosity and the Legacy of 'Gathering.'" *Nova Religio: The Journal of Alternative and Emergent Religions* 16 (3): 77–94.
Phillips, Rick, Ryan T. Cragun, Barry A. Kosmin, and Ariela Keysar. 2011. *Mormons in the United States 1990–2008: Socio-demographic Trends and Regional Differences*. Hartford: Institute for the Study of Secularism in Society and Culture.
Priest, Robert. 2003. "'I Discovered My Sin!': Aguaruna Evangelical Conversion Narratives." In *The Anthropology of Religious Conversion*, edited by A. Buckser, and S. Glazier, 95–108. Lanham: Rowman and Littlefield.
Prince, Gregory. 2016. *Leonard Arrington and the Writing of Mormon History*. Salt Lake City: University of Utah Press.
Prince, Gregory, and Robert Wright. 2005. *David O. McKay and the Rise of Modern Mormonism*. Salt Lake City: University of Utah Press.
Putnam, Robert, and David Campbell. 2012. *American Grace: How Religion Divides and Unites Us*. New York: Simon and Schuster.
Quinn, D. Michael, ed. 1992. *The New Mormon History*. Salt Lake City: Signature Books.
Radstone, Susannah, and Bill Schwarz, eds. 2010. *Memory: Histories, Theories, Debates*. New York: Fordham University Press.
Rambo, Lewis. 1993. *Understanding Religious Conversion*. New Haven: Yale University Press.
Riis, Ole, and Linda Woodhead. 2010. *A Sociology of Religious Emotion*. Oxford: Oxford University Press.
Robbins, Joel. 2004. *Becoming Sinners: Christianity and Moral Torment in a Papua New Guinea Society*. Berkeley: University of California Press.
Roberts, B. H. 1965. *History of the Church*. Salt Lake City: Deseret.
Roof, Wade Clark, and Shawn J. Landres. 1997. "Defection, Disengagement, and Dissent: The Dynamics of Religious Change in the United States." *Religion and the Social Order* 7:77–95.

Rosenlof, Celeste. 2014. "60% of Utahns LDS in 2013, Gallup Says." KSL Broadcasting, Salt Lake City. https://www.ksl.com/?sid=28799562.

Sass, Louis. 1994. *Madness and Modernism: Insanity in the Light of Modern Art, Literature, and Thought.* Cambridge: Harvard University Press.

———. 2001. "Self and World in Schizophrenia: Three Classic Approaches." *Philosophy, Psychiatry, and Psychology* 4 (8): 251–270.

Schutz, Alfred. 1967. *The Phenomenology of the Social World.* Evanston: Northwestern University Press.

Scott, Gini. 1994. *The Power of Fantasy: Illusion and Eroticism in Everyday Life.* New York: Carol Publishing Group.

Secular Priest. 2004. "So GBH Does Not Know What Happens after Death!!!" ExMormon .org, December 27, 2004. https://www.exmormon.org/mormon/mormon381.htm.

Seligman, Rebecca. 2010. "The Unmaking and Making of Self: Embodied Suffering and Mind-Body Healing in Brazilian Candomblé." *Ethos* 38 (3): 297–320.

Sells, Jeffrey, ed. 2005. *God and Country: Politics in Utah.* Salt Lake City: Signature Books.

Seminaries and Institutes of Religion Curriculum Services. 2009. *Book of Mormon Teacher Manual.* Salt Lake City: Church of Jesus Christ of Latter-day Saints.

Sherkat, Darren. 1991. "Leaving the Faith: Testing Theories of Religious Switching Using Survival Models." *Social Science Research* 20:171–187.

———. 1995. "Preferences, Constraints, and Choices in Religious Markets: An Examination of Religious Switching and Apostasy." *Social Forces* 73 (3): 993–1026.

———. 2014. *Changing Faith: The Dynamics and Consequences of Americans' Shifting Religious Identities.* New York: New York University Press.

Shipps, Jan. 1981. "The Mormon Past: Revealed or Revisited?" *Sunstone* 6:57.

———. 1987. *Mormonism: The Story of a New Religious Tradition.* Chicago: University of Illinois Press.

Shirky, Clay. 2011. "The Political Power of Social Media: Technology, the Public Sphere, and Political Change." *Foreign Affairs* 90 (1): 28–41.

Simmel, Georg. 1950. "*Unification of a Group in Opposition to the Ruler.*" In *The Sociology of Georg Simmel*, edited by K. Wolff, 192–193. Glencoe: Free Press.

Simon, Gregory. 2009. "The Soul Freed of Cares? Islamic Prayer, Subjectivity, and the Contradictions of Moral Selfhood in Minangkabau, Indonesia." *American Ethnologist* 36 (2): 258–275.

Smith, David, and Ronald McIntyre. 1982. *Husserl and Intentionality.* Dordrecht: Reidel.

Smith, Jesse. 2011. "Becoming an Atheist in America: Constructing Identity and Meaning from the Rejection of Theism." *Sociology of Religion* 72 (2): 215–237.

Smith, Joseph. 2007. *Teachings of the President Joseph Smith.* Salt Lake City: Church of Jesus Christ of Latter-day Saints.

Smith, Joseph Fielding. 1972. "Eternal Keys and the Right to Preside." LDS General Conference report. Church of Jesus Christ of Latter-day Saints.

———. 1984. *The Way to Perfection.* Salt Lake City: Deseret.

Southerton, Simon G. 2004. *Losing a Lost Tribe: Native Americans, DNA and the Mormon Church.* Salt Lake City: Signature Books.

Spiegelberg, Herbert. 1972. *Phenomenology in Psychology and Psychiatry.* Evanston: Northwestern University Press.

Spinoza, Benedict. 1985. *The Collected Writings of Spinoza.* Princeton: Princeton University Press.

Stack, Peggy F. 2012. "Mormons Confront 'Epidemic' on Online Misinformation." *Washington Post*, February 1, 2012. http://www.washingtonpost.com/national/on-faith/mormons-confront-epidemic-on-online-misinformation/2012/02/01/gIQApULJiQ_story.html.

Stark, Rodney. 2005. *The Rise of Mormonism.* New York: Columbia University Press.

Stark, Rodney, and Roger Finke. 2002. "Beyond Church and Sect: Dynamics and Stability in Religious Markets." In *Sacred Markets, Sacred Canopies: Essays on Religious Markets and Religious Pluralism*, edited by T. Jelen, 31–62. Lanham: Rowman and Littlefield.

Starrett, Gregory. 1995. "The Hexis of Interpretation: Islam and the Body in the Egyptian Popular School." *American Ethnologist* 22 (4): 953–969.

Stewart, Kathleen. 1996. *A Space on the Side of the Road: Cultural Poetics in an "Other" America*. Princeton: Princeton University Press.

Strassberg, Donald. 1998. "Force in Women's Sexual Fantasies." *Archives of Sexual Behavior* 27 (4): 403–415.

Streib, Heinz, Ralph Hood Jr., Barbara Keller, Rosina-Martha Csöff, and Christopher Silver. 2009. *Deconversion: Qualitative and Quantitative Results from Cross-Cultural Research in Germany and the United States of America*. Gottingen: Vandenhoeck and Ruprecht.

Stromberg, Peter. 1993. *Language and Self-Transformation: A Study of the Christian Conversion Narrative*. Cambridge: Cambridge University Press.

Sutton, David. 2001. *Remembrance of Repasts: An Anthropology of Food and Memory*. London: Bloomsbury.

Taira, Teemu. 2012. "New Atheism as Identity Politics." In *Religion and Knowledge: Sociological Perspectives*, edited by M. Guest and E. Arweck, 97–114. Farnham: Ashgate.

Taylor, Charles. 2007. *A Secular Age*. Cambridge: Belknap.

Thayne, Emma Lou. 2012. "The Mormon Moment." *Huffington Post* (blog). Last updated April 11, 2012. http://www.huffingtonpost.com/emma-lou-thayne/the-mormon-moment_b_1259873.html.

Toscano, Paul. 2007. *The Sacrament of Doubt*. Salt Lake City: Signature Books.

Trouillot, Michel-Rolph. 1997. *Silencing the Past: Power and the Production of History*. Boston: Beacon.

Turner, Rodney. 1992. "Unpardonable Sin." In *Encyclopedia of Mormonism*. Provo: Brigham Young University. http://eom.byu.edu/index.php/Unpardonable_Sin.

Turner, Victor, and Edward Bruner, eds. 1986. *The Anthropology of Experience*. Chicago: University of Illinois Press.

Ure, James, ed. 1999. *Leaving the Fold: Candid Conversations with Inactive Mormons*. Salt Lake City: Signature Books.

Valsiner, Jaan, and René van der Veer. 2000. *The Social Mind: Construction of the Idea*. Cambridge: Cambridge University Press.

Wacquant, Loïc. 2004. *Body and Soul*. Oxford: Oxford University Press.

Walker, Joseph. 2013. "Mormons Navigate Faith and Doubt in the Digital Age." *Deseret News*, July 26, 2013.

Walker, Ronald W., Richard E. Turley, and Glen M. Leonard. 2011. *Massacre at Mountain Meadows*. Oxford: Oxford University Press.

Washington Post. 2012. "Mormon Press Office: Church's Image Survived the Campaign." http://www.washingtonpost.com/blogs/election-2012/wp/2012/11/06/mormon-press-office-churchs-image-survived-the-campaign/.

Weber, Max. (1920) 1993. *The Sociology of Religion*. Boston: Beacon.

Werleman, C. J. 2014. "Atheists Have Their Number: How the Christian Right Is Hastening Religion's Decline." *Salon*, March 25, 2014. http://www.salon.com/2014/03/25/calling_the_christian_right_soon_you_will_be_outnumbered_partner/.

Whitmer, David. 1887. *An Address to All Believers in Christ*. Richmond.

Williams, Raymond. 1978. *Marxism and Literature*. Oxford: Oxford University Press.

Winell, Marlene. 1993. *Leaving the Fold*. Oakland: New Harbinger.

Woodruff, Wilford. 1983. *Wilford Woodruff's Journal: Typescript Volumes 1–9, 29 December 1833 to 2 September 1898*, vol. 9, edited by Scott G. Kenney. Midvale: Signature Books.

Wright, Stuart. 1988. "Leaving New Religious Movements." In *Falling from the Faith: The Causes and Consequences of Religious Apostasy*, edited D. Bromley, 143–165. Newbury Park: Sage.

Yafeh, Orit. 2007. "The Time in the Body: Cultural Construction of Femininity in Ultraorthodox Kindergartens for Girls." *Ethos* 35 (4): 516–553.

Young, Brigham. 1855. *Journal of Discourses*. Vol. 2. Salt Lake City: Church of Jesus Christ of Latter-day Saints.

———. 1997. *Teachings of Presidents of the Church: Brigham Young*. Salt Lake City: Church of Jesus Christ of Latter-day Saints.

Young, Neil. 2007. "'The ERA Is a Moral Issue': The Mormon Church, LDS Women, and the Defeat of the Equal Rights Amendment." *American Quarterly* 59 (3): 623–644.

Zivic, Claudio D. 2009. "Avoiding Personal Apostasy." *Ensign*, June 2009.

Žižek, Slavoj. 1989. *The Sublime Object of Ideology*. London: Verso.

———. 2007. *The Indivisible Remainder: On Schelling and Related Matters*. London: Verso.

———, ed. 2010. *Everything You Always Wanted to Know about Lacan but Were Afraid to Ask*. London: Verso.

Žižek, Slavoj, and Glyn Daly. 2004. *Conversations with Žižek*. Cambridge: Polity Press.

Zuckerman, Phil. 2009. "Atheism, Secularity, and Well-Being: How Findings of Social Science Counter Negative Stereotypes and Assumptions." *Sociology Compass* 3 (6): 949–971.

———. 2011. *Faith No More: Why People Reject Religion*. Oxford: Oxford University Press.

Zuckerman, Phil, Luke Galen, and Frank Pasquale. 2016. *The Nonreligious: Understanding Secular People and Societies*. Oxford: Oxford University Press.

Index

Page numbers in *italics* refer to figures.

About the Author

E. Marshall Brooks is an instructor in the Department of Family Medicine and Population Health and adjunct lecturer in the School of World Studies at Virginia Commonwealth University.